Bringing Science to Our Stories in Animal-Assisted Services

Animal-assisted professionals carry powerful stories of change – moments of connection, growth, and insight that unfold through human-animal interaction. *Bringing Science to Our Stories in Animal-Assisted Services* shows how those stories can become the foundation for clear, credible evidence. Through the SAGA process (Start with a story, Ask a question, Gather evidence, Act on your findings), this book guides readers in turning meaningful experiences into measurable insights without losing heart or humanity.

Using real-world examples and accessible tools, practitioners learn how to observe human and animal behavior, gather useful data, evaluate programs, monitor wellness, and communicate findings with confidence. By blending story with science, this book strengthens professional credibility, supports animal welfare, and invites practitioners to contribute to the growing evidence base of the field – one story at a time.

Angela K. Fournier, PhD, LP, is a professor, psychologist, anthrozoologist, researcher, and author specializing in equine-assisted services and the science of human-animal interaction.

Elizabeth A. Letson, MS, LPCC, is the founder of Eagle Vista Ranch & Wellness Center. She is a counselor, researcher, instructor, and author specializing in equine-assisted psychotherapy, learning, and coaching.

"*Bringing Science to Our Stories in Animal-Assisted Services* beautifully demonstrates that storytelling and science are not opposites – they're partners. With engaging examples and practical tools, this book empowers animal-assisted practitioners to ground their work in evidence while honoring the lived experiences that make it so powerful. This is a tremendous resource for our field."

Taylor Chastain Griffin, PhD, *executive director, Association of Animal-Assisted Intervention Professionals (AAAIP)*

"As a social worker, psychotherapist, and provider of equine-assisted services, I have witnessed countless experiences of healing that need to be measured in more than words alone. This book finally gives us a practical way to show what we know to be true: animals help people heal. It blends powerful stories with meaningful data, offering practitioners a roadmap to document outcomes, advocate for programs, and share our work with credibility. This book is a valuable resource for clinicians, researchers, and organizations committed to advancing the evidence base for animal-assisted services."

Rebecca Brown, MSW, RSW,
author of Break Free from Burnout

"This book bridges knowledge and real-world application and has taken the complex subject of data analysis and made it clear, practical, and immediately usable. By using story to close the gap between understanding and action, the authors have turned something intimidating into something empowering. I'm excited to put these insights into practice."

Lynn Moore, MA, LADC, *founder and CEO of Acres for Life Therapy and Wellness Center*

Bringing Science to Our Stories in Animal-Assisted Services

A Practitioner's Guide to Blending Anecdotes and Evidence

Angela K. Fournier and Elizabeth A. Letson

Routledge
Taylor & Francis Group
NEW YORK AND LONDON

Designed cover image: Cover photo by Jennifer Laitala, featuring Crackerjack and Peaches

First published 2027
by Routledge
605 Third Avenue, New York, NY 10158

and by Routledge
4 Park Square, Milton Park, Abingdon, Oxon, OX14 4RN

Routledge is an imprint of the Taylor & Francis Group, an informa business

ISBN: 978-1-041-07385-7 (hbk)
ISBN: 978-1-041-07382-6 (pbk)
ISBN: 978-1-003-64025-7 (ebk)

DOI: 10.4324/9781003640257

Typeset in Palatino
by KnowledgeWorks Global Ltd.

Access the support material at: www.bringingsciencetoourstories.com

This book is dedicated to the practitioners working where story and science meet. To those who witness meaningful change and feel curious about how it happens. To those who trust intuition and welcome evidence. To those who hold compassion and rigor side by side. May your questions stay alive. May you notice and measure what matters. And may you continue honoring the human and animal partners whose shared stories shape this work.

Contents

List of Figures

List of Tables

About the Authors

Angela K. Fournier, PhD, LP, holds a PhD in clinical psychology and works as a professor in the Department of Psychology at Bemidji State University. She is a licensed psychologist in Minnesota and certified in psychotherapy and learning incorporating horses. Dr. Fournier is the director of the Humanimal Interaction Laboratory. Her research interests are in human-animal interaction broadly, with specific interests in measurement and theory development in animal-assisted services, impacts of human-animal interaction on animal welfare, and mental health and well-being of those who work with animals (e.g., practitioners, shelter workers, etc.).

Elizabeth (Liz) Letson, MS, LPCC, holds a Master of Science in counseling psychology and is a licensed professional clinical counselor in Minnesota. Liz is the founder of Eagle Vista Ranch & Wellness Center, a private practice in Bemidji, MN. She specializes in equine-assisted psychotherapy, learning, and coaching, with a particular focus on supporting resilience in helping professionals. She is an adjunct instructor in the Department of Psychology at Bemidji State University. As a scientist–practitioner in animal-assisted services, she collaborates on studies, co-authors scholarship, and leads the translation of scholarly work for everyday practice.

Credits

Cover

Cover photo by Jennifer Laitala

Photographs

Photographs in this book were taken by the authors, unless otherwise noted. Images have been selected and, when necessary, adapted to protect the privacy and confidentiality of clients and participants. In some cases, scenes have been recreated for this purpose. Photographs accompanying field stories were provided by the authors or by contributing practitioners and are used with permission.

Field Stories

Several field stories, with accompanying photographs, were provided by practitioners for inclusion in this book:

Field Story 3 and Figure 3.1 provided by Tracy Parthun
Field Story 4 and Figure 4.1 provided by Glenna Wilson and Sarah Allen
Field Story 7 provided by Ashley Fullerton
Field Story 9 and Figure 9.1 provided by Quinci Schmidt and Caleb Scherber
Field Story 11 and Figure 11.1 provided by Lori Brama

Use of Artificial Intelligence (AI)

ChatGPT (OpenAI, GPT-5.3) was used as a tool for idea exploration and language improvement. All content was written and finalized by the authors. No AI-generated or manipulated images or figures were used.

Acknowledgments

Writing this book has been a deeply meaningful and rewarding journey. We are grateful to everyone at Routledge for the opportunity, guidance, and care that carried this project from proposal to publication. We extend our sincere thanks to Anna Moore for championing this book, thoughtfully shepherding us through the review and writing process, and offering steady encouragement along the way. We also thank the production team for their precision, expertise, and dedication in transforming our ideas, stories, and data into this finished work.

We are profoundly grateful to the practitioners who generously shared their field stories: Sarah Anderson, Lori Brama, Ashley Fullerton, Tracy Parthun, Caleb Scherber, Quinci Schmidt, and Glenna Wilson. Thank you for the extraordinary work you do alongside your animal partners and for trusting us with your stories. We are honored to include them and hold them with deep respect.

We extend sincere thanks to Rebecca Brown, Taylor Chastain Griffin, and Lynn Moore, who generously reviewed drafts and offered endorsements. Your thoughtful feedback and support helped strengthen this work.

To the animal partners of Eagle Vista Ranch & Wellness Center (EVR) – Crackerjack, Peaches, Pumpkin, Superman, King, Prince, Elvis, Buckwheat, Montana, Dakota, Cleo, Tilly, Miss Kitty, Sonic, Maverick, Anders, Bekka, Teddy, Red, Midnight, Bruce, Bronco, Aksel, Moose, Buck, Luna, Hillary, Honey, Ruby, and Buddy – thank you. Most of you have lived and worked at the ranch; others traveled there to participate in this work. Each of you welcomed guests, remained wholly yourselves, and shared your world with patience, honesty, and grace. Your presence shaped the story of this book.

To the many EVR clients, thank you for your trust, courage, and willingness to step into the pasture. Some inspired specific field cases; all deepened our understanding of animal-assisted services and sparked important questions.

We are grateful to the EVR employees and volunteers whose dedication sustained this work. We offer special appreciation to Jennifer Laitala, who has supported EVR from its earliest days as an equine specialist, photographer, animal caretaker, colleague, and friend. Special thanks to Tammy Schotzko, who has provided invaluable help with organization, program development, and marketing over the years. To Julia Montebello, Sharon Cooper, and Jill-Ann Walter – thank you for sharing your time, energy, and compassion. To Pamela St. Pierre, and Bailey Wethern - thank you for helping us better serve Indigenous community members and for leading important ceremonies honoring the animals' lives, health, and spirit. Miigwech.

This book grew from a longstanding collaboration between Bemidji State University and EVR. That partnership created the space where stories, science, clients, students, nature, and animals come together.

We have been fortunate to work with many college students over the years, which has shaped and inspired our work. To the psychology students who completed research projects and internships at the ranch: Kylie DeGrote, Megan French, Ally Gould, Joy Hanson, Kelli Hayes, Bekah Huff, Emma Pasiuk, Lauren Proels, Marybeth Wilkes, Lori Winston, Marissa Winterlin, Gracy Yang, Ashley Fullerton, and Shianne Judge. Thank you for showing up for both the human participants and the animals. Your work left something meaningful behind. To the Bemidji State University students who served as research assistants and participants, thank you for your time, care, curiosity, and respectful engagement. We are especially grateful to Dr. Emma Pasiuk. Watching your growth from learner to collaborator has been a joy. Your insights and contributions have enriched this work immeasurably.

We gratefully acknowledge community partners, referral sources, and collaborators, including Beltrami County, Bemidji School District, Bemidji State University, Boys & Girls Club of the Bemidji Area, Cass Lake-Bena Schools, Evergreen Youth & Family Services, Face It Together, Hope House, Leech Lake Tribal College, North Homes Children & Family Services, Northwest Minnesota

Foundation, Northwest Technical College, Northwoods Battered Women's Shelter, Oshki Manidoo Center, Peacemaker Resources, Red Lake Family & Children's Services, Red Lake MARS Program, Red Lake Nation College, Sanford Health and Behavioral Health, Stellher Human Services, United Way of Bemidji, Voyageurs Expeditionary School, White Earth Circle Back Center, Trek North High School, and Women's Wellbriety.

To our colleagues in the Psychology Department at Bemidji State University, thank you for your encouragement, curiosity, and support of this work.

Finally, we thank the practitioners, training organizations, students, and readers who continue to ask better questions, listen carefully to animals, and blend stories with evidence. This work moves forward because of you.

For Those Who Shaped Angela's Story

To Liz Letson, my co-author, collaborator, and dear friend, this work exists because of you. Your openness in inviting me into the equine-assisted field – not only as a scholar but as a practitioner and partner – made this book possible long before we began writing it. Over the past decade, our shared curiosity, conversations, questions, and reflections have shaped these pages. Thank you for your trust, generosity, and willingness to examine both successes and struggles. You have taught me what cannot be learned from books alone. Our partnership has been one of the great privileges of my professional life.

To Justin, my strongest supporter and steady anchor, thank you for the pep talks, honest feedback, patient listening, and for giving me the time and space to "horse around" and to write. You also help me maintain balance, reminding me – gently and often – that meaningful work is sustained not only by effort but by rest, laughter, and perspective.

To my son, Bleu, watching you grow into a kind, thoughtful, and curious young man has been the great joy of my life. Your love of animals, nature, and creative exploration continually inspires me. To Ray, sharing our home with you during this season of writing broadened my horizons and filled our home with laughter, curiosity, and joy. You are forever our Familienmitglied.

To my parents, Gary and Nancy Krom. Caring for animals and for nature is part of who I am because of you. You taught me responsibility, respect, and wonder for the living world. To my brother, Bryan, I have come to appreciate the ways you influenced my life. Your pride in me and my work continues to encourage me. You remain forever part of my story.

To Jack and Alice Fournier, I remain grateful for the love and care you both showed for animals and people, which continue to inspire me. To extended family, near and far, thank you for the many ways you have shaped my life and work.

To my dear mentors and colleagues, Dr. Thomas Berry and Dr. E. Scott Geller, thank you for your training, guidance, and lasting influence on how I think about behavior, observation, and science.

To close friends – Karen Little, Lisa Sheppard, Kelli England, Sarah Cronin, and Chana Monda – thank you for your laughter, encouragement, and grounding presence.

For Those Who Shaped Liz's Story

First and foremost, I acknowledge Dr. Angela Fournier. What began as a professor–student relationship grew into a deeply valued partnership and friendship. Working side by side in animal-assisted services, sharing curiosity, questions, and learning over time, has been one of the great privileges of my professional life. It is both an honor and a joy to co-author this book together.

To my husband, Tom, thank you for your patience, steadiness, and unwavering support. Your encouragement, understanding, and belief in this work sustain both my efforts and my spirit. To my sons and their families – Jake, Dana, and Miles; Donny, Morgan, Dean, and Kate – thank you for your love and encouragement. You remain a beautiful source of joy and inspiration in my life. What was once a "pipe dream" became a reality through the support that surrounded me.

I gratefully acknowledge my parents, Earle and Mariann Dickinson. Though they are no longer here, their guidance and influence continue to shape who I am and how I move through the world. Their tolerance for a household filled with animals allowed me to learn early on, and often vicariously, about human-animal relationships.

To my sister, Dianne Hoffbeck, and her husband, Dr. Steve Hoffbeck, thank you for your editorial support, thoughtful feedback, and encouragement throughout this process. Dianne, I am especially grateful for your contributions as a co-facilitator in equine-assisted sessions over the years. To my extended family and friends, thank you dearly for your support over the years.

To Ron and Linda Olson, thank you. Ron, thank you for introducing me to the quiet art of natural horsemanship – teaching me to listen first, to lead with softness, and to trust the language of the horse. "Be as gentle as possible, but as firm as necessary" remains a guiding mantra.

To Jennifer Laitala, thank you for your dedication, expertise, and tireless advocacy for animal welfare. Your care and commitment have strengthened both the ranch and the lives of the animals who call it home.

I express my appreciation to Dr. Gib Mouser, DMV, and farrier Dick Leonhardt for your consistent, skilled, and compassionate care. Thank you to Lia Sader for your guidance, support, and wisdom in caring for our equine partners, especially in difficult end-of-life decisions.

I extend sincere appreciation to leadership and mental fitness coach Lora Newman, and to the E3A Organization, for your leadership, trust, and continued support of this work and the broader field.

Finally, I thank God for the nudges that led me down this path and for the steady guidance that continues to sustain this work.

Part I
Start with a Story

1

Bringing Science to Our Stories in Animal-Assisted Services

Let's Start with a Story

We begin this chapter, and every chapter, with a story. We start with story because as practitioners we have the good fortune of collecting beautiful stories of the ways in which animals help people. We, the authors, often share our work through stories and we're guessing you do too. So, here's a story to get us started.

Field Story 1: Horses Help with Recovery

This is a story about how two horses – Crackerjack and King helped a young man change the trajectory of his recovery journey. A few years ago, we were working with a client we'll call Charlie who was in recovery from drug addiction. Charlie had been progressing on his recovery journey for two years but had experienced several relapses. He was having difficulty understanding why he kept relapsing and was beginning to feel stuck. His therapist referred him to equine-assisted psychotherapy, to see if doing something different could help him get unstuck. The session we're sharing here included Charlie, Liz and Angela as co-facilitators, and Crackerjack and King. We were all in an outdoor round pen on a spring day in the north woods. The session began with Charlie greeting the horses and making some

DOI: 10.4324/9781003640257-2

initial observations. While sharing his thoughts about the horses with us, we noticed a pattern begin to emerge. When King walked by and got a bit too close, bumping into him, Charlie stepped back and moved away. A little while later, something similar happened with Crackerjack. He was walking by Charlie and very subtly got close and bumped into him. Again, Charlie responded by moving out of the way. These moments unfolded while he was sharing about his relapse prevention plan, which we noticed was rather passive. His plan was to try his best to stay clean and avoid risky situations, but he had difficulty identifying specific situations or strategies. When we asked him to elaborate, he couldn't. We wondered aloud whether the passive way Charlie interacted with the horses was connected to the experiences he was having in recovery.

Near the edge of the round pen, there was an empty rubber feed pan that had been left from an earlier activity. Charlie picked it up while we were talking and began holding it as he continued to share. As we observed this, we wondered together whether the pan might represent something important to him – his sobriety – and what he might notice as he held onto it while interacting with the horses. Charlie stepped toward the horses holding the pan. The horses noticed him moving with the pan and began to walk toward him. As they came closer, Charlie appeared uneasy. He set the pan down and stepped out of the round pen. The horses moved toward the pan and sniffed it.

We joined Charlie and talked about what had just happened. He shared that he felt scared and thought the horses might "run him over," so he put the pan down and left. As we continued talking, Charlie told us about a recent relapse. He described a visit from his brother who still used substances and offered him some. Charlie refused initially, but his brother persisted and eventually he gave in. When asked about another relapse, a similar pattern emerged – this time involving his father. Charlie started to understand a pattern – he had difficulty standing up to family members and this was putting him at risk for relapse. He wanted help to be more assertive with his father and brother. The three of us brainstormed how the horses could help Charlie work on being more assertive.

With this new insight, Charlie was interested in trying the activity again. This time, he chose to view the horses as people he associated with relapse and the pan as his sobriety. We set up the activity the same as before, but with this new symbolism – Charlie was working on being assertive, protecting his *sobriety* (pan) from his *father* (King) and *brother* (Crackerjack). Before re-entering the round pen, we talked about what it might look like to stand his ground, both with the horses and with his family. Charlie generated ideas – standing tall, staying present, making a clear decision not to give in, and asking for help if he needed it.

When Charlie returned to the round pen, something had shifted. He looked different than before. He was standing taller and had a serious, confident presence. The horses noticed him and began walking toward him. As they moved in, Charlie remained steady. When they got close, he raised the pan above his head and held his position. The horses slowly walked up to him, sniffed the pan, and then moved past him. This moment is illustrated in Figure 1.1.

He did it! Charlie had protected his *sobriety*. He was visibly energized – excited and proud – and spoke about feeling more confident. The experience helped him see his relapse pattern in a new

FIGURE 1.1 "Charlie" standing up to family pressures to use.

way and gave him a felt sense of what it might be like to respond differently. From there, he worked with his regular psychotherapist to develop a more assertive relapse prevention plan, including strategies for handling family pressure.

We love this story because it highlights the unique way that engaging with animals can help us see things differently. It's also a great description of what equine-assisted psychotherapy might look like – clients in an equine environment working on therapeutic goals. Because it is interesting and descriptive, we often use this story to describe our work. To enhance the story's impact, we usually follow it up with some science. We share about the evidence we have gathered to find out how often the kind of symbolism employed in this session – horses representing important parts of clients' lives – occurs, and whether there are patterns in the kinds of things horses symbolize for clients. We gathered evidence by asking clients after sessions to rate on a ten-point scale, from *"not at all"* to *"completely"* how much they agree with the statement, *"The horses represented something in my life."* For example, Charlie may have written something like what you see in Figure 1.2. We can see the rating scale gives us two pieces of information or data. We get a number indicating quantity – *how much* horses represented something – 7. We also get information about *how* horses represented something – the horses were symbols for family members. After gathering this type of data over time from many different participants, we found some patterns. Scores ranged from 0 to 10 and the average rating was 6.41. The most common ratings were 0, 5, and 10. This is helpful

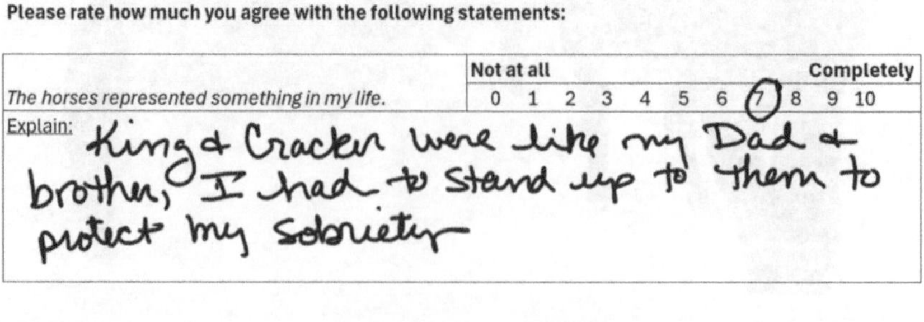
Please rate how much you agree with the following statements:

	Not at all ... Completely
The horses represented something in my life.	0 1 2 3 4 5 6 (7) 8 9 10

Explain: King & Cracker were like my Dad & brother, I had to stand up to them to protect my sobriety

FIGURE 1.2 Rating scale created to learn about animal symbolism.

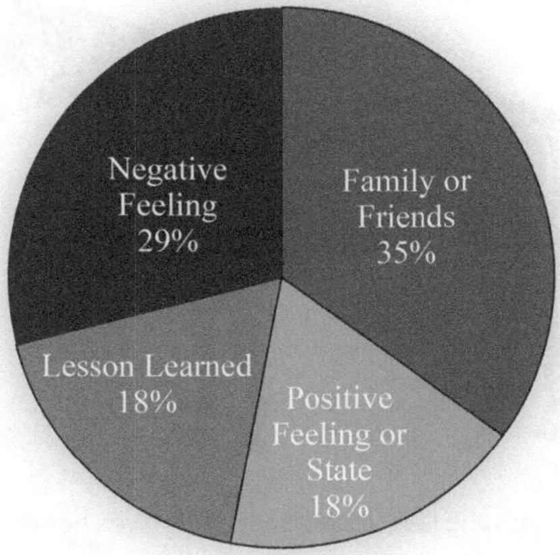

FIGURE 1.3 Pie chart showing what horses represented in equine-assisted sessions.

information to share with an audience. Sharing about your findings is even more impactful when illustrated with charts. Let's look at Figure 1.3.

This is a pie chart summarizing the written comments from our rating scale. When asked to explain their rating of *"horses represented something in my life,"* respondents wrote a variety of things, but there were four main themes. The horses most often represented a friend or family member, such as Charlie who saw King as his brother. A significant proportion also labeled horses as some kind of negative feeling or state during their session – *fear, anxiety, depression, guilt*. Tied for third place were lessons learned (e.g., *"I'm not alone"*) and positive feelings or states (e.g., *fun, peace, a bright future*). The pie chart in Figure 1.3 is a nice way to summarize the data so that readers can quickly get a snapshot of the information. The downside to a chart like that is we lose some of the interesting details. Family or friends made up 35% of responses, but the family and friends category is quite broad. It would be nice to have a little more detail. Therefore, we might complement the pie chart by pairing it with another visualization such as the infographic in Figure 1.4.

This is an image of a horse with textboxes of specific labels from our data. You can see that family and friends included *"Mom"* and *"Partner"*; positive feeling or state included *"fun"* and *"peace,"* and negative feeling or state included *"illness"* and *"grief."* An image like this is unique and interesting. It might

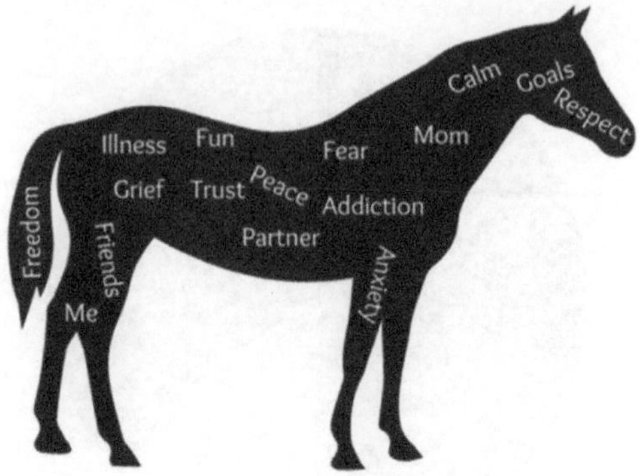

FIGURE 1.4 Infographic showing labels participants have given horses during equine-assisted sessions.

draw a viewer in, get their attention. It provides rich context for your work. The combination of all these images – the photo, rating scale, pie chart, infographic – can complement a powerful story. You end up giving a more detailed look into what you do, while also increasing your credibility because you have data to support what you are saying. We have found this combination of story and science – blending anecdotes and evidence – to be a powerful way of communicating our work to a variety of different audiences. Supporting a story with evidence has helped us secure grant funding, increase referrals, and acquire new partners for collaboration. That, in combination with requests we receive to help animal-assisted practitioners with the *what*, *when*, and *how* of measuring their work, has led us to write this book.

If you would like to read more about this data we've described, you can read the journal article where we published the findings. Reading the article will give you more background information on equine-assisted services and specifically why it makes sense to ask about horses serving as symbols for participants. The article will also provide more details on the findings, the study's limitations, and our recommendations for future research. The level of information we have provided here is sufficient to make our point, but if you're interested in the finer details and you'd like to get into the weeds, so to speak, reading the article would be a good step. Information on the article – *Human-Animal Interaction and Metaphor in*

Equine-Assisted Psychotherapy (Fournier et al., 2018) – is provided in the Bibliography at the end of the chapter. You can type the title into your browser and find the publication online. This example illustrates one way story and science can work together. Zooming out, it's helpful to consider how story functions more broadly across the animal-assisted services field.

The Role of Story in Our Field

Within the field of animal-assisted services, story appears in several forms. Some frameworks use story implicitly or explicitly as a facilitation strategy within sessions, while others describe story as a central mechanism of change. For example, equine-assisted story transformation theory (Esposito & Fournier, 2023) proposes that interactions with horses help clients recognize, explore, and revise personal narratives as part of the therapeutic process. This idea aligns with broader narrative perspectives in psychotherapy (White & Epston, 1990). This approach highlights the important role that story can play in how change unfolds during animal-assisted work.

Story also plays a significant role at the practitioner level. Practitioners routinely use stories and anecdotes to describe what happens in sessions, to share their work with others, and to make sense of their own experiences in practice. These stories often inform decisions about programming, facilitation choices, or perceptions of effectiveness. This reliance on story is important; it reflects the relational, experiential nature of animal-assisted work.

Stories alone can be incomplete, reflecting well-documented limits of intuitive judgment and narrative reasoning (Bruner, 1991; Kahneman, 2011). Anecdotes capture meaningful moments, but they do not always reveal patterns, boundaries, or alternative explanations. The focus of this book is on this practitioner-level use of story – helping practitioners add evidence to the equation so that the stories they already tell can better support learning, decision-making, and communication through systematic observation, measurement, and informed reflection.

Purpose of the Book

This book is a practical, accessible guide to help you build the science-based skills needed to make data-driven decisions in your animal-assisted work – by thoughtfully blending compelling anecdotes with evidence. If you're a helping professional in fields like mental health, education, or coaching and you partner with animals in your work – such as animal-assisted therapies, learning, or recreation – this book is for you. We address a common gap: you are already skilled in your discipline and trained to work with animals, and you appreciate the importance of making decisions based on experience and data-based evidence, and perhaps you need tools to collect, analyze, and interpret data effectively.

This book fills a gap by teaching you, dear reader, how to combine the emotional power of your stories with concrete evidence, creating a more credible and persuasive way to illustrate the impact of your work. Through the SAGA method (Start with a story, Ask a good question, Gather your evidence, Act on your findings), the book will guide you through a dynamic, repeatable framework for data-driven practice. Figure 1.5 illustrates the SAGA steps – a path from story to data-driven action.

Inspired by the word "saga," meaning a long, detailed story of heroic achievements (Merriam-Webster, n.d.), this method

FIGURE 1.5 Steps of the SAGA process.

begins with a story, an engaging anecdote to inspire curiosity. It then progresses to asking empirical questions, gathering data through observations and self-reports, and analyzing and acting on the findings. Importantly, the method includes taking informed action based on the evidence, ensuring that you not only *understand* your results but also *apply them meaningfully*. The process comes full circle by revisiting and sharing your story – now enriched with evidence and actionable insights, transforming it into a modern-day saga of impactful, data-driven work. By linking stories to evidence, you can elevate your work and engage stakeholders in a way that is both relatable and credible.

> Each saga is an evolving story, shaped by the questions you ask and the evidence you gather.

Throughout this book, we also use *saga* to describe the ongoing data story for a particular focus area. For example, a Wellness saga tracks the well-being of the animal–handler team over time. Superman's saga might document patterns related to one specific animal partner – a horse named Superman who you will meet soon enough. Charlie's saga could capture a client's journey across sessions.

We – the authors, Dr. Angela Fournier and Ms. Elizabeth (Liz) Letson – are scientist-practitioners (Belar & Perry, 1992), meaning we are helping professionals who are trained in scientific method and apply research findings to our professional practices. This book draws on our extensive backgrounds in research, practice, and teaching in the field of animal-assisted services. With over a decade of providing services, teaching, conducting research, and presenting at national and international conferences, we blend inspiring stories from our practice with empirical research to model the blending of anecdotes and evidence. This guidebook offers a critical toolkit for professionals like yourself who seek to elevate practice, strengthen communication with stakeholders, and advance the field of animal-assisted services by combining stories with science. Speaking of stories, we'd like to share a bit of our own story so you can get to know us and understand why we wrote this book.

Our Stories

Angela's Saga

My (Angela) saga starts on a small hobby farm in rural North Dakota. I grew up with my parents and brother, as well as several pets – dogs, cats – and many farm animals – chickens, geese, cows, pigs, and a horse-goat pair that I've heard stories about. Growing up in the country, surrounded by nature and animals, I developed an early appreciation and respect for our furry and feathered relatives. I've had animal friends for as long as I can remember. I've always been curious about livestock and wild animals, loving the rare opportunity to connect with a squirrel or a cow. I was fortunate to do well in school and was especially interested in science courses, curious about animals, nature, and how the living world works. I was the first person in my immediate family to attend college. I studied psychology as an undergraduate, kind of by accident. I was exploring allied health fields and took several psychology classes. A wonderful psychology professor – Dr. Thomas Berry – introduced me to the *science* of psychology, inviting me to help with research. He encouraged me to apply to graduate school. I was fortunate again to be accepted into the clinical psychology doctorate program at Virginia Tech to work with Dr. E. Scott Geller, a leader in applying psychology to promote healthy people and places. Both Dr. Berry and Dr. Geller are behavioral scientists, focusing on observable behavior – what we can *see* people and animals do. They taught me to be a researcher – to ask good questions, to gather data that can answer my questions, to analyze and interpret my findings, and to act on those findings. While I was conducting research with Dr. Geller, I was learning clinical psychology theory and developing psychotherapy skills. I was fortunate to conduct my dissertation research on an animal-assisted service within the prison system. Upon completion of my PhD, I began work as a university professor. I have been a professor in the Department of Psychology at Bemidji State University since 2008.

In 2013, an enthusiastic graduate student in our Master of Counseling program – Liz Letson, co-author of this book – was interested in writing her thesis on equine-assisted services. She knew I had done some animal-related work and asked me to serve on her thesis committee. She told me fascinating stories about growing up with horses and how spending time with horses had been healing for herself and others. As an animal person, I loved the stories and believed in the healing power of the animals. As a researcher and someone with very little experience with horses, I was curious about just *how* horses help people heal. To learn more, I attended a training on equine-assisted psychotherapy and learning. The training involved having my own experience with equine-assisted learning. I had a very powerful experience and witnessed other trainees having experiences as well. I came away from the training even more curious about the process. As a researcher, I was thinking about what to measure to better understand the process. As a clinician, I wanted to develop my skills and become an actual practitioner of equine-assisted services. I completed certification in equine-assisted services and began working with Liz. Over the next ten years we would work together on many projects, some as clinicians, some as researchers, and some as course instructors. I'm grateful for this saga. These experiences have led me here – to writing this book in support of the wonderful work you and your animal partners do.

Liz's Saga

I (Liz) grew up in Bemidji, MN, in the country, lucky to have horses, cats, dogs, rabbits, parakeets, hamsters, gerbils, guinea pigs, goldfish, etc., as a child. These experiences with animals of all types would shape me and the future work I do as an animal-assisted practitioner. When I was very young, I dreamt of becoming a veterinarian. But in actuality, I worked as a flight attendant and then substitute teacher, in addition to being a wife and raising my two sons. Through it all, I was connected to animals; horses, dogs, and cats have been a constant in my life. In 2009 I heard about equine-assisted services – incorporating horses into psychotherapy and learning. Since then, I have worked as an adjunct psychology instructor, licensed professional clinical counselor, equine specialist, author, and healer, incorporating animals into my private practice. Throughout this journey, Angela and I created the Human-Animal Interaction

Scale (introduced in Chapter 8) to help understand the power of animals in human transformation and healing. This journey has been dynamic, challenging, and rewarding. I went from being research-phobic initially to being a believer. Through trial and error, I have found animal-assisted services to be my area of expertise. You see, being in nature with animals, I can truly connect with my inner self. This has forged the foundation for my work in the human-animal arena.

Our Saga as Partners in Animal-Assisted Services and Science

At the time of this writing, we (Angela and Liz) have been working together for nearly 15 years, partnering our organizations – Eagle Vista Ranch & Wellness Center, a private practice in the community providing animal-assisted counseling, learning, and coaching and the Humanimal Interaction Laboratory, a team of faculty and student researchers in the Department of Psychology at Bemidji State University – to make a positive impact on the animal-assisted services field. Together, we have been productive, serving clients and students, receiving grants, conducting research, presenting at conferences, and publishing our work. The reason we've been successful is that we have a unique combination of strengths – Liz working primarily as a practitioner and being a great connector and storyteller and Angela working primarily as a teacher/researcher, curious about how animal-assisted services help people and how to understand it better through science.

We are both practitioners – we provide animal-assisted services – and researchers – we conduct research to inform the field. We've applied our strengths when presenting together at conferences – Liz will tell a story about a session out at the ranch, an anecdote that illustrates a process or outcome, and Angela will share about data we collected at the ranch that helps us understand that story. These two things combined – a story about a clinical case and data relevant to the story – create a compelling experience. The combination of story and science draws people in, helps them understand our work, and gives them faith in our competence.

When we present our work, we always have both researchers and practitioners who ask questions, who want to know how to do what we do. We have been mostly approached by practitioners – people providing animal-assisted services. Like you, they are passionate about partnering with animals to provide health, healing, and happiness for people in need. They appreciate the need for research on the field, and they are curious about science-related topics. They understand the importance of measuring outcomes to find out if what they are doing is working. They want to support science by providing information and data on what they do. But they are not scientists themselves, and they do not necessarily know animal-assisted scientists to work with. They ask great questions, like *"What should I measure?"*, *"How can I show others that this works?"*, and *"Have there been any studies on what I'm doing that I can share with my board/agency/potential clients?"*

It's clear that individual practitioners and clients, as well as the animal-assisted field in general, would benefit from more user-friendly science-based resources. And so, here we are! This guidebook is our way of sharing what we think has worked well in our partnership – telling *effective* stories and *gathering and acting on relevant data*. We are both teachers as well, with a combined 35 years of teaching experience. So, dear reader, you are in good hands. We welcome you on this learning and practicing journey with us.

After reading and working through this guidebook, you will have the skills to share your anecdotes in the most effective way. From selecting the right story for your purpose to telling the story in the most interesting and compelling way, you'll come away from this book a better storyteller and ambassador of your work. The other key set of skills you will learn is data-driven practices, which is a fancy way of saying you'll learn to ask good questions, answer those questions by making your own observations, act on your findings, and ethically share your data story with others.

The Field's Evolving Evidence Saga

Up to this point, we have focused on individual stories – tales of clients, animals, practitioners, and our own journeys as scientist-practitioners. Each of these stories matters. But none of them exist in isolation. Just as a saga is a long, unfolding story made up of many chapters, the evidence base of animal-assisted services is an evolving story shaped by many contributions over time. Each question the field asks – about outcomes, processes, animal welfare, or fit – develops gradually as different forms of evidence are added.

Some of that evidence comes from formal research studies conducted by universities or research teams. Other evidence comes from practitioners who systematically learn from their own work by noticing patterns, asking questions, and gathering data in real-world settings. Together, these forms of evidence shape the field's understanding. In this book, we use the word *saga* not only to describe individual data stories – such as a client's journey or an animal's wellness over time – but also to describe the broader, collective evidence story of animal-assisted services.

> The field's saga is not written all at once, and it is never finished. It grows through accumulation, refinement, and shared inquiry.

The SAGA method you will learn in this book is designed to support that process. Early chapters focus on shaping individual data stories. Later chapters show how those stories connect to the field's evolving evidence base. **We intentionally use the phrase *practitioner–science evidence base* to emphasize that evidence in animal-assisted services often begins in practice and is strengthened, refined, and tested through science.** When practitioners thoughtfully blend anecdotes and evidence, their work does more than inform individual decisions – it becomes part of the field's evolving story. Later in the book, we return to this idea and make it more explicit. For now, we invite you to hold this perspective as you move forward: **the skills you are about to learn are not only tools for your own practice, but ways of contributing to something larger**.

How to Use This Book

As a practitioner's guide, this book is designed to be user-friendly and very applied. Our goal is to give you the information you need and help you develop and apply skills to strengthen your animal-assisted work.

We begin each chapter with the first step of the SAGA method. We start with a story and then apply it to the topic of the chapter. Then we introduce relevant background content and teach a new skill. Chapters end with a recommended activity, where you apply the chapter content to take the next step in the data-driven process.

The book is separated into four parts, based on the four steps of the SAGA process. Part I – Start with a Story – includes Chapters 1–3, which together will give you tools to strengthen your stories. Here in Chapter 1, we have given you an example of blending anecdotes with evidence and introduced you to the SAGA method. Chapter 2 is all about storytelling. We review content on writing and storytelling to help you refine the stories and anecdotes you tell about your work. In Chapter 3 we distinguish between three processes where data are gathered – assessment, evaluation, and research. After reading the chapter you will be clearer on the differences between these three processes and know how they apply to your work. Ultimately this chapter will help you determine which data story you are telling.

Part II is all about asking good questions. In Chapter 4 we discuss the importance of asking empirical questions about our work and then help you develop SMART questions. In Chapter 5 you will learn terms and concepts that are essential for asking good questions, as well as using the language of data-driven work. We want to help you walk the walk *and* talk the talk of data-driven animal-assisted services.

Part III is the heart of the book, where we cover evidence-gathering skills. We begin with Chapter 6, which covers gathering evidence through behavioral observation. You will learn about and practice naturalistic observation. Then Chapter 7 covers systematic observation – selecting specific behaviors to observe and record. Chapter 8 names the concept of human-animal interaction as a key variable to measure in animal-assisted work. We introduce a standardized tool for measuring human-animal interaction and share how to use it in your work. Chapter 9 addresses self-report data – journals, inventories/questionnaires, tests, and interviews. We cover deciding what to measure, how to find a measurement tool, and answer the popular question, *"should I create my own test or survey?"*.

Part IV will help you analyze and act on your findings. First, you will learn basic data analysis in Chapter 10. This includes instructions for simple summaries and comparisons that anyone can do. We also provide guidance on using your data analysis results to make informed decisions on your work. Then in Chapter 11 you learn how to share your data story with others. We cover some basic tips on effective written and oral communication and then dive into technical messaging through data visualization. Chapter 12 covers the ethics of working with data. These are concepts that you are likely familiar with through your animal-assisted work – confidentiality, integrity, resolving ethical dilemmas – applied specifically to working with data. Chapter 13 addresses gathering evidence related to the wellness of your animal-handler team. We define and give examples of animal welfare and wellness and connect you with published standards for the field (e.g., IAHAIO, 2018). Then we provide examples of data-gathering related to animal-handler wellness. Finally, Chapter 14 ties everything together, summarizing the content, providing a clear example of blending anecdotes and evidence, and offering an invitation to join a larger SAGA movement.

For Current and Future Practitioners

We've written this book for people in the animal-assisted services field. This includes professionals currently incorporating animal partners in their work, professionals working in their scope of practice and thinking about incorporating animals, facilities who host animal-handler teams, as well as students who plan to provide animal-assisted services in the future. Because this is a wide audience with varying levels of experience and training, we have purposely written the book at a novice level, keeping the language and concepts beginner friendly. In doing so, we acknowledge that some might find sections or chapters unnecessary for them. In that case, feel free to skip to the parts of the book most relevant for you. You can always go back later to pick up material you skipped if you find that you need it. For anyone who considers themselves brand new to data-driven work, we recommend starting at the beginning and working your way through each chapter.

Adapted Stories

Chapters are formatted to begin with a story relevant to animal-assisted services, then introduce a data-driven topic, followed by an activity for you to complete in order to apply the material to your work. The stories we share are loosely based on real animal-assisted cases. Identifying details have been changed to protect privacy and confidentiality of the humans involved. The names of animal partners have been kept, with their caretaker's permission, in order to honor the important work they have done. Real data that we share are all de-identified and in aggregate; we never share individual data on people we have worked with. When sharing about published data, we provide the citation at the end of the chapter for anyone who wants to learn more about that particular data story.

Language Matters

Every field has its own language, and an important part of data-driven practices is being able to use technical terminology. Therefore, each chapter includes key terms or phrases you can use in your practice. We encourage you to add this language to your professional repertoire and share it with your colleagues. For easy reference, we include a Glossary at the back of the book.

> The way we talk about our work shapes how we think and act.

A Working Companion

You will get the most out of the book if you read the chapters *and* do the activities. Rather than putting this book on your bookshelf, we suggest you keep it on your desk or in your backpack, saddlebag, or vehicle and think of it as a working companion. Once you've been through the book once, completing the activities, it should be a reference for you going forward. Each time you decide you need evidence to help tell your story or make a decision, pull it out and use it to get ideas, refresh your skills, and tell a strong story by blending anecdotes and evidence. To set the stage for the next chapter, ask yourself – what drives you and your work? What motivates you to provide animal-assisted services, and perhaps what made you pick up this book? Below are just some of the possible motivators for animal-assisted professionals:

- Passion for the work
- Passion and appreciation for animals
- Wanting to do good and make a difference
- Wanting to serve your community
- Wanting to solve a problem
- Intuition

With these motivators in mind, think about the reason(s) you picked up this book. Are you hoping to address a concern you have, or answer curiosity? Perhaps you need numbers to go along with your stories when pitching your services to new clients or funders. Whatever the reason, we know that bringing science to your stories will enhance your work. We're excited to go on this journey with you, and we thank you for stepping up to learn data-driven practices.

Companion resources, templates, and updates are available online at www.bringingsciencetoourstories.com

Try It! Prepare to SAGA

To get started on your SAGA journey, answer the following questions. We recommend recording your answers somewhere – start creating a SAGA file, notebook, or journal. This step is important; set an intention for why and how you will use the book. Like Charlie creating a more active plan for success, step into the pasture alongside us, knowing where you stand on your story–science journey – and begin your SAGA work with clarity and purpose.

1. What is your goal in reading this book? Think about what caused you to start reading this book, and has it changed since reading this introductory chapter?
2. Where are you on the story-science continuum, and where would you like to be?

3. What is your goal in learning about data-driven practices?
4. What might be some concerns you have or challenges you foresee in doing SAGA work?

Bibliography

Belar, C. D., & Perry, N. W. (1992). The national conference on scientist–practitioner education and training for the professional practice of psychology. *American Psychologist, 47*(1), 71–75. https://doi.org/10.1037/0003-066X.47.1.71

Bruner, J. (1991). The narrative construction of reality. *Critical Inquiry, 18*(1), 1–21. https://doi.org/10.1086/448619

Esposito, N., & Fournier, A. K. (2023). *How change happens in equine-assisted interventions: A theory of horses, humans, and psychotherapy.* Routledge.

Fournier, A. K. (2019). *Animal-assisted intervention: Thinking empirically.* Palgrave MacMillan.

Fournier, A. K., Letson, E., & Berry, T. D. (2017). *HAIS: Human-animal interaction scale and manual.* Angela Fournier.

Fournier, A. K., Letson, E., Berry, T. D., & Pasiuk, E. (2018). Human-animal interaction and metaphor in equine-assisted psychotherapy: Empirical support for the Eagala model. *Human-Animal Interactions, 6*(1), 47–63.

Hosey, G., Melfi, V., & Pankhurst, S. (Eds.) (2023). *The Routledge international handbook of human-animal interactions and anthrozoology.* Routledge.

International Association of Human-Animal Interaction Organizations (2018). *The IAHAIO definitions for animal-assisted intervention and guidelines for wellness of animals involved in AAI.* IAHAIO.

Kahneman, D. (2011). *Thinking, fast and slow.* Farrar, Straus and Giroux.

Kazin, A. E. (2008). Evidence-based treatment and practice: New opportunities to bridge clinical research and practice, enhance the knowledge base, and improve patient care. *American Psychologist, 63*(3), 146.

Letson, E. A. (2021). Scientist-practitioner approach: Harnessing the power of equine-assisted psychotherapy and animal-assisted interventions in private practice. In L. R. Kogan & P. Erdman (Eds.),

Career paths in human-animal interaction for social and behavioral scientists (pp. 153–155). Routledge.

McAdams, D. P. (2001). The psychology of life stories. *Review of General Psychology*, *5*(2), 100–122. https://doi.org/10.1037/1089-2680.5.2.100

Merriam-Webster. (n.d.). *Saga*. In *Merriam-Webster.com dictionary*. https://www.merriam-webster.com/dictionary/saga

Nisbett, R. E., & Ross, L. (1980). *Human inference: Strategies and shortcomings of social judgment*. Prentice Hall.

White, M., & Epston, D. (1990). *Narrative means to therapeutic ends*. W. W. Norton & Company.

Wood, W., Alm, K., Benjamin, J., Thomas, L., Anderson, D., Pohl, L., & Kane, M. (2021). Optimal terminology for services in the United States that incorporate horses to benefit people: A consensus document. *The Journal of Alternative and Complementary Medicine: Paradigm, Practice, and Policy Advancing Integrative Health*, *27*(1), 88–95.

2

Stories with Strength

Sharing Anecdotes and Evidence

Field Story 2: A Place to Start

It was late afternoon at our local youth and family services agency. At the time, Liz was working as a youth counselor and sometimes worked with her therapy dog Aksel – a calm, lumbering 175-pound Saint Bernard (pictured in Figure 2.1). Liz and Aksel were finishing up the day, and on the way out, they passed by the drop-in center. This is a space where young people could come without an appointment to receive help with food, housing, mental health, or other services.

That day, a young woman – whom we'll call Kaya – sat quietly in one of the chairs. She was new to the center. When staff asked her how they could help, she said she wasn't sure. She was quiet and seemed nervous, fidgeting and avoiding eye contact. As Liz and Aksel walked by, Kaya looked up. Her attention immediately shifted to Aksel. She stood, walked over, and asked if she could pet him. As she reached out, her demeanor changed. She smiled, her eyes lit up, and her voice became more animated. She asked simple questions at first – his name, his age, how big he was – and Aksel stood beside her, steady and calm. Liz paused. What had been a brief pass through the space became something special. She decided she and Aksel would stay a while.

Kaya moved to the floor beside Aksel, sitting close to him and continuing to pet him as they talked. The interaction slowed the

DOI: 10.4324/9781003640257-3

FIGURE 2.1 Aksel, a therapy dog, pictured with Liz's son Jake.
Source: Photo by Jennifer Laitala

moment down, beginning as small talk and gradually becoming something more. As she remained there, grounded next to Aksel, Kaya began to share pieces of her story. She had grown up in foster care and was now a young adult navigating unemployment, temporary housing, and food insecurity.

As the conversation unfolded, Liz introduced Kaya to a drop-in center staff member who joined them. Sitting together on the floor, with Aksel in the center, they began to talk about her situation. Kaya shared that she needed help but didn't know where to start. The staff member began sharing about the available resources. Kaya continued petting Aksel as she listened, asked questions, and shared more about her situation. She became more open to receiving services. She agreed to take the next step and scheduled a counseling session with Liz. In the weeks that followed, she returned for services and began making progress toward her goals.

This young woman had come in looking for help but was unsure how to begin. In a moment, Aksel's presence shifted the experience – creating a point of connection and making it easier to engage with Liz and the staff who could support her. It was a place to start.

This story highlights several ways an animal can assist in human services. Aksel's presence changed the conditions of the interaction – shifting attention and creating a point of connection. This made it easier for the young woman to engage, share her story, and take a first step toward getting help. Most importantly, Aksel helped her feel safe enough to share her needs with a helping professional and ask for help. How did he do it? We asked that same question in a study a few years back.

We asked dog-handler teams to answer some questions after individual dog visitation sessions (Fournier, 2019). Through Pet Partners, we were able to recruit 100 practitioners to complete over 700 reports, sharing what the animal did during an animal-assisted session. One of the questions we asked was how they (the animal handler) thought their dog helped the person they were visiting. People gave a range of responses, which fit into several categories.

The most common response, by quite a bit, was that the dog helped improve emotion in the client. For some visits, this meant the person felt calmer and more relaxed, while for others, the person seemed happier and more excited. Overall, we got the sense that dog visits helped people feel a little bit better for a little while. And feeling a little bit better is a pretty big deal, especially when someone is struggling with loneliness, fear, or physical pain. The dogs brought relief, brightening the people and places visited. This was true for dogs visiting hospitals, nursing homes, schools, and community centers.

Anecdote, Story, or Saga – Which Are You Telling?

The answer to the question above may be – all of them! If you are an animal-assisted professional and anything at all like us and the professionals we have worked with, you've had wonderful experiences witnessing your animal(s) helping others. We're willing to bet that sharing these experiences is an important part of the way you explain to others what you do. Giving examples of your experiences may be the way you describe your work to potential clients and funders, as well as community members, family, and friends. After all, animal-assisted work can mean many things. Some people have never heard of it, and many people have never experienced it firsthand. So, telling a story about a powerful experience you've had is a natural way to share what you do. And we humans are natural storytellers; we've been telling stories forever. In this chapter, we provide some clarity on different types of narrative and how they can come together to best communicate about animal-assisted work. First, let's learn some of the language, defined in Table 2.1. An **anecdote** is a short, amusing, or interesting story about a real incident or person, perhaps told to illustrate a point. For example:

> Last week, we were in the pasture providing equine-assisted learning to a group of high schoolers. The energy in the pasture was very calm. Participants were petting and brushing the horses while the horses soaked up the sun, almost falling asleep. Suddenly Aksel, a therapy dog who lives at the ranch, joined the session by chasing and barking at a bird outside of the pasture. Very quickly the energy of the group shifted, and the topic of the session changed from mindfulness to coping with change.

This is a good example of an anecdote. It's brief, factual, and useful in illustrating a point – in this case, that you never know what you're going to get when working with animals. In contrast, **stories** tend to be a bit more developed, can be fiction or non-fiction, and tend to have some key components like characters, setting, conflict, and resolution. In this book, we use the word

TABLE 2.1 Distinguishing between anecdote, story, and saga

Term	*Definition*	*Example*
Anecdote	Brief factual account of an event or observation, meant to illustrate a point	*"People are often surprised when Aksel, a St. Bernard, is kind and gentle. It leads to discussions of first impressions."*
Story	A longer, more developed narrative, with clearer structure, may be fiction or nonfiction	*"During one session with Aksel, a young woman looking for help was able to connect with him. It all started when Liz and Aksel…"*
Saga	An extended, often heroic, story focusing on a prolonged series of events	*"The story of Aksel and all of the clients he helped spans more than ten years…"*

story for the rich, lived accounts that draw us into this work – the moments that stay with us. We begin each chapter with one of these field stories. A **saga**, on the other hand, is a long, layered narrative that may span generations and show growth or transformation. We (Angela and Liz) think of our work bridging science and stories as a saga. If you have been doing animal-assisted work for years, you could think of the overall story of your work or business as a saga.

Ok, now we are going to shift gears away from terminology and toward strengthening your anecdotes and stories. In this chapter, we focus on stories as a way of communicating about practice, rather than on story as a facilitation strategy or mechanism of change within sessions. We do this by referring to the literature on stories and storytelling.

Stories Matter

Research indicates that storytelling is universal. Across time, space, and cultures, humans tell stories. We use stories to communicate our history, values, and beliefs. Many cultures have an origin story. For example, we live in northern Minnesota, the current and ancestral homeland of the Ojibwe and Dakota peoples. The Ojibwe creation story tells of the beginning of Turtle Island, otherwise referred to as North America. As Edward Benton-Banai, Ojibwe elder and scholar, writes in *The Mishomis*

Book (1988), the story of how Turtle Island came to be is more than a story. It is a cultural compass. Passed down from generation to generation, it teaches about humility, interdependence, and the sacredness of the earth. If you aren't already, become familiar with the origin stories relevant to you and your work – stories from your own heritage, the populations you serve, and the land on which you are located. Doing so will enrich your work and allow you to better serve your clients and community.

In his book The *Storytelling Animal: How Stories Make Us Human* (2012), Jonathan Gottschall discusses our inherent attention to and propensity to believe and even create stories. He makes the case, citing psychological research and cognitive science, that stories are essential to our understanding of the world. Whether it be tenets of the major world religions or scientific theories, information is communicated through stories. And that is because we think in stories. Stories make sense to us; we understand the world in terms of stories.

In his book *Storycraft: The Complete Guide to Writing Narrative Nonfiction*, Jack Hart (2021) summarizes literature on storytelling and brain research. He makes nine points on the importance of story, stating that: (1) story dominates human existence, as shown by the amount of time we spend watching television and other media, daydreaming, dreaming in our sleep, and storytelling, (2) human storytelling has ancient roots, with evidence dating back to cave drawings, (3) storytelling has clear survival value in hunter-gatherer societies, (4) the brain is hard-wired for story at a deep level, (5) mirror neurons in the brain echo emotions created by story, (6) young children organize play around storytelling, (7) characters are what motivates audience members to follow a story, (8) story is more important to maintaining audience interest than writing quality, and (9) we construct our own identities from the stories we tell about ourselves.

So, it makes sense that your natural inclination to share your animal-assisted work is through storytelling. Sharing examples of your experiences, in the form of storytelling, probably comes naturally to you, and listening to stories is a natural way for your stakeholders (i.e., audience) to learn about and get inspired by what you do.

What's Your Go-To Story?

Before learning some important content on stories, we'd like you to think of a story that you tell about your animal-related work. If you are not doing the work yet, think of a time when you experienced the power of animals firsthand. Maybe it was a childhood pet who got you through a difficult time, or maybe it was last week when you came home from work all stressed out. Whatever it is, bring that story to mind.

Next, think about the *reason* you share this story. Do you tell the story to describe or explain something? Do you mean to evoke a particular emotion or response in the listener? Why did you choose *that* story? We doubt it's the only story you could share about animals or your animal-assisted work. So why did you pick that one?

Finally, as far as you can tell, does the story have the effect you want? Maybe you share a story to entertain someone – is the story entertaining? Or perhaps you share a story to describe or explain your animal-assisted service – does the audience end up having a better picture or understanding of your work? Sometimes we tell a story to evoke emotion, increase curiosity, or sell an idea – does the story do those things? Maybe you haven't asked these questions before. That's ok. Take some time to reflect and answer the questions as best you can.

We believe answering these questions and reflecting on your storytelling is good practice; it will make your storytelling more intentional and effective. We are not here to tell you which story to share or why to share a particular story. You know what you're doing there. We want to validate your inclination to tell stories and help you do the *best possible job* of telling those stories.

In the next section, we share information about the key ingredients of stories and tips for telling a strong story. This section is helpful whether you are new to storytelling or are a master storyteller. If you're already a great storyteller and your stories are working well for you, keep doing what you're doing. Reading the rest of the chapter may validate why your stories are working so well. And perhaps you will learn ways to make your stories even stronger. On the other hand, if you think you could benefit from improving your storytelling skills, then this next section is especially important for you. Read it carefully and complete the activities. We want you to have some great stories to tell along with the supporting evidence you'll be collecting as you move through this book.

Key Ingredients

Because people are storytellers and people have been storytelling forever, some very smart folks have written about what makes a good story and how to deliver a story to be most effective. We summarize some of that work here. The bibliography at the end of the chapter lists additional resources in case you want to learn more than the basics we cover.

Hart (2021) describes the key ingredients of a story as (1) a sequence of events, (2) a sympathetic character, (3) a complication, and (4) a resolution. These are the key pieces or ingredients we mentioned earlier when distinguishing stories from anecdotes. We will spend a bit of time explaining these key pieces because each is important when fine-tuning the stories you share about your work.

A Sequence of Events + A Sympathetic Character +
A Complication + A Resolution

A Sequence of Events

Stories include a sequence of events, meaning several things happen and happen in a particular order. In this chapter's field case, first, Aksel and Liz were leaving the office, the young woman entered the drop-in center, seeming anxious and uncertain, then Liz and Aksel walked by and engaged with her, and so on. In the story you have recalled, what is the sequence of events? What happened first, second, etc.?

Characters

Stories have one or more characters who want something, are faced with challenges or difficulties to get it, overcome the challenges, and achieve the goal (or not, in which case they are overcome or defeated by it). In Hart's key ingredients, he calls for a sympathetic character, someone the audience can identify with and root for. We could also call this individual the protagonist, which is someone who makes things happen. Who are the characters in your story? Who is the protagonist, the one making things happen, or who the audience is rooting for? In the field cases we have shared with you so far, the recipient of the animal-assisted service was the main character or protagonist. The desired outcome of the service (e.g., help with relapse prevention, connecting an individual with important resources) was the goal. And engaging with the animal facilitated achieving the goal. This formula may fit many of the stories you tell about your animal-assisted work. Of course, the animal(s) you work with can be characters in any given story, and in many cases, an animal might be the protagonist.

Before you share your go-to story again, think about the character(s). Are there any details you've been leaving out that would change how an audience receives the story? Or details you have included but aren't necessary, or that take away from the story? Of course, communicating about our work ethically means we never share personal, identifying details of the people we serve. Finding the right level of detail, while changing identifying features to protect privacy and confidentiality, is an important skill.

A Complication, Problem, or Crisis

The third key ingredient is a complication, problem, or crisis. In stories about animal-assisted services, the reason for the service might be the clearest complication, problem, or crisis. A young man in recovery from addiction, trying to understand his relapse pattern. An emerging adult needing to get started with support services. A group of working mothers seeking help with burnout. A veteran adjusting to life after active duty. In clinical terms, we might call these the "presenting problem," the reason someone seeks services. The presenting problem is a good candidate for your story's complication, problem, or crisis. In many cases, our go-to stories are about an individual session. In that case, the crisis might be what we call the "peak" of the session - the moment when things shift or change.

Resolution

In the resolution phase, something happens so that the protagonist achieves the goal, the major problem is solved, or the complication of the story is somehow settled. In our stories of animal-assisted services, engaging with animals is key to the resolution. In Field Story 1, Charlie solved the mystery of his relapses by engaging with the horses and identifying key situations and behaviors. In Field Story 2, Aksel is a bridge between the young woman and the services she needs. Think back to your go-to story. How did the resolution happen? What is the clearest, most compelling way you can describe that resolution process?

Stories Have Structure

In addition to the key ingredients discussed so far, stories have structure. Their description of the setting, characters, and sequence of events tends to follow an arc with key points moving the characters from problem to solution, or from conflict or crisis to resolution. This is the place where you can do the most revision of your stories to make them as effective as possible. Keep in mind the story you recalled earlier and be ready to work on it as you read through this section.

The Story Arc

In the mid-19th century, Gustav Freytag (1894) developed what is called Freytag's Pyramid, an illustration of the stages of a story. The stages create the shape of a pyramid or arc, where action rises and falls as a story progresses. The pyramid was adapted by Jack Hart in *Storycraft*. We have further adapted it here for our purposes. Figure 2.2 shows the Story Arc we suggest you use to think about, revise, and tell stories about your work.

The stages of the story arc, in order, are:

1. **Context** – background information told at the beginning of the story. In this stage, we share details about the characters, setting, and anything else the audience needs to know. This stage ends with or leads into a complication.

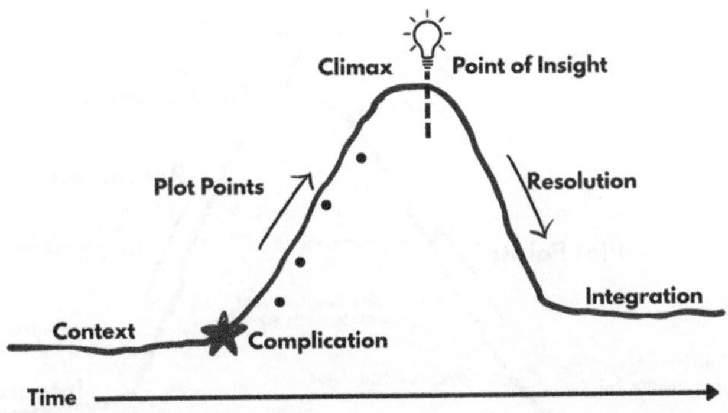

FIGURE 2.2 The story arc illustrates how experiences often unfold across time – from context, triggered by a complication, through plot points to a climax, altered by a point of insight, then shifting to resolution and integration.

2. **Complication** – an event or experience that sets the story in motion.
3. **Plot Points** – multiple events that change the direction of the story. Tension builds with each plot point, leading toward a climax.
4. **Climax** – a point of heightened intensity that brings the story to a head.
5. **Point of Insight** – the character undergoes a transformation and understands or experiences the world differently.
6. **Resolution** – intensity fades, pace slows, and the story winds down. Remaining questions are answered.
7. **Integration** – the final stage, where the story concludes and things are different than before.

Writers often map out their stories before writing them. Sometimes we create a simple outline with bullet points in a particular order. It helps us organize our thoughts. We can take it further by mapping the story outline onto the story arc, as we did for this chapter's field story about Liz, Aksel, and Kaya (Figure 2.3). Our focus is on how practitioners might tell the story of a session, rather than on how change occurs within the session itself.

Mapping a story in this way can help you see if your story follows an arc, a straight line, or several concentric circles. Generally, it is recommended that your story follow an arc shape,

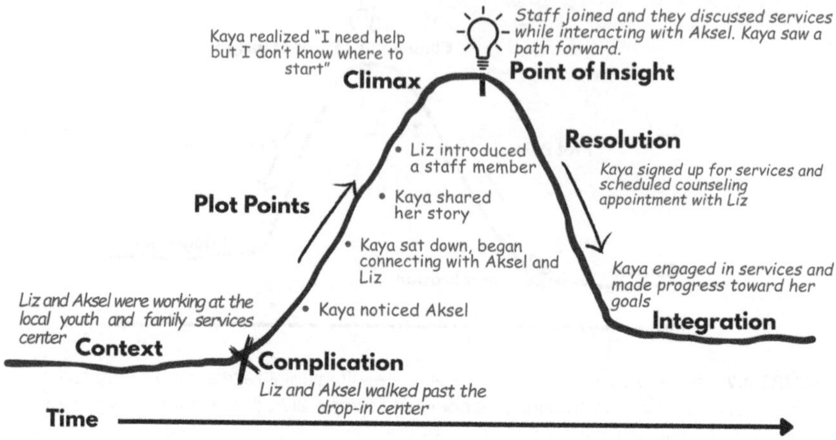

FIGURE 2.3 The story arc applied to Aksel and Kaya's field case.

with rising and declining energy or tension, split by some kind of climax or peak (Hart, 2021). The plot points build curiosity and suspense; the audience wants to keep reading or listening to find out what happens. The climax is dramatic; things come to a head. The point of insight provides a sense of satisfaction; the audience gets to see a transformation. The resolution brings the audience back down, clears things up, and lets them know the story is ending, and integration gives clarity to the end of the story and a feeling of closure for the audience.

We recognize that storytelling is personal and often shaped by culture, tradition, and lived experience. Not all stories follow a single arc, and not all audiences expect them to. If you have a way of telling stories that reflects your cultural background, professional training, or personal style, that is valuable. The narrative arc described here is one approach, and it can be a helpful tool for some people in some situations. We offer it as a guide, not a rule.

If you map your favorite animal-assisted anecdote or story onto the story arc, you may find ways to strengthen the story. Or perhaps you find that you're telling the story consistently with the arc – that can be validating and perhaps explain why that is a favorite story for you or your audience. An interesting activity could be to pick two stories you have shared before – one that worked well and one that did not. A story working well could mean that you received verbal or nonverbal feedback. Recall incidents where you shared animal-assisted or other animal-related stories. What was your intent in sharing the story, and did it work? Liz has told the story of Aksel and Kaya often. The reason for sharing it is to connect with the audience and give them a concrete example of how her dog Aksel interacted with people and helped them get started in counseling or other services. She knows the story has been effective when people stop asking questions about how or why and start sharing their own stories about the power of animals. Does mapping your stories onto the story arc help you understand what works or doesn't work?

Tips for a Strong Story

In his book *On Writing Well* (1980), William Zinsser teaches about writing nonfiction by way of writing good English. The book provides great information for the interested writer. You may or may not think of yourself as a writer. But if you are sharing anecdotes and personal stories of your work with an audience (e.g., clients, referral sources, funders, community members, family, and friends), then you are a writer – nonfiction writer, to be precise. Below are three tips from Zinsser on writing nonfiction:

1. **Keep your writing simple.** Avoid long sentences, long words, fancy jargon, unnecessary adverbs, etc. Good writing is simple and straightforward. The same can be said for sharing a story orally. Think ahead about what you want to say and say it as simply as you can. The audience will be more likely to continue reading/listening.
2. **Don't write for the audience; write for yourself.** You have anecdotes/stories about your work that you might share with any number of audiences – health professionals, schools, community members, potential funders. The audience might influence which story you choose to share, but the story itself should be told by you, in your own style, consistently. You've chosen the story because it's a

good one – it will get their attention, or it's a great example of what you do, or it evokes the kind of emotion you're looking for. Your story will work out best if you tell it in your own voice and style. Tell it the way you like it. If it involves humor, include that. If you feel the need for a dramatic pause, take one.

3. **Unity is the anchor of good writing.** Unity, or consistency, helps the audience follow the story, which makes it more appealing. You can have unity in the point of view – speaking all in the first person or third person. You can have unity of tense – speaking all in the past, present, or future tense. Stories of your work will likely be in the past tense, and we suggest telling stories completely in the past tense. Skipping between past and present can leave the audience confused. Unity of mood is another factor. Will you share the story in a happy, chatty style or in a serious, subdued tone? Although some stories might call for a mix, Zinsser suggests generally choosing a mood/tone and sticking with it.

Chip and Dan Heath wrote the book *Made to Stick: Why Some Ideas Survive and Others Die* (2007). The book is full of wonderful examples of "sticky" stories and ideas, supported by research on what makes something stick with us. Sticky ideas are ideas that stay with us. This could be a word, phrase, jingle, or story. For our purposes, we are interested in *stories* that stick. Early in the book, the authors share six principles of successful – sticky – ideas. The first letter of each of the six principles together spells out SUCCESS – simplicity, unexpectedness, concreteness, credibility, emotions, and stories. As you think about the stories you tell in your own work, one or more of these principles may help you make a story more memorable.

1. **Simplicity** – Identify the essential core of the idea and strip away anything extraneous. Proverbs are a useful model: simple, yet profound. A single sentence – such as *treat others as they want to be treated* – can be so rich that someone could spend a lifetime trying to live it.

2. **Unexpectedness** – Capture attention by violating expectations. Saying something counterintuitive or surprising creates alertness and curiosity. You can deepen engagement by opening a gap in the audience's understanding and then deliberately filling it.
3. **Concreteness** – Be specific and grounded. Describe observable actions and sensory details. Concrete images – such as a participant standing tall while holding an empty grain pan above their head – help listeners picture what you mean. Metaphors can also add clarity, such as describing someone as standing "solid like a tree."
4. **Credibility** – Help people believe the idea by allowing them to test it for themselves. While numbers and statistics have their place, relying on them too heavily can backfire. Quoting evidence alone does not guarantee trust – and may even disengage some audiences.
5. **Emotions** – Make people care. Stories that evoke emotion – whether awe, concern, fear, or warmth – are more likely to be remembered. We are wired to respond to others (two-legged, four-legged, feathered, or scaled), not abstractions, so finding the right emotional entry point matters.
6. **Stories** – Stories prompt action by allowing listeners to mentally rehearse. When people imagine themselves in a situation, they are better prepared to respond when something similar arises in real life.

None of these suggestions requires special expertise. In fact, they are largely intuitive. Because humans are natural storytellers, you may already be using many of these principles without realizing it. Most of us tell stories throughout our lives with no formal training at all – and that is precisely why people tell the stories they do.

This may also explain why there are a growing number of books devoted entirely to stories from animal-assisted work. For example, Lori Kogan's book *The Gifts We Receive from Animals: Stories to Warm the Heart* (2022) brings together narratives from animal-assisted services, with each chapter highlighting ways animals contribute to human healing. Similarly, memoirs such as

Jean Baur's *Joy Unleashed: The Story of Bella, the Unlikely Therapy Dog* (2026) offer personal accounts of how relationships with animals have shaped and supported human lives. These stories are abundant in the literature for a reason. They stick.

Moving Beyond Anecdotes

Now that we have covered ways to strengthen your stories, let's look at another important term we use throughout the book – evidence. **Evidence** is information that indicates whether a belief or proposition is true or valid. In the context of animal-assisted services, this topic typically comes up in discussions of whether services are effective or whether interacting with animals leads to specific outcomes. We can have different kinds of evidence. For our purposes, we distinguish between *anecdotal evidence* and *empirical evidence*.

Anecdotal Evidence

Anecdotal evidence is evidence based on – you guessed it – anecdotes, personal accounts. For example, we might support the proposition that dogs help people feel safe and calm by sharing the story at the beginning of this chapter – the personal account of Aksel in the drop-in center, creating a bridge to services for Kaya. Anecdotal evidence – like our story of Aksel and Kaya – is compelling and relatable. But it has limitations. An anecdote is just one instance, and it may not be representative of the broader field. In addition, an anecdote is told by someone close to the story who may be biased. Whether we are conscious of it or not, as animal-assisted professionals, we are biased toward the animals we work with and may only remember or share stories where there were positive outcomes (Herzog, 2011). We may forget or intentionally leave out experiences where there were no outcomes or negative outcomes. When making claims about the success of our work, anecdotes are important. They paint a picture of what we know is a very complex process; stories help others see what we do and understand how animals can help people. But anecdotes are not enough alone.

Empirical Evidence

We also need more objective, generalizable evidence. **Empirical evidence** is information about whether a claim is true or valid that is based on direct observation, measurement, or experimentation. The Pet Partners data that we shared earlier in the chapter is an example of empirical evidence. Beyond an individual story about one dog visit, we gathered data from 100 people, and they shared about multiple dog visits. Because there were many accounts, we can speak more generally about the effects of dog visits. While sharing evidence like this is important for generalizability, the message may not be relatable or moving. Findings and figures are not enough alone. They are strengthened when combined with relevant stories provided as examples.

After reading and working through this book, you will have everything you need to gather your own empirical evidence, making direct observations from your work. In addition, there is a second way you can support your anecdotes with empirical evidence – referring to evidence gathered by others.

Empirical Evidence in Published Research

Referring to the definition of empirical evidence, it includes direct observation, measurement, and experimentation. Research conducted by scientists and published for public use is an excellent source of empirical evidence to share alongside your personal stories and anecdotes. For example, we could support Liz's anecdote of Aksel helping Kaya open up to get started with services by referring to a research article on dogs facilitating disclosure:

> The experience of Aksel helping Kaya is consistent with research on the effects of dogs on disclosing negative thoughts and feelings. Researchers at the University of Lincoln, in the United Kingdom, surveyed 286 dog-owners about their willingness to disclose to their dog. The participants reported being more willing to disclose to their dog, compared to their human confidant, feelings of depression, anxiety, and fear.
>
> (Evans-Wilday et al., 2018)

This is a scientific study published in the peer-reviewed journal *Anthrozoös*. We found it by searching on Google Scholar. We show you how to find this type of empirical evidence – published research – in Chapter 9 and Appendix A.

Anecdotes + Evidence = A Powerful Story

This is a field-tested formula. We have found, and will argue throughout this book, that a combination of both anecdotal *and* empirical evidence is the best way to communicate your work to others. The beautiful, heart-warming, or messy and challenging stories of people engaging with animals (anecdotal evidence), blended with observations or other measurements that you make (empirical evidence), or descriptions of published research conducted by scientists (empirical evidence), will help stakeholders picture the process and believe in its power. To keep it simple, we refer to these as anecdotes (your personal accounts) and evidence (your data or published research) throughout the book. Each chapter teaches a skill for each step of this process of blending anecdotes and evidence. And by the end of the book, you will have the skills to blend your own anecdotes and evidence, strengthening the stories you share about your animal partners. Part of strengthening your stories is knowing which stories to share and when. In the next chapter, we cover three different kinds of anecdote + evidence stories and help you discern which best fits your needs.

Try It! Start Your SAGA with a Story

To get started on your SAGA journey, refer to the story you recalled earlier in the chapter. Use a recording device to record yourself telling the story. Then listen to the recording and answer these questions:

1. How long is the story, in minutes/seconds?
2. What are your favorite parts of the story and why?
3. What are your least favorite parts of the story and why?

4. Map the major parts of the story onto the story arc shown in Figure 2.2.
5. After answering these questions and reflecting, what adjustments, if any, will you make to the way you tell the story? For each of these, does it need more, less, or no change?
    - Context (background information)
    - Complication (a challenge or problem)
    - Plot Points (events that build tension in the story)
    - Climax (the height of the problem)
    - Point of Insight (main character sees things differently)
    - Resolution (tension declines as the story draws to a close)
    - Integration (story ends, and things are different from before)

Bibliography

Baur, J. (2016). *Joy unleashed: The story of Bella, the unlikely therapy dog.* Skyhorse Publishing.

Benton-Banai, E. (1988). *The Mishomis book: The voice of the Ojibway.* Indian Country Communications.

Evans-Wilday, A. S., Hall, S. S., Hogue, T. E., & Mills, D. S. (2018). Self-disclosure with dogs: Dog owners' and non-dog owners' willingness to disclose emotional topics. *Anthrozoös, 31*(3), 353–366.

Fournier, A. K. (2019). Studying animal-assisted intervention through citizen science. In: *Animal-assisted intervention: Thinking empirically* (pp. 95–118). Springer Nature.

Freytag, G. (1894). *Freytag's technique of the drama: An exposition of dramatic composition and art* (E. J. MacEwan, Trans.). Scott, Foresman and Company.

Gottschall, J. (2012). *The storytelling animal: How stories make us human.* Houghton Mifflin Harcourt Publishing Company.

Hamilton, V. (1988). In *the beginning: Creation stories from around the world.* Harper Collins.

Hart, J. (2021). *Story craft: The complete guide to writing narrative nonfiction* (2nd ed.). University of Chicago Press.

Heath, C., & Heath, D. (2007). *Made to stick: Why some ideas survive and others die*. Random House.

Herzog, H. (2011). The impact of pets on human health and psychological well-being: Fact, fiction, or hypothesis? *Current Directions in Psychological Science, 20*(4), 236–239.

Kogan, L. R. (Ed.) (2022). *The gifts we receive from animals: Stories to warm the heart*. Routledge.

Letson, E. A. (2022). Aksel to the rescue. In: *The gifts we receive from animals: Stories to warm the heart* (pp. 129–131). Routledge.

Zinsser, W. K. (1980). *On writing well* (2nd ed.). Harper & Row.

3

Assessment, Evaluation, or Research

Which Data Story Are You Telling?

Field Story 3: Comfort with Gentle Belle

Tracy and her Golden Retriever, Belle (pictured in Figure 3.1), were participating in a canine-assisted reading program at the local Boys and Girls Club. During one session, a child asked whether her friend could simply watch rather than read, explaining that her friend was afraid of dogs. The friend – a small, quiet nine-year-old – stood several feet away as Tracy and Belle settled onto a mat with the reader. Belle lay stretched out on her side, relaxed and still, as the child read aloud. Tracy noticed the observing girl gradually inched closer – first kneeling several feet away, then sitting nearby. After several minutes, the girl reached out and briefly touched Belle with one finger, quickly pulling her hand back. She repeated this cautious touch several times, each contact lasting slightly longer than the last. Eventually, she began petting Belle with her whole hand and moved closer, sitting directly beside her. When Belle shifted her position or stretched her legs, the girl occasionally flinched and leaned back, but she remained nearby. After some time, she selected her own book, lay down next to Belle, and rested her head on Belle's abdomen while reading quietly. Later, Tracy learned that the girl had

DOI: 10.4324/9781003640257-4

FIGURE 3.1 Belle, a therapy dog in the Bemidji Area Reading Canines (BARC) program.
Source: Photo provided by Tracy Parthun

been bitten by a dog when she was younger, explaining her initial nervousness with Belle. Over the course of approximately twenty minutes, Tracy observed a clear change in the child's proximity, contact, and comfort around Belle.

Moments like this are why many people are drawn to animal-assisted work. Tracy didn't intervene, rush the interaction, or push the child beyond her comfort level. Instead, she watched carefully – tracking proximity, touch, startle response, and choice – allowing the interaction to unfold at the child's pace. It would be easy to tell this story as proof that animal-assisted reading programs reduce fear of dogs. But before we decide what this moment *means*, it helps us to step back and ask a different question: *What kind of data story are we telling here?*

Three Types of Data Stories

Tracy's observations focus on one child, in one session, at one point in time. The purpose of noticing and remembering these details was to understand what was happening for that child in that moment – not to evaluate the program as a whole or to draw conclusions about how animal-assisted reading works in general. That makes this an example of assessment, specifically informal assessment, where careful observation guides practice.

In this chapter, we unpack the differences between assessment, program evaluation, and research and explain why knowing which story you are telling matters. The goal is not to diminish powerful moments like this one but to help you tell them in ways that are accurate, ethical, and useful – both for your clients and the field at large.

Doing data-driven work creates a data story – there are characters (client, program, animals, business), a complication (things happen that cause you to ask a question), a sequence of events (getting the data you need and interpreting it), and a resolution (responding to the evidence). There are three types of data stories, or genres, that we can create – assessment, evaluation, and research. Each of them has the major components of a story but will have different purposes and audiences. Assessment stories are created for the client. Evaluation stories inform a program. The audience for research is broad – the world at large. Table 3.1 highlights the differences between these three data story genres.

TABLE 3.1 Distinguishing between Assessment, Program Evaluation, and Research

Genre	*Conducted By*	*Unit of Focus*	*Primary Audience*	*Primary Purpose*
Assessment	Practitioner	Individual client or group	Client/ practitioner	Understand and guide decisions for a specific case
Program evaluation	Practitioner/ Organization	Program/ Service system	Organization/ Stakeholders	Evaluate the effectiveness of services
Research	Researchers/ Scientists	Sample/ Population	Scientific Community	Generate general knowledge

Assessment – Data on a Client for the Client

Put simply, **assessment** is gathering data on an individual or group for that individual or group – human or animal. This is a single case, which is an individual or group of humans or animals that you are working with. A case could be an individual psychotherapy client, a corporate group receiving coaching, an animal providing a service, etc. This may mean watching and recording behaviors or administering tests or questionnaires, both types of information we will talk about in later chapters. In assessment, we are gathering this information from an individual, and it is to serve that individual. For example, with an equine-assisted coaching participant, we might gather data to determine whether the individual we are coaching has reached their learning goals. In a canine-assisted reading program, we might gather data to know whether an individual student has improved their reading ability. For an animal-assisted counseling, social work, or physical therapy client, we can gather data to determine whether an individual client's symptoms are decreasing or if functioning is improving. For all these scenarios, we would gather data from one person or group, share that information only with that group, and use the information to make decisions about or with the individual or group. The data would help us work together on their education plan, treatment plan, etc. We address more details on which data to gather, how to gather it, and what to do with it throughout the book. For now, we are just defining these processes and helping you determine which process meets your needs. Below we have an example of assessment in animal-assisted services – incorporating data on a human participant and an animal partner.

Informal and Formal Assessment: The Individual Story

In the genre of assessment, we tell the story of a single case – one client or one human-animal pair – to understand what is happening and what might help. However, not every assessment story has the same purpose or the same level of formality.

Formal assessment follows established procedures and uses standardized, validated tools. These assessments are designed to inform diagnosis, treatment planning, or clinical decision-making. Because of their technical and interpretive demands, formal assessments require specialized training and, in many professions, appropriate credentials or licensure. For example, a psychologist or licensed counselor may administer and interpret validated measures of anxiety, mood, or functioning.

Informal assessment, by contrast, is more like a structured set of field notes. Practitioners gather observations, ratings, reflections, and descriptions that help them notice patterns, monitor progress, and guide day-to-day decisions. These methods are not diagnostic and are not intended to replace formal clinical or educational evaluation. Instead, they add context, depth, and practical insight into what unfolds during sessions. The same case may include both formal and informal assessment data.

Assessment Example

Joel is a licensed counselor who incorporates his therapy cat, Whiskers, into counseling sessions. Joel has been working with Alec, a 23-year-old experiencing generalized anxiety. As part of his formal assessment plan, Joel administers a standardized anxiety screening measure, the Generalized Anxiety Disorder 7-Item scale (GAD-7) (Spitzer et al., 2006), at intake and every two weeks. These scores provide a structured indicator of Alec's anxiety symptoms over time.

Alongside these formal measures, Joel gathers informal assessment data. Before and after each session, Alec rates their anxiety on a 1–10 scale. After sessions, Joel records brief notes describing Whiskers' arousal and proximity to Alec during the session.

Figure 3.2 illustrates both forms of data. The GAD-7 scores show that Alec's anxiety was elevated at intake and, although fluctuating slightly, appears to be gradually declining across weeks. The dashed line marks the commonly used cutoff score indicating clinically significant anxiety. While Alec's scores are trending downward, they remain above the threshold, suggesting continued treatment is appropriate.

The informal notes tell a complementary story. Session observations describe Whiskers as initially alert and distant, later

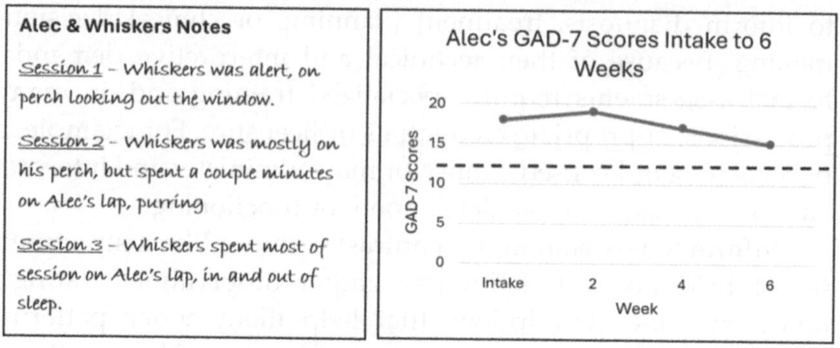

FIGURE 3.2 Informal (left) and formal (right) assessment data.

spending more time relaxed and in close proximity to Alec. These informal data help Joel and Alec reflect on the therapeutic process and the possible role of the animal in sessions.

Together, these assessment approaches provide different kinds of insight. Formal measures offer standardized, comparable indicators. Informal measures capture lived experience, context, and moment-to-moment patterns. Both contribute to understanding the case, but they serve different functions and require different levels of training. In this way, assessment becomes both rigorous and realistic – informed by observation and grounded in the realities of practice. Formal and informal assessments are different lenses on the same unfolding story.

Genre Tip: Know Your Role as the Data Storyteller

Practitioners credentialed in assessment may ethically integrate both approaches, using formal tools to anchor decisions while drawing on informal observations to enrich interpretation. Practitioners without formal assessment training can still gather meaningful informal data to guide practice. When informal observations begin to suggest the need for diagnosis or formal evaluation, consultation or referral to a qualified professional is warranted. *Informal assessment* is the story you can tell from careful observation and reflection. *Formal assessment* is the story that requires specialized training and credentials. Know which genre you're working in before you start collecting data.

Program Evaluation – A Program Story

Program evaluation is defined as gathering data on your program or business to inform your program or business. Rather than gathering data on just one client and informing your work with them, program evaluation gathers data about a whole program or business. A program might be a counseling clinic or an animal shelter, or some other organization that serves multiple individuals. With program evaluation, we are wondering about that organization as a whole. Or we can tell a data story about a smaller program within the organization. In either case – the whole organization or a program within the organization – we want to know something about the services to inform our decisions about the program or services. For example, an animal-assisted social worker might wonder whether their clients are meeting their goals overall. For animal-assisted learning, perhaps we wonder if children, overall, benefit from our canine-assisted reading services. As an example of a smaller program within an organization or business, maybe we wonder whether a particular curriculum we've been using is helpful. In that case, we are not gathering data on all recipients, just those experiencing that curriculum. Of course, gathering this information is relevant to individual clients, but with program evaluation, the ultimate end user of the information is the program/organization.

You probably already gather evidence relevant to program evaluation if you are an established animal-assisted professional. Data gathered for program evaluation can be very basic, such as the number of no-shows in a clinic per month. On the other hand, it can be more complex, like comparing scores on a symptom checklist for all clients before they begin treatment and after three months. Let's look at a hypothetical example of program evaluation.

Program Evaluation Example

The Pawsitively Impressive Reading program is a hypothetical canine-assisted reading program for elementary school students. One of several dog-handler teams visits the local library on the first Saturday of the month. The dog-handler team visits library patrons, and children who are interested can work on their skills by reading aloud to the dog. Let's imagine the director of the program is wondering (1) whether the program is influencing the number of people who visit the library and (2) in what ways the program helps children with their reading. She decides to gather data to answer these questions. To understand the effect of the program on library attendance, she asks the library for the number of visitors to the library every Saturday for the past six months. To determine how the program helps children with reading, Pawsitively Impressive Reading dog handlers ask the parents of children who read with the dogs to complete a short form, where they give their perspective on how the program helps their child. Figure 3.3 shows an example of this type of form, with hypothetical responses.

How has reading with the dogs helped your child?

My child has improved their	Not at all			A Great Deal
Interest in Reading				✓
Confidence in Reading				✓
Pronunciation	✓			
Fluency		✓		

Colmments

Thank you so much. My child loves reading now!

Thank you for sharing your feedback with us!

FIGURE 3.3 Example of an informal tool created for program evaluation.

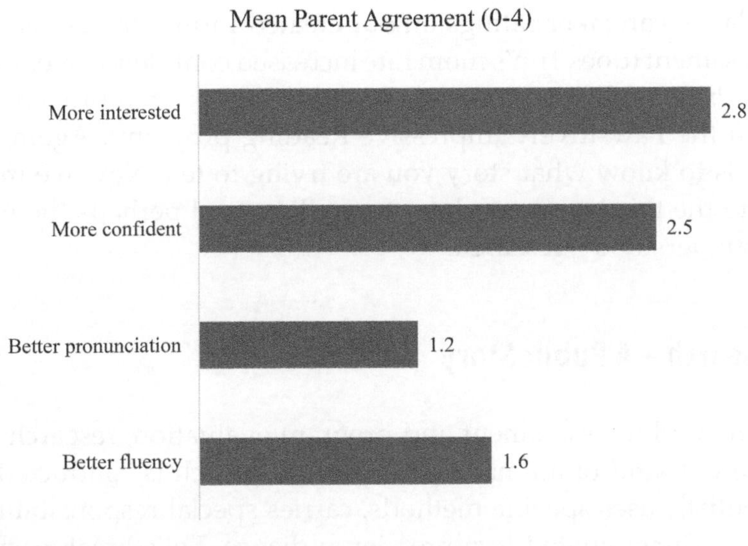

FIGURE 3.4 Hypothetical reading program evaluation data.

Figure 3.4 shows hypothetical data from the parent-report forms. A total of 30 parents completed the form, reporting on ways the program did or did not help their child with reading. These data show that the mean parent agreement ratings ranged from a low of 1.2 (Better pronunciation) to a high of 2.8 (More interested in reading). It looks like, from the data gathered so far, parents see improvements in all areas, with more Interest and Confidence having the strongest outcomes. The Pawsitively Impressive Reading program could compare these data with their desired outcomes and make changes where needed. We will address how to collect and use data like this as we move through the book.

This is a good example to discuss how the same type of data could be used in more than one data-story genre. We have reported the parent ratings at the program level – we can see how the Pawsitively Impressive Reading program is doing overall. We could use that same type of data for assessment. For example, perhaps there is one specific child that we are curious about. Maybe his teachers specifically referred him to the program to help build his reading confidence. We could ask his caretaker(s) to complete the same rating form every 2 weeks and look at just his scores to see if they change over time. This same kind of data – caretaker ratings on our created form – can be used in assessment (does Tim's mom rate increased confidence over time) and Program Evaluation (are caretakers reporting improvements from the Pawsitively Impressive Reading program). Again, the key is to know what story you are trying to tell. Now we move on to the third genre of data storytelling, and perhaps the most misunderstood – research.

Research – A Public Story

Compared to assessment and program evaluation, research is a different kind of animal, so to speak. Research is conducted by scientists, uses specific methods, carries special responsibilities, and is disseminated to a broader audience. Let's break each of those down.

Conducted by Scientists

Refer to Table 3.1 and note that the person or team telling the data story is different for research compared to assessment and program evaluation. So far, we've discussed evidence collected by practitioners or members of their teams. Assessment and program evaluation are practitioner-driven activities, designed to inform client care or improve a program or organization.

Research, on the other hand, is conducted by scientists – people trained in the scientific method, measurement, and experimental design specific to their field. This training typically occurs at the university level, and those who lead research projects usually hold an advanced degree, such as a master's or doctorate.

Most animal-assisted practitioners are not also researchers (we can't all be good at everything, right?). This is important to acknowledge because it relates to a common misunderstanding about data. Many people equate *gathering data* with *doing research*, using the term "research" for any activity that involves collecting and analyzing information. That's a mistake. Gathering data is not research; it's simply gathering data. It becomes research when the purpose is to generate new knowledge, and the findings are intended for public consumption (for example, through publication or presentation). The goal of research is not to decide what to do about one client or one program. It's to deepen our understanding of a phenomenon and share that story with the scientific community and, ultimately, with the world.

An example of a research question might be *What are the outcomes of equine-assisted learning?* Another example could be *Is canine-assisted psychotherapy effective in treating PTSD?* Or *does adaptive riding result in improved balance and coordination for children with physical disabilities?* Notice that these questions tell us the research is about a broader group than an individual client or individual organization. Rather than asking whether canine-assisted psychotherapy is effective in treating one person's PTSD (assessment) or whether one program is effective in treating a group of clients' PTSD (program evaluation), it is more open (Is canine-assisted psychotherapy effective in treating PTSD?). Regarding the welfare of therapy animals, we are not asking about the effects of a canine-assisted reading program on one dog (assessment) or all the dogs in one organization (program evaluation), but on dogs doing this work in general (research).

Even if you don't identify as a researcher and aren't designing and leading research studies, research is relevant to you – as a consumer and a contributor. We discuss that later in the chapter. First, let's learn a little more about why research is different from the other data genres.

Data Are Gathered on a Sample to Inform the Population

As mentioned earlier, research is conducted to deepen our understanding of a phenomenon, and research results are shared broadly to contribute to collective knowledge. Research findings are part of the data-driven process – but at a broader level. People beyond the immediate data team use research results to make decisions that can affect many others. For example, research studies on medications or medical treatments can lead to national or global changes in health recommendations (e.g., physicians prescribing or discontinuing certain treatments). Similarly, research on environmental effects on mental health can inform policies or influence how communities are designed.

Because research can have such far-reaching effects, scientists need to be confident that their findings are both accurate and applicable beyond the specific people or animals they studied. This introduces the concept of a *sample* versus a *population.* Whenever we collect data from people or animals, we're working with a **sample** – a smaller subset of a larger group we're curious about.

For example, when the Pawsitively Impressive Reading Program asks parents of children at the library to complete a feedback form, they're collecting data from a *sample* of parents. When a counselor asks a client to complete a mood checklist, they're collecting a *sample* of that client's mood. The sample represents the specific data you collect or the individuals who provide it. We gather samples because we want to learn something bigger – to make inferences or draw conclusions about a **population** (the broader group the sample represents). Researchers are trained in great detail to apply methods that help ensure a study's findings can be applied to a population. And if they can't (studies have limitations, errors can be made), then researchers are skilled at critically analyzing their study and reporting what can and cannot be inferred from the data.

Research Carries Special Responsibilities

Research involves drawing conclusions about larger populations and sharing those findings publicly. And participation in research can place both humans and animals in positions of vulnerability to manipulation or unintended harm. For these reasons, research carries distinct ethical responsibilities.

> Researchers must follow established ethical guidelines and obtain appropriate approvals before collecting data.

In Chapter 12, we discuss the ethics of data-driven work, addressing the ways that harm can be done when gathering, interpreting, and sharing findings from data. Essentially, there are dos and don'ts of data-driven work that relate to doing good and doing no harm. Researchers have additional ethical standards to meet. For example, participation in research must be voluntary, participant data must be protected, and participants must be informed of the purpose of the research and consent to participating in it. It is beyond the scope of this book to go beyond these basics, but the interested reader can find a wealth of information about research ethics online. In the United States, research is regulated by the U.S. Department of Health and Human Services' Office for Human Research Protections. You can find federal regulations for research involving human subjects on their website.[1]

These regulations are implemented by institutions within which the research takes place. Most institutions have an Institutional Review Board (IRB), which is a group of people trained in research ethics who review research proposals. Their role is to review the research plan and determine whether any potential harm to the participants outweighs the benefits of the research. Before any research with human participants can begin, it must be reviewed and approved by an IRB. This generally means the researchers submit a document outlining the details of the study they would like to conduct. The committee reviews the plan and approves, denies, or gives feedback for revision. Conducting human subject research without IRB approval is unethical and can have significant consequences for the researcher, including reprimand, sanctions, loss of employment, and legal consequences.

And what about the animals involved in animal-assisted research? Do they have special protections? Yes, they do! Animals are even more vulnerable and potentially at risk for harm in research, so they are protected by ethical codes and legal regulations. As a counterpart to the IRB, institutions can have an Institutional Animal Care and Use Committee (IACUC). The process is like that of the IRB – researchers submit a proposal outlining their plan and any potential for harm to animals. Again, research involving animal subjects cannot begin until approved by an IACUC. Doing so can result in serious consequences for the researcher. Similar to research involving humans, there is a wealth of information on the ethical standards and regulations for research involving animals. In the United States, the interested reader can seek information from the National Institutes of Health Office of Laboratory Animal Welfare.

In summary, research is quite different from assessment and program evaluation. It is conducted by scientists with specific training and is governed by special ethical standards and regulations.

Research studies are intended to produce generalizable knowledge and must be reviewed by ethics committees charged to protect humans and animals.

Below we have an example of research from a study that our team conducted.

Research Example

In 2018, we conducted an experiment to compare the effects of experiential learning that incorporated a horse, a dog, or a stuffed animal (Fournier et al., 2021). The study was planned by us, the authors, as a collaboration between Angela's institution – Bemidji State University – and Liz's private practice – Eagle Vista Ranch & Wellness Center. We submitted our research proposal to the university's IRB and IACUC; the study was approved by both committees. Through an announcement in undergraduate psychology classes, we recruited 28 adult volunteers to participate in the research. In groups of 2–6, the student volunteers participated in a group experiential learning activity on problem-solving. The indoor horse arena was used as our laboratory. The students were to decide on a goal and use props in the arena to create a path toward their goal. Then they were to bring the "four-legged" in the space to the goal. We randomly assigned sessions so that the four-legged was either Montana, a Paint horse; Bronco, a Yellow Labrador; or a stuffed rocking horse. The research team observed as the participants followed instructions and eventually worked with the horse, dog, or stuffed animal to bring it to their goal. Afterward, the students completed several questionnaires, reporting on their emotions, and sharing what they learned about problem-solving. The results of the study showed that sessions with the horse and the dog resulted in greater positive emotions than sessions with the stuffed animal, with the dog sessions resulting in the highest positive emotions. The study provided some evidence that a group activity with an animal, especially a dog, may have greater effects on student emotion than a group activity without an animal. The results were published in a journal article for other researchers and the public to read. You can see this process had the components of research – the goal was to answer a broad question about animal-assisted services, the study was first reviewed by an IRB and IACUC, data were gathered on volunteer research participants, and the findings were disseminated to the public. If you'd like to read more about this study, the citation is in the Bibliography at the end of the chapter.

Being a Consumer of Research

Although you may not be a researcher conducting studies like the one just described, you do have a connection to research as an informed animal-assisted practitioner. You can be a consumer of research and a contributor to research. Being a consumer of research means that you integrate published research into your work. You may learn about studies relevant to your work by reading journal articles or books, listening to podcasts, or attending conferences or trainings where research is discussed. You can use research to guide your data-driven process, influencing the kinds of questions you ask, the measurement tools you choose, and the interpretation of your findings. Wherever possible, lean on published research to strengthen your data story. We cover how to find and use published research relevant to your work in Appendix A.

Being a Research Contributor

The second way you can connect with research is to be a research contributor. A growing number of researchers are studying animal-assisted services. Common research directions address (1) whether a given service is effective, (2) for whom this service is effective, (3) the effects of the service on the animals involved, and (4) in general, how the service works to result in outcomes. Scientists who conduct these studies need YOU. They can benefit from your wisdom and experience. Sharing stories of your work can inform their research questions. Research studies need participants, who could be practitioners or clients. Either way, you are the gateway to their human subjects. Additionally, you could contribute data from your practice. This last one requires additional steps – see the extras discussed above – but after working through this book, you will be better equipped to collaborate with researchers to contribute to their studies on animal-assisted services. Our experience has shown us that there are many animal-assisted professionals who appreciate the need for research and would love to contribute to it. Appendix B provides more details on connecting with universities to collaborate on research and student experiences.

Research Myths

To conclude this section, we highlight common myths about research – misconceptions we've encountered frequently in our work with animal-assisted practitioners and echoed by the general public. By understanding and addressing these myths, you can help clarify the nuances of research and promote more accurate, ethical, and informed data practices.

Myths about Research

- **If you are collecting data, you are conducting research – False**. Collecting data is not the same as conducting research. Research is much more involved, requiring special training, methods, and approval.
- **If something is labeled research, it must be true – False**. Researchers can make mistakes and be biased. All research has limitations. We should practice skepticism and think critically when learning about research.
- **Research gives us facts – False**. Research gives us findings, and those findings can be accurate or inaccurate and often lead to more questions. Think of research as providing evidence for or against something rather than determining facts.
- **One study can prove a point – False**. In research, a single study rarely tells us very much. Findings become meaningful when multiple studies examine the same question and arrive at similar results. That's why researchers tend to use careful language such as "the evidence suggests"

or "the results are consistent with." Be wary of anyone claiming they have "proven" something based on one study.

It takes multiple studies demonstrating consistent outcomes before we can say there is general evidence of a service's effectiveness. A single study reflects the work of one researcher or team, with one group of participants, in a specific setting, using a particular method, at a particular point in time. Many variables can influence the results. For example, if a client named Shelby shows reduced PTSD symptoms after working with a horse named Prince, that's promising. But we don't know whether the improvement was due to the horse, the setting, Shelby's readiness for change, the therapist, or other factors. It could be any one of these, or a combination. While this complexity may seem frustrating, it's important to acknowledge it.

Understanding the distinctions between assessment, program evaluation, and research is essential for telling accurate and ethical data stories in animal-assisted services. Each genre serves a different purpose, requires different tools and training, and reaches a different audience. Whether you're gathering data to support an individual client, improve a program, or contribute to scientific knowledge, knowing your role as a data storyteller helps ensure your work is both meaningful and responsible.

Try It! Choose Your SAGA Genre

The next step in the SAGA process is to determine which SAGA genre you are working in. As mentioned earlier, we imagine you are reading this book for help with assessment or program evaluation, and probably both at different times. To begin:

1. Select a topic you are most interested in or curious about.
2. Review the material in this chapter to decide which genre it fits.
3. Keep the topic and genre in mind as you move on to Chapter 4, where you will develop a specific question to guide your SAGA process.

Note

1. The U.S. federal law that regulates research with human subjects is 45 CFR 46. At the time of this writing, this legal code can be found at www.hhs.gov/ohrp/regulations-and-policy/regulations/45-cfr-46/index.html

Bibliography

American Educational Research Association, American Psychological Association, & National Council on Measurement in Education. (2014). *Standards for educational and psychological testing*. American Educational Research Association.

Anastasi, A., & Urbina, S. (1997). *Psychological testing* (7th ed.). Prentice Hall.

Binfet, J. T., Green, F. L., Godard, R. J., Dahlman, M. L., & Basiri, Z. (2026). Head, middle, or tail-end? A pilot examination of the differential effects of interacting with different parts of a therapy dog on college student well-being. *Human-Animal Interactions, 14*(1), 0009.

Connell, C. G., Tepper, D. L., Landry, O., & Bennett, P. C. (2019). Dogs in schools: The impact of specific human–dog interactions on reading ability in children aged 6 to 8 years. *Anthrozoös, 32*(3), 347–360.

Donabedian, A. (1988). The quality of care: How can it be assessed? *JAMA, 260*(12), 1743–1748. https://doi.org/10.1001/jama.260.12.1743

Fine, A. H. (Ed.). (2019). *Handbook on animal-assisted therapy: Foundations and guidelines for animal-assisted interventions* (5th ed.). Academic Press.

Fournier, A. K., Berry, T. D., Letson, E. A., Laitala, J., Proels, L., & Kavanagh, K. (2021). The anodyne-agent model: A framework for understanding animal-assisted intervention. *Human-Animal Interactions, 9*(1), 55–75.

Hall, S. S., Gee, N. R., & Mills, D. S. (2016). Children reading to dogs: A systematic review of the literature. *PLOS One, 11*(2), e0149759.

Howell, T., Leanne O. N., Clare T.-P., et al. (2022). Defining commonly used terms for animals working in support roles for vulnerable people. *Animals, 12*(15), 1975.

International Association of Human-Animal Interaction Organizations. (2025). *Minimum standards for research in animal-assisted services (AAS), human-animal interaction (HAI), and the human-animal bond (HAB)*. IAHAIO. https://iahaio.org/minimum-standards-for-research-in-aas-hai-hab/

Kazdin, A. E. (2011). *Single-case research designs: Methods for clinical and applied settings* (2nd ed.). Oxford University Press.

Kerlinger, F. N., & Lee, H. B. (2000). *Foundations of behavioral research* (4th ed.). Harcourt College Publishers.

Kolarić, A. (2024). *Reading in the EFL in the company of therapy dogs: Literature review* (Master's Thesis, University of Zagreb). Repository, University of Zagreb Faculty of Teacher Education. https://urn.nsk.hr/urn:nbn:hr:147:560700

Kruger, K. A., & Serpell, J. A. (2010). Animal-assisted interventions in mental health: Definitions and theoretical foundations. In A. H. Fine (Ed.), *Handbook on animal-assisted therapy* (3rd ed., pp. 33–48). Academic Press.

Lentini, J. A., & Knox, M. S. (2015). A qualitative and quantitative review of equine facilitated psychotherapy (EFP) with children and adolescents. *Open Complementary Medicine Journal*, *7*, 1–16. https://doi.org/10.2174/1876391X00901010051

O'Haire, M. E. (2013). Animal-assisted intervention for autism spectrum disorder: A systematic literature review. *Journal of Autism and Developmental Disorders*, *43*, 1606–1622. https://doi.org/10.1007/s10803-012-1707-5

Patton, M. Q. (2008). *Utilization-focused evaluation* (4th ed.). Sage Publications.

Pioneer Staff Report. (2025, June 14). *Someone special volunteers: Boys and girls club nominates Tracy Parthun and Michele Brielmaier.* Bemidji Pioneer. https://www.bemidjipioneer.com/community/someone-special-volunteers-boys-and-girls-club-nominates-tracy-parthun-and-michele-brielmaier

Pioneer Staff Report. (2025, June 21). *Someone special volunteers: Hope house nominates Ethan Larson and Tracy Parthun*. Bemidji Pioneer. https://www.bemidjipioneer.com/community/someone-special-volunteers-hope-house-nominates-ethan-larson-and-tracy-parthun

Rossi, P. H., Lipsey, M. W., & Henry, G. T. (2019). *Evaluation: A systematic approach* (8th ed.). Sage Publications.

Serpell, J. A., McCune, S., Gee, N. R., & Griffin, J. A. (2017). Current challenges to research on animal-assisted interventions. *Applied Developmental Science, 21*(3), 223–233. https://doi.org/10.1080/10888691.2016.1262775

Shadish, W. R., Cook, T. D., & Campbell, D. T. (2002). *Experimental and quasi-experimental designs for generalized causal inference.* Houghton Mifflin.

Spitzer, R. L., Kroenke, K., Williams, J. B. W., & Löwe, B. (2006). A brief measure for assessing generalized anxiety disorder: The GAD-7. *Archives of Internal Medicine, 166*(10), 1092–1097. https://doi.org/10.1001/archinte.166.10.1092

Part II

Ask a Good Question

4

Moving from Curiosity to Empirical Question

Field Story 4: Rest Assured at Bent Anchor Ranch

On a clear autumn day in East Texas, Glenna and Sarah prepared for their session with Clara, a young client participating in equine-assisted psychotherapy at Bent Anchor Ranch. The facilitation team included Glenna, an equine specialist; Sarah, a licensed mental health professional; and two equines: Bingo, a black miniature john mule; and Stormy, a red-roan mare. Glenna transported the animals to Sarah's facility, parking the horse trailer inside the arena – a familiar and intentionally chosen environment for that day's work. Inside the trailer sat a well-known item affectionately called the "box of wonders," a container of props and materials that often sparked curiosity among participants.

Clara had been referred for services due to behavioral concerns at school. In earlier sessions, the team had begun to understand that Clara was navigating ongoing stress within her family environment. She arrived that day with her father. Although he described things at home as "fine," Clara appeared noticeably fatigued. After greeting them, Sarah and Glenna accompanied Clara into the arena. Clara moved toward a shaded area, Bingo and Stormy meandering nearby. As the session began, Sarah gently checked in. Clara hesitated, then spoke quietly. "I just can't get any rest at home." She went on to describe living circumstances that made

DOI: 10.4324/9781003640257-6

sleep difficult. Sarah reflected an observation from prior sessions – Clara often carried responsibilities beyond what would typically be expected of someone her age. Clara nodded in agreement. The facilitators asked Clara what she needed most at that moment.

Without hesitation, Clara replied, "Rest." She then turned and walked toward the trailer. Glenna and Sarah followed at a respectful distance, maintaining awareness of both Clara and the equines. Clara stepped inside the trailer, climbed onto the box of wonders, and lay down. The facilitators remained nearby, quietly attentive, supporting Clara in getting what she needed from the session.

Bingo and Stormy slowly walked over to the trailer, all eyes on Clara. After a few moments, Bingo, pictured in Figure 4.1, made an unexpected but calm choice. He walked into the trailer, unhurried and relaxed, positioning himself near Clara's feet. At intervals, he gently nudged her with his nose. Stormy remained just outside, standing quietly.

Gradually, the arena grew still. Clara rested. The animals rested. The facilitators held a steady, watchful presence. In a session that began with concerns about behavior, what unfolded instead was

FIGURE 4.1 Bingo, a miniature mule who held space for a client to rest.
Source: Photo provided by Glenna Wilson

an experience of pause and restoration. Clara identified what she needed and acted on it. Supported by a steady environment, attentive practitioners, and attuned equine partners, she received something she had been missing – rest.

Experiences like this might lead animal-assisted professionals to describe certain sessions as "different." Stories like this are meaningful – and they are also the starting point for important questions. What, specifically, was different during this session? A client lying down to rest is different and perhaps so was the animals' response. How might we describe these differences in observable terms? And how could we begin to document patterns in ways that honor the humans, the animals, and the story while supporting data-informed practice?

In Part 1 of the book, we introduced data-driven concepts and practical skills to strengthen your stories of animal-assisted work. We've introduced the SAGA method, distinguished between anecdotes and evidence, and defined three different genres of data storytelling. Now in Part 2, we address the second step of the SAGA method – asking good questions.

In this chapter, you will learn skills to ask questions that fit your purpose and can be answered with a realistic data-gathering plan. This information is meant to support animal-assisted practitioners who are guiding their work with assessment and/or program evaluation. Remember from Chapter 3 that research is a very different animal, one that we leave to scientists with special training and resources.

Lean into the Language of Measurement

Measurement is not something to fear or avoid. It is a foundational concept for anyone working in animal-assisted fields. When we ask good questions and want to answer them with accurate information, we need a way to describe what we are noticing. That is what measurement allows us to do.

In this chapter, we begin by defining measurement and several related terms, using examples drawn directly from animal-assisted work. These concepts may feel technical at first, but they are simply a shared language that helps us communicate clearly about our observations, outcomes, and decisions. Using this language well strengthens your credibility with important stakeholders – clients, colleagues, funders, organizations, and the broader field. Just as you learn the language of your human clients and your animal partners, learning the language of data-driven practice helps you communicate your work to others.

> We measure because we care about what is happening and want to respond thoughtfully.

Measurement exists because things change. To **measure** something means to quantify or qualify it so that we can notice patterns, track change over time, or inform decisions. You already measure many things in everyday life. You measure ingredients when you cook. You step on a scale to measure your weight. You measure a window before buying new curtains. These measurements help you make choices. The same is true in animal-assisted work.

The things we measure are called **variables**. A variable is simply something that can vary. Body weight varies. The amount of flour in a recipe varies. Window sizes vary. In animal-assisted services, we might measure psychological variables such as self-esteem, attitudes, or symptoms in order to understand change over time as someone participates in a service. We may also measure variables related to our animal partners. For example, we might track how often a dog lies down during an occupational therapy session, how frequently a horse walks away during equine-assisted learning, or how barn cats interact with donkeys before, during, and after sessions. These are all variables – features of the interaction or environment that can change and therefore be observed. Table 4.1 highlights examples of variables commonly encountered in animal-assisted work across human, animal, and environmental domains. Many practitioners already attend to these factors informally; naming them simply allows us to be more intentional and communicative about what we are noticing.

Once we measure a variable, the information we gather is called *data*. **Data** are the units of information we collect. When you measure a window in inches, the number of inches is data.

TABLE 4.1 Potential variables to measure in animal-assisted work

Human	*Animal*	*Environment*
Demographics (age, gender, race)	Demographics (age, breed, sex)	Setting, weather
Test scores	Health indicators (heart rate, food intake)	People present
Interactive behavior	Interactive behavior	Animals present

When you calculate a score on a symptom checklist, that score is a data point (or datum). When you collect multiple scores across time or individuals, those points together form data.

For some people, words like *measurement*, *variable*, and *data* can stir up discomfort or old anxieties about math, science, or school. These terms may feel like they belong to laboratories or to people with advanced degrees. But in reality, they describe activities you already engage in as a practitioner – observing, tracking, comparing, and making informed decisions. Learning and using this language does not change who you are or how you practice. It simply gives you tools to describe your work more clearly. Being able to measure, gather data, and talk about what you observe helps you care for yourself, your clients, and your animal partners – and it helps move the field of animal-assisted services forward.

The Power of Asking a Good Question

We start the evidence-gathering process by asking a question. And that question holds great power. It shapes the data we collect, how we interpret it, and how we respond to it. Asking an erroneous question could send us in the wrong direction. Sometimes we can even ask a question that is impossible to answer with data, or at least with the data we have access to. Believe it or not, there is a skill to asking questions. And this step is critical. We can't jump right into looking for a measurement tool. We first need a clear question, because that determines what and how we measure. Reading and working through this chapter will give you what you need to ask great questions about your work.

Types of SAGA Questions

Curiosity is the spark of investigation. Let's begin with your natural curiosity about your work. What do you want to know about your animal-assisted work? This could be something about the humans in your work or the animals. It could be about an individual, a group, or a program. There is no right or wrong answer here. Your natural curiosity is important. You know your work, and your natural curiosity is likely related to a meaningful aspect of your work that could benefit from the data-driven process. Take a minute to reflect on your curiosities, and write them down on a notepad. Your curiosity probably fits into one of the categories in Table 4.2, which provides types of questions that you might ask. They may look familiar, as they are probably questions you have asked yourself or others have asked you about your work. For example, people unfamiliar with equine-assisted services often ask us, when they hear that we offer psychotherapy and learning at the horse ranch, "what do people do out there with horses?" This is an example of a descriptive question.

As with all of our examples, this is not an exhaustive list but a sample of different kinds of questions you can ask about your animal-assisted work. These examples, combined with your natural curiosity, may lead you to a good empirical question, something that you can answer with data. Next, we refine that question by making it a smart question.

There is one important group left out of the question list in Table 4.2 – you! There are many important questions about animal-assisted practitioners, and they can be relevant to description, outcomes, or process. One especially important topic for practitioners is wellness – studying things like balance and burnout among the team. Because of its importance, we dedicate a whole chapter to team wellness in Chapter 13.

Asking SMART Questions

Once you have leaned into curiosity and have a question in mind, we recommend turning that question into a SMART question. SMART is an acronym that stands for Specific, Measurable,

TABLE 4.2 Types of questions we can ask in animal-assisted services

Focus Area	*Question Type*	*Representative Questions*
Human Participants	Describing	What does the service look like? Who are the participants? What behaviors or interactions are observed?
	Examining outcomes	Do measures differ before and after the service? Are there single-session effects? Are there multi-session effects? What is the effect of X on Y?
	Examining process	What are the key ingredients? What leads to change? How does X affect Y?
Animal Partners	Describing	What characterizes the animal partner? What are the animal's baseline behaviors? What traits or training are relevant?
	Examining outcomes/ Effects	Are there changes in behavior or arousal? Are there indicators of stress or relaxation? Are maintenance behaviors changing? Are physical welfare measures changing?
	Examining process	How does the animal engage across sessions? What interaction patterns emerge? How does arousal fluctuate? Does the animal respond differently with different participants or tasks?
Environment/ Context	Describing	What defines the setting? What physical, sensory, or social features are present? How predictable or novel is the environment?
	Examining outcomes	Do participant or animal responses vary across settings? Are outcomes different in different contexts?
	Examining process	How might setting variables influence interaction? How does context shape engagement or behavior?

Achievable, Relevant, and Time-Based. This may seem familiar to you, as it is adapted from Doran's original work on goal setting in management (1981). The SMART or SMARTS acronym has been applied in a variety of settings (e.g., Geller, 2015) and is perfect for helping us ask good questions within the SAGA framework. Let's go through each of these characteristics, with examples of meeting and not meeting the characteristic:

S – Specific

Smart questions are specific. As we alluded to in the previous section, there are various levels of specificity at which you can ask a question. A good question is specific enough to answer the question and guide decision-making. Here is an example of a question you might have, applying the characteristic of specificity.

Is the client who is receiving canine-assisted counseling improving?

This question is not specific enough. We cannot tell from the question what evidence we should gather. *Improvement* could mean many things. A more specific question would be – Are the client's *anxiety symptoms* improving? This is better because it clearly leads to evidence we could gather – anxiety symptoms. Regarding animals, a non-specific question might be *"Are animal-assisted sessions negatively affecting my animal partner?"* There are many ways that sessions could negatively affect animal partners; there could be effects on their physical health, emotional health, or behavior. A more specific question could be: *Are animal-assisted sessions causing stress for my animal?* Although this is somewhat specific – it suggests we should gather evidence on stress – there is room for improvement. A more specific question might be *"Does my dog yawn more than usual during sessions?"* Yawning behavior can be a sign of stress or just sleepiness, so it's not the best question either. But it is more specific – getting at something you could gather data on – a specific behavior.

> Not Specific – *Is the Client Improving? Is the work affecting my animal partner?*
>
> Specific – *Are the client's anxiety symptoms improving? Is my dog's yawning behavior different during animal-assisted work compared to non-work?*

M – Measurable

Smart questions are measurable. They tell us exactly what we will measure and how we will measure it. Let's continue with the question we've been working on. Our improved, more specific question is *Are the client's anxiety symptoms improving?* While this is specific, it does not tell us everything we need to make it measurable. We can tell from the question we are measuring anxiety symptoms. But we need more. *How* will we measure anxiety symptoms? To make it measurable, we spell out exactly what we are going to measure. For instance, we could measure anxiety symptoms with the Beck Anxiety Inventory (BAI) or the Generalized Anxiety Disorder 7-Item Screener (GAD-7). Then our question would be – Are the client's scores on the GAD-7 improving? This gives us clarity on what we are measuring. As the practitioner, it leads you to your next action – measure symptoms with the GAD-7.

> Not Measurable – *Are the client's anxiety symptoms improving?*
>
> Measurable – *Are the client's scores on the GAD-7 improving?*

A – Achievable

A good question should be achievable. This means we are asking a reasonable question and not something that is too difficult or unrealistic. This is most likely to come up when measuring change, such as improvement in symptoms or behavior. An example of a poor question might be – Are the client's anxiety symptoms gone? Or has the problem behavior stopped? Eliminating symptoms or problem behaviors altogether may not be achievable, but reducing symptoms or problem behaviors is. So how do you know what is achievable and what isn't? This will require you to lean on your experience – what kinds of changes have you seen in your participants in the past? You can also lean on the experience of others – ask colleagues what change has looked like for their participants. Another source of information can be reading the literature connected to your measurement tool. If you are using the GAD-7 to measure anxiety symptoms, you can read about the GAD-7, and see what the research says about difference scores or pre-post scores. You can do

> Not Achievable – *Have the client's anxiety symptoms been eliminated?*
>
> Achievable – *Have the client's anxiety symptoms been reduced from severe to moderate?*

this by searching online or reading the manual if you have it. If you use artificial intelligence (AI) tools, you can ask your AI source for an achievable change score for a given population. For example, if you are working with adult women, you could ask AI, "*What is an achievable change score for adult women receiving outpatient services to reduce anxiety symptoms, measured with the GAD-7?*" Appendix C provides guidance on using AI in your data-driven work. Of course, beware that AI can introduce bias and must be used with a critical eye (Sargsyan et al., 2025).

There is an additional aspect of the achievable criterion to discuss. In addition to ensuring that the outcome we are measuring is achievable (it really is possible to see a reduction in anxiety from moderate to minimal), we need to be sure that the data collection process we are planning is achievable. It is possible to have a great data-driven question, but the method of gathering the data is too involved, takes too much time, or cannot be gathered reliably. In that case, we need to revise the plan. We want to set ourselves up for success – create a data-gathering plan that is achievable. An example of a data plan that is not achievable might be planning to count, as a measure of happiness that pets bring their caretakers, every time a caretaker smiles in the presence of their dog. That might be a lot of smiles! It is probably not feasible to observe a person all day, every day, for a whole week and count every time they smile with their pet. Phew, we get tired just thinking about it! Instead, we could gather a smaller sample – observe the number of smiles in an hour, once a day, for five days. That is much more achievable.

> Not Achievable – *measuring the number of smiles in a pet caretaker all day, every day for a week*
>
> Achievable – *measuring the number of smiles in a pet caretaker in one hour, once a day, for five days.*

R – Relevant

Good questions are relevant, meaning they are useful and will lead to action. For any given animal-assisted service, there are many questions you could ask. As mentioned earlier, you could ask questions about the humans involved, the animals, or the environment. For each of those, you could ask about a multitude of variables. For a human recipient of animal-assisted psychotherapy, for example, you could ask about the person's emotions, thoughts, behaviors, or physiology. Each of those can be broken down further (related to our previous discussion on being specific). It is important to remember that the question you ask will move you in a particular direction. From the question, you create a plan to gather data and then eventually respond to that evidence. You will use the evidence to make a decision about your work. Asking a question that is not relevant to your overall objective(s) can be misleading, taking you in the wrong direction.

Let's stick with our example of working with someone to treat anxiety symptoms. Maybe we have a practitioner who gives their clients a battery of questionnaires to complete at intake – three different instruments that measure anxiety, depression, and self-esteem. Measuring anxiety symptoms is relevant, but measuring depression and self-esteem may not be relevant. Other variables that may be interesting, but not relevant, could be things like personality traits, sleep quality, work satisfaction, etc. Humans and animals are interesting. Human-animal interaction is interesting. Because it is so interesting, we could get sidetracked by asking questions that are interesting but not necessarily relevant to the task at hand or the service objectives.

Measurement can take time and energy – for the practitioner and the respondent. And measurement should lead us in a specific direction in the decision-making process. Measuring the wrong variable can lead us in the wrong direction and take up a client's time and energy while not really helping them. So it's imperative, in order to do good work for our human recipients and our animal partners, that we measure something relevant. A hint that you may not be sticking to the "relevant" criterion is if you are measuring many different things. The more variables you are measuring, the more likely you are straying from the intended focus of the SAGA process and measuring things that are irrelevant.

> Not Relevant – *measuring too many variables, measuring variables that are interesting but not directly related.*
>
> Relevant – *measuring exactly what you are targeting in your SAGA process.*

T – Time-based

Smart questions are time-based, meaning they name a specific time period for data collection. Asking whether a client is improving is too vague. Instead, we could ask, are the client's anxiety symptoms lower today than they were six weeks ago? Comparing today and six weeks ago makes the question time-based. No improvement from one day to the next is not very meaningful or surprising. But no improvement over six weeks might indicate a problem with the treatment plan and thus lead to an important adjustment. The time-based criterion often overlaps with the Specific criterion for smart questions because asking about time makes the question more specific. For the example question about animal welfare, we could ask about the number of yawns we observe in our animal during a one-hour session, compared to one hour at the same time of day on non-working days. This is more specific and will give us a better comparison.

> Not time-based – *Is my dog yawning more during animal-assisted sessions than other times?*
>
> Time-based – *Is my dog yawning more during one-hour animal-assisted sessions compared to the same one hour, at the same time of day, during nonworking days?*

Putting It All Together

Putting it all together, we now provide examples of questions that are not so SMART and revise them to be SMART. Again, the reason for doing this is to develop the skill of asking a question that can be answered with data and then used to make important decisions about your work. First, putting it all together, here is a super SMART question, applying all the criteria into one question:

> ***Did <u>anxiety symptoms</u>* (Specific) *measured with <u>GAD-7 scores</u>* (Measurable), *decrease from <u>severe to moderate</u>* (Achievable & Relevant) *between <u>intake and six weeks</u>* (Time-Based)*?***

We can see all five criteria are met. We are specifically interested in anxiety symptoms; we will measure them with the GAD-7. A decrease from moderate to minimal is achievable and relevant, and we're asking about a specific time period. For the remainder of the chapter, we share examples of starting with a common question and turning it into a smart question. Let's imagine the following hypothetical scenario:

Shawna lives at Maple Ridge, a nursing home with a facility animal. Isaac the cat lives at the facility and visits residents at his leisure. We will develop several smart questions for this scenario – one for assessing an individual resident, one for evaluating a whole program, and one for assessing the effects on the animal partner.

Assessment of an Individual Resident

- Is Shawna benefiting from the facility cat?
  - Is the facility cat increasing Shawna's social behavior?
    - ☐ Is the facility cat increasing Shawna's visits with other residents?
      - Do the staff observe Shawna talking to the other residents more when the facility cat is present than when the facility cat is not present?

Here we went from the vague question of a resident benefiting from the animal to a specific type of benefit – increased visiting with other residents – and a time-based comparison – when the cat is present compared to when the cat is not present. The question will then lead to developing a method for quantifying visiting behavior and a timeline for making observations.

Evaluation of a Program in the Facility

- Does the facility cat influence attendance at Maple Ridge events?
  - Does the facility cat influence attendance at resident social hours?
    - ☐ Is the number of residents in attendance at weekly social hours different when the facility cat is present than when the cat is not present?

In this series of questions, we move from a vague question about the cat influencing event attendance to a specific type of event – social hours. Our last question gives us the specific data to be collected – number of residents in attendance at weekly social hours – and a time-based comparison to make – when the cat is present compared to when the cat is not present.

Assessment of the Animal Partner

- How is being a facility animal affecting Isaac's health?
  - How is being a facility animal affecting Isaac's physical health?
    - ☐ Is interacting with residents affecting Isaac's diet and weight?
      - Do residents report giving Isaac cat treats and human food in-between meals?
      - What is Isaac's weekly weight in ounces?

Notice that we have two final questions here. We asked about interactions with residents and the effects on the cat's diet and weight. That is getting at two different pieces of evidence – residents feeding the cat and the cat's weight – so we have a separate question for each. We could gather both types of data simultaneously, or if that is too difficult, we could prioritize and gather the data one type after the other.

Try It! Ask a SAGA Question

Now return to the question you thought of earlier in the chapter and run it through the process to create a SMART question.

1. Make it specific, measurable, achievable, relevant, and time-based.
2. Practice doing this with a variety of questions you have about your work. We recommend creating a list of SAGA questions and adding to it on a regular basis. You'll see that once you are on your SAGA journey, empirical questions will come to mind frequently.
3. Record all of your curiosities; no question is a bad question to get you started.
4. When you are ready to act on it, develop it into a SMART question.

Get into the habit of being specific and thinking about the *what, when,* and *how* of measurement. And now that you understand conceptual measurement – how to develop a smart question, we will help you with practical measurement – how to actually do the measuring that can answer your question. Get ready to make your question measurable in Chapter 5.

Bibliography

Anastasi, A., & Urbina, S. (1997). *Psychological testing* (7th ed.). Prentice Hall.

Doran, G. T. (1981). There's a S.M.A.R.T. way to write management's goals and objectives. *Management Review, 70*(11), 35–36.

Geller, E. S. (2015). Seven life lessons from humanistic behaviorism: How to bring the best out of yourself and others. *Journal of Organizational Behavior Management, 35*(1), 151–170.

Kazdin, A. E. (2008). Evidence-based treatment and practice: New opportunities to bridge clinical research and practice. *American Psychologist, 63*(3), 146–159.

Locke, E. A., & Latham, G. P. (2002). Building a practically useful theory of goal setting and task motivation. *American Psychologist, 57*(9), 705–717.

Pasiuk, E. L., Rudd, C., Webberson, E., Anderson, N. C., Hall, N., Stellato, A. C., & Schroeder, K. (2023). Investigating human experiences and perceptions of unmounted activities commonly practiced in equine-assisted services. *Human-Animal Interactions, 11*, 1–11.

Popper, K. (1959). *The logic of scientific discovery*. Routledge.

Sargsyan, A., Weierbach, F. M., Horn, F., & Beebe, L. H. (2025). Artificial intelligence applications to aid qualitative research in animal-assisted therapies with farm animals. *Western Journal of Nursing Research, 48*(4) 423–430.

Serpell, J. A., McCune, S., Gee, N. R., & Griffin, J. A. (2017). Current challenges to research on animal-assisted interventions. *Applied Developmental Science, 21*(3), 223–233.

5

Making Questions Measurable

Field Story 5: Our Measurement Saga

After spending time with the animals at the ranch, people often pause before leaving. Sometimes it happens after brushing Peaches, a Paint mare, in the warm corner of the pasture, her body leaning gently into the rhythm of the brush. Other times it follows a quiet moment cuddling with Red, a barn cat who settles in close, kneading and purring. The experience may not be dramatic, yet people frequently exhale, smile, or say something like, *"I don't know how to explain it, but that was amazing."* Early in our work, we captured these moments by listening and documenting participants' reflections in therapy notes or learning-session summaries, where they described feeling calmer, lighter, more grounded, or simply "better." Over time, we wanted to better understand what was happening across sessions, so we began gathering evidence. In Figure 5.1, you can see us testing an observational method with our four-legged partner Peaches.

We started measuring participant responses with a simple 1–10 distress rating scale, which often showed decreases in distress after the session. But the measure quickly revealed its limits, as people did not all feel "better" in the same way. Sometimes the shift was toward calm or reduced anxiety; other times, it was feeling uplifted, happy, or less sad. To address that, we began using two separate rating scales – one for anxiety and one for mood. This small change helped clarify that animal interactions were associated with more than

DOI: 10.4324/9781003640257-7

FIGURE 5.1 Liz and Angela practicing measurement at the ranch. Liz is connecting with Peaches, a therapy horse, and Angela is recording observations.

one type of emotional shift. When we later moved into more formal data collection, we wanted to use published, validated measures. We began with the Mood States in Daily Life Scale (Wilhelm & Schoebi, 2007), which assesses mood state across three domains: calm, valence, and well-being. This was a meaningful step forward and allowed us to ground our work in established measurement tools. At the same time, we found that the three domains still did not fully explain what participants were experiencing. The data showed change, but the *quality* of that change remained somewhat vague.

We eventually turned to the Modified Differential Emotions Scale (mDES), which measures specific positive and negative emotions rather than broad mood categories (Fredrickson, 2013). This shift allowed us to see differences between feeling happy, content, loved, calm, or hopeful – distinctions that mattered in understanding participants' experiences. Alongside the rating scales, we also added three brief open-ended questions so participants could describe outcomes in their own words.

Together, this progression helped us better understand what we now describe as the *anodyne effect* (Fournier, 2019) of engaging with animals. This is a temporary, meaningful shift in emotional state that is often hard to articulate and best captured when our measures evolve alongside what people and animals are experiencing. This case illustrates that making something measurable is not about finding one perfect tool, but about listening carefully to what is happening in practice and allowing our questions – and our measures – to evolve alongside it.

Types of Data

We defined the term data in the last chapter, and now we are ready to discuss the different types of data you might have access to or that you may want to create. There are three major categories of data that we see animal-assisted professionals gathering and using – records, self-report data, and observable behavior. We define them briefly here and then cover them in separate chapters later in the book.

Records

One type of data that you probably already have is your records. You keep records on the humans in your work, for example, therapy clients, learning students, or executive team members. You may also keep records on your animal partners, like health records and behavior records. These records contain data that you might use to answer important questions in your SAGA work.

Self-Report

Self-report data is what it sounds like; these are data that are created by an individual reporting on themselves. Self-report data are often question-and-answer types of data or paper-and-pencil questionnaires or surveys. With a self-report tool, we ask an individual something about themselves, and they report it back to us. A classic example would be an individual in counseling who completes a self-report instrument that measures anxiety symptoms at intake. The self-report instrument asks questions about anxiety. Participants reflect on their experiences and respond to the items, often using numerical ratings that are combined into a score representing their level of anxiety. Self-report is a very common type of evidence that we often collect, and in Chapter 9, we will talk about the best ways to plan, gather, and use that evidence.

Observable Behavior

Observable behaviors are actions we can directly see someone do. These data often involve behaviors that are counted, such as the number of times a therapy dog lies down during a session or the number of times a person speaks to a horse. This book includes two chapters devoted to observable behavior data: Chapter 6 on naturalistic observation and Chapter 7 on systematic observation. Many practitioners already make these kinds of observations in their work; the difference is learning to record them intentionally and use them more systematically.

Making a Variable Measurable

Now that we have introduced the different types of data we can gather, let's move through the process of making a variable measurable. We take you through four steps – choosing your variable, learning about your variable, deciding what data format will answer your question, and finding a way to measure your variable.

Choose Your Variable

The first step in measurement is to identify the variable you intend to measure. A variable is simply what you are trying to understand or track. In animal-assisted services, variables usually reflect the outcome you care about most – what you hope will change because of the interaction.

So far, research in animal-assisted services has examined a wide range of outcome variables, such as self-esteem, communication, anxiety, relationship skills, depression, and empowerment. In practice, an individual client typically has a specific goal. To evaluate whether that goal is being met, we need to measure the variable most closely aligned with it and track change over time. This is where the *relevant* criterion of the SMART question framework becomes especially important. Therefore, you **identify your variable by asking yourself what the goal of the service is.**

For example, when an individual participating in animal-assisted learning was asked why they presented for services, they said, "*I want to talk to my spouse without yelling*." From that, we know that the intended outcome of the service is to improve communication. So, the variable that we are going to measure is communication, or more specifically, communication skills. This is a key formula for your work:

Goal	*Disagree without yelling*
↓	↓
Outcome	Improved communication
↓	↓
Variable	Measure communication skills

Here is another example: a teen is participating in counseling services that incorporate Red, the therapy cat. The teen is asking for help with social anxiety. From that, we might assume the desired outcome is a reduction in anxiety, and therefore, the variable we need to measure is anxiety symptoms. Let's apply the formula again:

Goal	*Help with social anxiety*
↓	↓
Outcome	Decrease in anxiety symptoms
↓	↓
Variable	Measure anxiety symptoms

Table 5.1 provides more examples following this formula. If you are unsure what the reason for the animal-assisted service you're providing is, spend some time discussing it with your client/participant and reflecting on it. If you're providing a service that someone else requested (e.g., the county is sending a group of underserved youth to spend time with animals), ask the referral source what their goal is. Or maybe you know what the goal of the service is, but you're having difficulty linking that with a specific variable. That's ok! Spend a little time getting help with that. You could Google the topic, ask an AI source (refer to our suggestions on using AI in Appendix C), or ask a friend or colleague for ideas.

TABLE 5.1 Examples of moving from service goal to measurable variable

Goal (Reason for service)	*Outcome (What you want)*	*Variable (What to measure)*
A dog visitation program is intended to uplift nursing home residents.	Improved mood	Mood state Positive affect
The library hosts a dog reading program, aimed at helping elementary students feel more confident in their reading.	Improved confidence in reading	Reading confidence Reading self-efficacy Oral reading volume
A woman participates in psychotherapy incorporating horses; she is being treated for depression.	Reduction in depression symptoms	Symptoms of depression Increased energy
A corporate group attends equine-assisted learning as a team-building exercise.	Increased group cohesion, improved communication	Group cohesion Communication skills
The university counseling center is sending a group of students out to the ranch for some rest and relaxation with the animals.	Reduced stress Relaxation	Perceived stress Arousal

The goal is to be intentional, which means taking just a little bit of time beforehand to do your homework.

Learn about Your Variable

The second step in the measurement process is to learn about your variable. At this stage, the goal is not to choose a specific measurement tool but to better understand what kind of information the variable represents and how it fits within your SAGA process. Measurement in animal-assisted services is not always about demonstrating change; often it is about understanding what is happening during sessions, how experiences unfold, or how people and animals are responding in context. Two considerations are especially helpful at this point.

What role does this variable play? Some variables represent outcomes we hope will change, such as mood, anxiety, or confidence. Others help us understand processes, experiences, or patterns – what occurs during an interaction, how an activity is experienced, or how animals and people respond to one another over time. Clarifying the role of the variable helps ensure that what you measure aligns with what you are trying to learn.

If a change is expected, how changeable is the variable? When a variable is intended to capture change, it is important to consider whether that change is realistic within the time frame and context of your service. Some variables are relatively stable and unlikely to shift quickly, while others fluctuate from moment to moment. Understanding a variable's changeability helps you decide whether it makes sense to measure it before and after a session, across multiple sessions, or simply to describe it as it occurs.

When choosing a variable you expect to change, it is important to ask whether the variable is a trait or a state. **Traits** are relatively stable characteristics that do not change easily over time or across situations, such as personality factors like introversion or extroversion. A **state**, in contrast, is a temporary condition that can change from moment to moment or day to day, such as mood, arousal, or situational anxiety. Because traits are slow to change, we should not expect them to shift meaningfully after a brief animal-assisted session – or even a short series of sessions. For that reason, traits are rarely good outcome variables when we are looking for change related to animal-assisted services. Below, we provide some examples of traits and states.

Traits – stable, difficult to change

- Introversion/Extroversion
- Agreeable/Disagreeable
- Type A Personality/Type B Personality

States – dynamic, more easily changed

- Mood
- Arousal
- Situational Anxiety

Another helpful way to think of variables is along a **continuum of malleability**. Some variables are less malleable (harder to change) than others. Personality traits, intelligence, and species-specific characteristics tend to be slow to change, while mood state and activity level can shift quickly and frequently. Variables

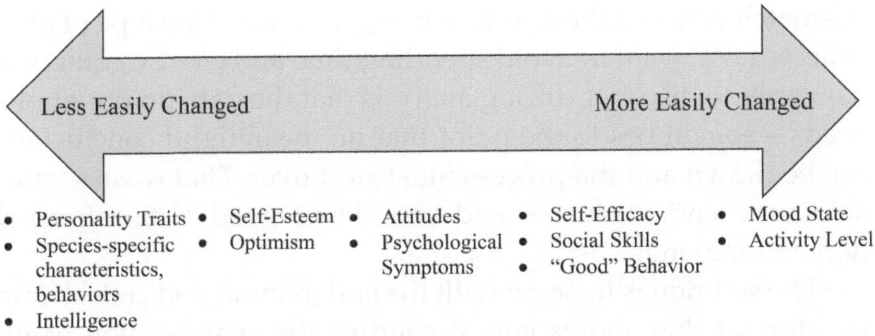

FIGURE 5.2 Continuum of malleability.

such as self-esteem, optimism, attitudes, and self-efficacy often fall somewhere in between. Figure 5.2 illustrates this continuum of malleability. While exact placement is approximate and can vary across individuals, variables tend to cluster within a general range. Traits should never be expected to change rapidly, and highly transient states should not be interpreted as lasting outcomes. The key is matching the variable to the time frame and goals of your service.

Decide Which Data *Format* Will Answer Your Question

Begin with the End in Mind (Covey, 1989). We recommend writing this phrase somewhere you will see it every time you work on your data-driven practice. Always begin with the end in mind. Usually, when we plan to gather data, it is because we have a goal or intention. Maybe we want to make a data-informed decision (yay – that's awesome!), or maybe we want to use data in a grant application or a presentation to stakeholders. These are all excellent reasons to collect data, and, in many cases, you will be motivated by more than one of them. We suggest that early in the process, you imagine the type of evidence you hope to showcase in that proposal or presentation. Are you picturing a table with percentages, a bar chart comparing two groups, or a word cloud illustrating the range of participant comments?

Chances are, you already have an idea of the kind of evidence you want and the kinds of statements you would like to be able to make (for example, "student ratings increased from the first session to the last"). This matters because there is sometimes a mismatch between the question being asked and the type of data collected. We want to avoid spending time and energy gathering data only to discover during analysis that the data do not fit our needs – sometimes to the point that no meaningful conclusions can be drawn and the process must start over. That wastes valuable time and resources and can derail good data-informed decision-making.

The solution is to begin with the end in mind and collect data in a format that allows you to conduct the analyses you want. There are two main ways we categorize quantitative data – categorical and continuous – which, at a basic level, come down to whether you have numbers or not. Categorical data place people, animals, or items into groups, with no inherent order or magnitude (for example, gender, race, grade level, species, or breed). You can count how many cases fall into each category, but you cannot perform mathematical operations beyond counting. Continuous data, by contrast, are true numerical variables that can be added, subtracted, multiplied, and divided, making statistical analyses possible – such as calculating averages, comparing groups, examining correlations, or identifying ranges. Although numbers are a powerful form of evidence, they are not the only kind. Later in the book, we introduce qualitative methods for working with non-numerical, word-based evidence. For now, however, we will focus on quantitative data, since many practitioners imagine answering their questions with numbers – presenting averages, bar graphs, or correlations to a board of directors or other stakeholders.

Choose a Strong Measurement Tool

Once you have chosen a potential variable, learned about it, and found that it is indeed something that makes sense for you to measure (e.g., you want to demonstrate change, and it is a variable that can potentially change), then you are ready to find an actual measurement instrument or method. You do not need to, and in most cases should not, reinvent the wheel. This is true for many things, including measurement. Chances are, you are NOT the first person to want to measure your variable. Even though you are super awesome and unique and no one does the

There are many excellent instruments, and it is better to use an existing instrument that has been shown to be strong than to create your own.

awesome things that you do just like you, people have been measuring variables for a long time, and there is a good chance the instrument you need is out there.

To get started, begin learning about the measurement of your variable. You can do this by simply googling "measures of [insert name of variable]." We cover the process of finding an instrument in much more detail in Chapter 9. When you find a measurement instrument or method you think might fit your needs, then you should learn about that instrument. Gosh – the work is never done, right?! Hang in there. It is a lot of work, but it is important work, and you can do it. Putting in the effort to choose the right variable and measure it with a good instrument will pay off in better, more accurate evidence. And more accurate evidence will lead to a better understanding of your work and improve your ability to make data-driven decisions for your clients, your animals, your business, and yourself. So, how do we know if the measurement tool (e.g., test, survey, checklist) we found is a good one? Great question! This leads to two very important terms – *reliability* and *validity* – that you may have heard of or used, but perhaps not in the context of measurement.

Reliability – You Can Count on It

When we say someone is reliable, we mean they are consistent – we can count on them. Reliability in measurement applies this same idea to a tool. A **reliable** measurement tool works the same way each time and produces consistent results. A common example used to explain reliability is a bathroom scale. If I step on the scale ten times in ten minutes and my weight has not actually changed, I should see the same number each time. That consistency tells me the scale is reliable. If the number changes every time I step on it, the scale is unreliable – it's not something I can count on.

When you measure anything for your practice – learning outcomes, symptoms, participant satisfaction, or behavior – you want information you can trust. If a tool is not reliable, the data it produces are unlikely to be accurate. Reliability is established through testing, where researchers examine whether a tool produces consistent results across people, time, or situations. Because this process is complex, it's usually best to use existing instruments that already have evidence of reliability rather than creating your own. With reliability in mind, we can now turn to the next essential question: even if a tool is consistent, is it measuring what we want to measure? That brings us to validity.

Validity – Measuring What Is Intended

In the context of measurement instruments, **validity** refers to whether a tool measures what it is intended to measure. A depression inventory with good validity actually measures depression. A satisfaction survey with good validity measures participant satisfaction. A good-dog behavior checklist measures good-dog behavior. Validity matters because many of the things we care about in animal-assisted services – emotions, attitudes, well-being – are abstract and cannot be observed directly. Because we can't physically locate or measure something like self-esteem, we rely on questions we believe reflect that construct. But it's possible to miss the mark. For example, a measure designed to assess self-esteem might instead capture optimism or general mood. In that case, something is being measured, but not the variable we intended. That would be an example of poor validity.

There are different ways researchers gather evidence for validity, involving comparisons between tests and related data, and that process can be complex. For our purposes, what matters is understanding the core idea: a valid tool measures what it claims to measure, and any instrument you use should have evidence supporting that claim. In Chapter 9, we'll walk through how to find measures with strong evidence of both reliability and validity.

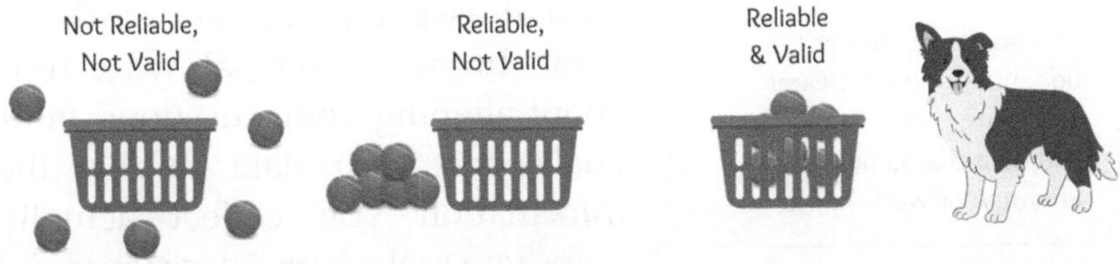

FIGURE 5.3 Representation of the relationship between reliability and validity. Reliability is Ruby getting the tennis balls in the same place each time (being consistent). Validity is getting the balls in the basket (hitting the target).

Reliability and Validity Together

To wrap up our discussion of reliability and validity, it helps to think about how these concepts work together. Ideally, we want our measurement tools to be both reliable and valid. In practice, tools vary in the strength of evidence supporting each, and while reliability and validity are related, they are not interchangeable. Figure 5.3 shows Ruby, who loves to retrieve tennis balls and is working on putting them in the basket.

On the left, the balls are scattered and not in the basket – neither reliable nor valid. In the center, the balls are consistently placed in the same spot but still outside the basket – reliable but not valid. On the right, the balls are consistently placed *in* the basket – both reliable and valid. This is the goal: a tool that measures consistently *and* measures the right variable.

Once you have identified a variable, learned about how it behaves and changes, and selected a measurement tool with evidence of both reliability and validity, you are ready… drum roll, please… to begin gathering data.

Ready to Measure without Losing Meaning

Making something measurable means slowing down long enough to be intentional about what you are trying to understand, why it matters, and how you will know if change is happening. As this chapter's field story illustrates, even well-designed measures can miss the mark. Measurement is not about proving that

The goal is not perfection, but progress: clearer questions, better-fit measures, and data that genuinely inform your work.

animal-assisted services "work" in some broad, universal way. It is about aligning your questions, your goals, and your data so that the information you collect actually helps you make better decisions – for your clients, your animals, and your practice. In the chapters that follow, we move from theory to application, showing you how to locate, select, and use specific measurement tools.

Try It! Name and Measure a SAGA Variable

To continue with the SAGA process:

1. Recall the SMART question you developed in Chapter 4. What is the variable you need to measure to answer that question? If you can't tell, revisit your question. It may not be specific enough.
2. Learn what you can to answer these questions about the variable:
   - What role is the variable playing (outcome, process, description)?
   - How changeable is it?
3. Think of three different ways you could measure the variable, and do your homework to decide which one is best for your SAGA process.

Bibliography

American Psychological Association Presidential Task Force on Evidence-Based Practice. (2006). Evidence-based practice in psychology. *American Psychologist*, *61*(4), 271–285. https://doi.org/10.1037/0003-066X.61.4.27

Anastasi, A., & Urbina, S. (1997). *Psychological testing* (7th ed.). Prentice Hall.

Conjointly. (n.d.). *Research methods knowledge base*. https://conjointly.com/kb/

Covey, S. R. (1989). *The 7 habits of highly effective people*. Free Press.

DeVellis, R. F. (2016). *Scale development: Theory and applications* (4th ed.). Sage.

Fournier, A. K. (2019). Animals as anodyne. In *Animal-assisted intervention: Thinking empirically* (pp. 53–74). Springer International Publishing.

Fournier, A. K. (2019). HAI dose in animal-assisted intervention. In *Animal-assisted intervention: Thinking empirically* (pp. 31–51). Springer International Publishing.

Fredrickson, B. L. (2013). Positive emotions broaden and build. *Advances in Experimental Social Psychology*, *47*, 1–53.

Furr, R. M. (2021). *Psychometrics: An introduction* (4th ed.). Sage.

Gee, N. R., Fine, A. H., & McCardle, P. (Eds.). (2017). *How animals help students learn: Research and practice for educators and mental-health professionals*. Taylor & Francis.

Grandin, T. (1995). *Thinking in pictures*. Vintage.

Johnston, J. M., & Pennypacker, H. S. (2009). *Strategies and tactics of behavioral research* (3rd ed.). Routledge.

McCrae, R. R., & Costa, P. T. (1994). The stability of personality. *Current Directions in Psychological Science*, *3*(6), 173–175.

Nunnally, J. C., & Bernstein, I. H. (1994). *Psychometric theory* (3rd ed.). McGraw-Hill.

Pasiuk, E. L., Rudd, C., Webberson, E., Anderson, N. C., Hall, N., Stellato, A. C., & Schroeder, K. (2023). Investigating human experiences and perceptions of unmounted activities commonly practiced in equine-assisted services. *Human-Animal Interactions*, *11*, 1–11.

Sacks, O. (1985). *The man who mistook his wife for a hat*. Summit Books.

Schön, D. A. (1983). *The reflective practitioner*. Basic Books.

Skorupiński, P. M. (2015). American Educational Research Association, American Psychological Association, National Council on Measurement in Education, Standards for Educational and Psychological Testing. *Kwartalnik Pedagogiczny*, *238*(4), 201–203.

Spielberger, C. D. (1983). *Manual for the State–Trait Anxiety Inventory (STAI)*. Mind Garden/Consulting Psychologists Press.

Wilhelm, P., & Schoebi, D. (2007). Mood states in daily life scale. *European Journal of Psychological Assessment*, 23(4):258–267.

Part III
Gather Your Evidence

6

Watching with Purpose

Observing Natural Behavior

Field Story 6: Bucking Bronco

On a cool morning in November of 2017, we found ourselves in the indoor arena at Eagle Vista Ranch, each of us doing what we do best. Liz was co-facilitating a group session with Jen Laitala, an equine specialist at the ranch. Angela was collecting data. In the arena was a group of four university student "participants," three other university students helping with data collection and a dog named Bronco (pictured in Figure 6.1). The student clients were there to learn about problem-solving and Bronco was helping them as part of the facilitation team. Angela and the student data collectors stood back and quietly observed.

Liz and Jen invited the participants to think of a group goal and a couple of barriers to reaching that goal. They asked the students to use props in the arena to create a physical representation of their goal and barriers and then create a path to the goal with the barriers along the way. They were told that once their path was built, they should bring the four-legged (i.e., Bronco) through the path to their goal. Like the good students they were, the participants went to work on their assignment, huddling up to discuss and plan. Bronco was off-leash in the arena, casually walking around and sniffing. He would occasionally walk up to the participants, the facilitators, or the data collectors and sniff and wag his tail. After a few minutes,

DOI: 10.4324/9781003640257-9

FIGURE 6.1 Bronco, a loyal family member, therapy partner, and hunting companion.

the participants had their plan and went to work. They placed a traffic cone at the far end of the arena and used a recipe card and marker to label it "*Graduate*." They then used pool noodles to create a path from one part of the arena to the traffic cone. They placed large barrels on the path; these were their barriers, labeled "*Time management*" and "*Finances*."

With their path complete, the participants called Bronco over. He came running, tail wagging, looking very excited. He ran around them, sniffing, panting, and wagging his tail. They tried to guide him through their path without a collar or leash and although he was engaging with them, he wasn't really doing what they asked. He was full of energy, running around and through the path, circling the group. They petted him and played with him a little, laughing. Suddenly, Bronco picked up the pool noodle labeled *Time Management* and started running around with it in his mouth. This made the students laugh at first. But then they tried to get it from him and couldn't; they seemed to get a bit frustrated, looking to the facilitators for help. Liz and Jen walked over to discuss.

Together, they brainstormed different options. During this brainstorm, Bronco began chewing up the pool noodle, essentially destroying their path to graduation. Liz and Jen coached the participants on commands that Bronco knew "*sit, stay, drop it*" and he released the pool noodle. During the debrief, the students shared what they learned about problem solving – that "*you have to have patience and persistence*," and "*sometimes you have to know when to ask for help along the path to graduation*."

Why That Animal?

You may be familiar with this question. Animal-assisted practitioners are often asked why they work with a particular species, breed, or individual animal. It's a good question, one that you probably have an answer for, and one that researchers are working to help us understand at a broad level. One thing we have long been curious about is the gifts that different species bring to animal-assisted services. We can all agree that a wonderful therapy dog is the result of some complex combination of species characteristics, breed characteristics, individual genes, temperament, learning history, and physical and emotional health. These factors, along with trust in and connection with their handler, can make a great therapy dog. We could say the same about a great therapy horse. Horses possess species-specific characteristics, influenced further by breed traits, individual histories, and lived experience. Most of us would acknowledge that dogs and horses can be good therapy animals and that while they may share some similarities, they bring different talents to the table. Whatever species you work with, or plan to work with eventually, write your thoughts on what makes that species a good candidate for animal-assisted services. As you write, consider which of these qualities you could *observe* directly during a session, and which you tend to assume.

Because we each had varied experiences with horses and dogs, we grew curious about how they compare in their interactions with humans. That curiosity led to the study and the experience described in this chapter's field story (the study was also referred to in the Research section of Chapter 3). We held sessions like the one we described with Bronco. And we held the same kind of session with a horse named Montana. We gathered all kinds of data on these sessions, looking to make comparisons and increase our understanding of how sessions are similar or different when they incorporate a dog versus a horse – the two most common therapy animals. One of the key methods of data gathering was observation.

What Is Observation?

Observation is a wonderful tool for data-driven work and something that you already do all the time. As humans, we are social creatures. We engage with others and we also are fascinated by others. Because of this, we spend time watching others. In a restaurant, maybe you spend some of the time watching people at other tables or watching the staff. At home, you probably spend a good amount of time watching your animal companions and other family members. And as an animal handler who partners with animals to help humans, you probably observe the interactions between your animal partner and the humans you serve.

In Chapter 5, we described three different types of data – records, observations, and self-reports. All of these can be valuable in your data-driven process. We recommend using observational data first, if possible, because it can have greater reliability and validity – two concepts you now know and care about. But first, let's start in a familiar place – with some definitions.

Behavior

Behavior can be defined as the way in which an animal or person acts in response to a particular situation or event. Put more simply, behaviors are things that we *do*. We classify behaviors into two categories – *overt* and *covert*. **Overt behaviors** are behaviors you can see someone do. Walking, talking, petting, panting – these are behaviors we can watch happen. **Covert behaviors** are things we do that are not directly observable. Thinking about something, solving a math problem in your head, feeling sad and reflecting on why – these are examples of covert behavior.

In this chapter, we focus on overt, observable behaviors. When developing your smart, empirical questions for data-driven practice, try to ask a question about observable behavior where possible, especially when asking a question about animals. Because animals can't speak to us and tell us what they are thinking or feeling, overt behavior is the best way to gather evidence on their experience and well-being. And although humans may be able to verbalize their thoughts and feelings, observable behavior still has fewer limitations and will likely be more reliable than asking them to tell you what is happening or did happen. Of course, there will be questions that you need to ask, and evidence you need to gather, that cannot be done through direct observation. That's okay. We discuss how to work with other types of data in the next few chapters. Just don't lean too heavily on self-report or forget to record observable behavior as part of your data-driven process.

As we discussed in Chapter 5, data can be **qualitative** – rich descriptions, written or spoken – or **quantitative** – numbers, calculations. Behavioral observations can be recorded qualitatively or quantitatively. Figure 6.2 provides an image to illustrate the difference. The image shows how we could record different animals' interactions with human participants. On the left, the qualitative data consists of written descriptions of

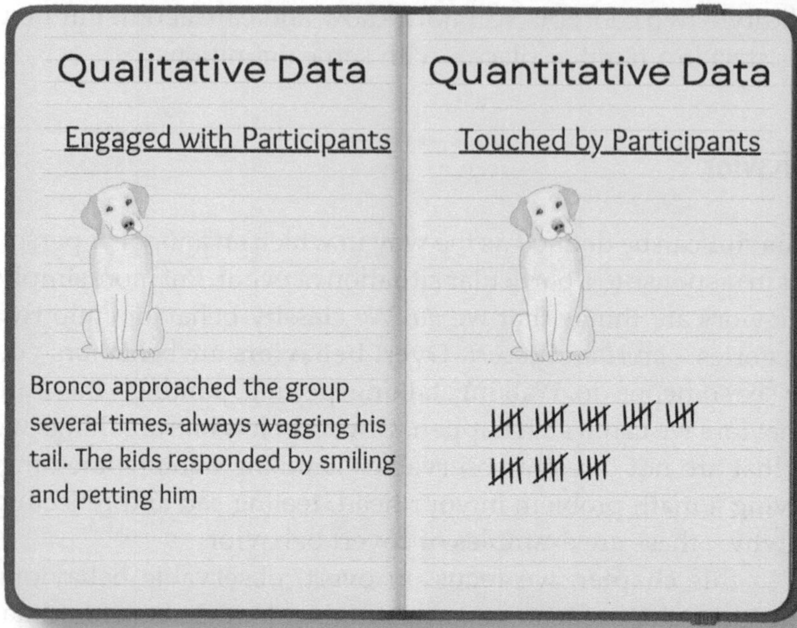

FIGURE 6.2 Distinguishing between qualitative data and quantitative data.

what it looked like when Bronco engaged with participants. Qualitative data can also be drawings. Sometimes you need to sketch what you see and then put it into words later. On the right of the figure, the quantitative data shows the frequency count for the number of times Bronco was touched by participants.

Both types of data could fall under the category of human-animal interaction, but they give us very different information. Ideally, our data-driven processes should include a combination of quantitative and qualitative data. Together, they give us a more complete picture of whatever it is we're studying. Table 6.1 provides examples of behavioral data you could collect for animal-assisted services, including behaviors elicited by humans, by animals, and interactive behavior between humans and animals.

Let's take the first behavior in the table. Body posture in humans during a session could be an indication of engagement, affect, or any number of other things. You can record a person's

TABLE 6.1 Examples of behavioral data

	Example Behaviors	*Possible Interpretation*
Human Behavior	**Body posture/orientation** – open vs. closed posture	Engagement or avoidance
	Facial expressions – smiling, frowning, neutral, tearful	Affective state or change
	Verbal tone or content – soothing, harsh, silent	Interpersonal tone
Animal Behavior	**Approach or avoidance** – moves toward or away	Comfort, curiosity, stress
	Ear, tail, or body posture – relaxed, alert, tense	Arousal, emotional state
	Vocalizations – nickering, barking, sighing, silence	Communication, distress, arousal level
Human-Animal Interaction	**Mutual gaze/attention** – both look at each other	Shared attention, connection
	Approach-response – who starts an interaction, how the other responds	Connection, avoidance
	Mutual arousal – both relax or tense together	Mutual regulation or contagion of emotion

body posture by describing what you see – *the participant initially sat with arms crossed and did not make eye contact, but when the cat approached him, he opened his arms and patted his lap*. This is an example of qualitative data. On the other hand, to collect quantitative data, you could record the human's posture as closed (arms across the body) or open (arms open or at sides) – by simply writing a hashtag for the corresponding category in a notebook several times throughout the session. This would give you the number of times you observed the person's posture as open versus closed. And maybe you could track that data to see if it changes from session to session. The list of behaviors in Table 6.1 is not exhaustive. The interpretations listed are possible meanings, not definitive conclusions. You are the author of your data story; you ask your SMART question and then gather the evidence you need to answer that question.

There are two major ways to record behavior – naturalistic observation and systematic observation. Naturalistic observation allows us to record a rich description of a behavior and factors that may influence the behavior, such as the environment and what happens before and after the behavior. On the contrary, systematic observation involves observing and recording specific behaviors, carefully defined. We cover systematic observation in Chapter 7. For the remainder of this chapter, we walk you through naturalistic observation.

Naturalistic Observation

Naturalistic observation is what it sounds like; you make observations of the natural situation without manipulation and with as few preconceived expectations as possible. Of course, complete neutrality is impossible; the goal is to remain open to what occurs rather than only what we expect to see. This type of observation is best when first studying a behavior. We need to see the behavior as it naturally occurs. Then, once you have made some observations, you may have a more specific question that can be answered with systematic observation.

Naturalistic observations can be recorded by hand, by writing notes, or by typing into a computer. Speaking into an audio recording about what you observe is another possibility, if speaking aloud will not interfere with the behavior being observed. Videorecording is a third way to conduct naturalistic observation.

> You can record behaviors occurring naturally on a phone or mobile device for later review.

Next, we share an example of naturalistic observation we conducted on our work.

Naturalistic Observation Example

Refer to the field case at the beginning of this chapter. Bronco helped students learn about patience and perseverance when he disrupted the path they had created. As part of the study, we video recorded those sessions and then made naturalistic observations to answer our question – How are human-animal interactions with a dog similar to or different from those with a horse? First, we watched the videos all the way through. We had no predictions or expectations beforehand; we tried to watch as if we were seeing humans and dogs and horses interact for the first time. We were guided only by our question –How is human-animal interaction similar or different with dogs compared to horses? Then we watched them again, taking notes on anything we saw that seemed related to our question.

We noticed the sessions were made up of instances of human-animal interaction and quite a bit of time when there was no interaction happening. We also noticed that the kinds of interactions that happened most noticeably and frequently were humans approaching the animal and the animal then responding in some way. We watched the recordings several times and noticed that although the humans showed similar behaviors when initiating interactions with the horse and dog (called them by name, walked over to, and petted them), the dog and horse responded to the humans differently. Figure 6.3 shows the sequence of events for people approaching Bronco, illustrated on the left, and Montana, illustrated on the right.

You can see that the interaction with Bronco was more involved than the interaction with Montana. When the students called Bronco, he ran over to them with his tail wagging. The students would smile and laugh and pet and talk to him. In response, he would wag his tail more (imagine a Labrador-whole-body wag) and circle the group. This would increase the students' energy and they would laugh more, pet him more,

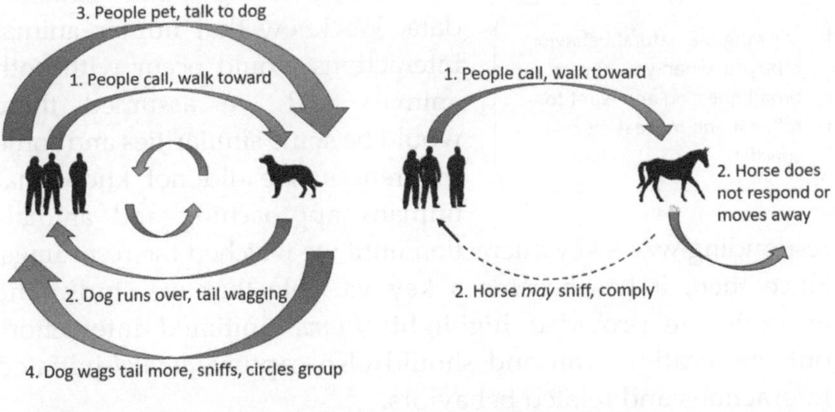

FIGURE 6.3 Different response patterns when comparing a horse and dog.

etc. The concentric circles in the middle of the human-dog interaction represent a reciprocal, escalating interaction loop between the students and the dog. This was a consistent finding across the different groups that interacted with Bronco.

The picture on the right of Figure 6.3, with Montana, looks quite different. In these instances, when the students approached Montana, his most common response was no apparent response at all. He would stand still, like a statue. Sometimes he would respond by moving away from the students, walking away, or turning his body away. In a small proportion of cases, he would respond affirmatively by moving toward them, sniffing them, or complying with their request. Even when this happened, he was subdued and the energy of the human–horse group stayed calm and quiet. There were no moments of reciprocally building energy with Montana, quite different from interactions with Bronco.

Start Broad and Get More Specific

We gathered these naturalistic observations because we were curious what interaction looked like with the two different animals. We did not know what we would find and didn't have any clear predictions. This is important because if we observe with something specific in mind, we might look for and record just that, missing other valuable data. We knew that human-animal interactions would occur with both animals and we assumed there would be some similarities and some differences. We did not know that humans approaching and animals responding was a key interaction until we watched the recordings. Since then, it has become a key variable that we study. The example we provided highlights *human*-initiated interaction, but observations can and should also capture *animal*-initiated interactions and related behaviors.

> Viewing the natural behavior is helpful when you have a broad question and want to refine it and make it more specific.

About Behavior

Readers curious about behavioral perspectives may find it rewarding to explore the work of B. F. Skinner, a pioneer in the study of observable behavior. Skinner was an experimental psychologist who focused on what organisms actually do – behaviors that can be seen, described, and measured. While he conducted much of his research with animals, he consistently reminded us that humans are subject to many of the same behavioral processes (Skinner, 1938; 1953). Skinner believed that careful behavioral analysis could improve not only individual lives but also society more broadly. He even expressed this idea through fiction in *Walden Two* (Skinner, 1948), a novel depicting a community shaped by behavioral science.

Try It! Make Naturalistic Observations

Follow these steps to start making naturalistic observations with your team.

1. Return to the question you wrote down earlier – what are you curious about? Think about how you could observe what you are wondering about. For this activity, it needs to be something you can see, not an internal thought or feeling.
2. Next, decide when and where you will make your observations and gather your recording materials (phone or tablet, pen and paper – whatever works for you). Choose tools that allow you to sketch if that is helpful. When we first reviewed recordings from our dog–horse sessions, we drew lines back and forth between the animal and people to make sense of what was happening and to begin describing patterns of interaction. Begin with the end in mind. How will you store these observations so you can return to them later? Who might you share them with? That might dictate the format you choose.

3. Take lots of notes, including questions that arise as you watch. There are no right or wrong notes – record anything that seems relevant.
4. Afterward, review what you wrote and reflect on the experience, adding new observations, ideas, or questions that emerge.

Make this a regular part of your work: notice when you are already observing and shift toward doing so intentionally. In later chapters, we will help you turn these rich observations into evidence. But first, in the next chapter, we move to systematic observation and provide concrete guidance for building it into your data collection plan.

Bibliography

Altmann, J. (1974). Observational study of behavior: Sampling methods. *Behaviour, 49*, 227–267.

Angrosino, M. (2007). *Doing ethnographic and observational research*. Sage.

Bekoff, M. (2024). *The emotional lives of animals: A leading scientist explores animal joy, sorrow, and empathy – and why they matter* (Revised Edition). New World Library.

Fine, A. H. (Ed.). (2019). *Handbook on animal-assisted therapy: Foundations and guidelines for animal-assisted interventions* (5th ed.). Academic Press.

Fournier, A. K., England, K. J., & Larson, K. (2016). Actively caring for our children. In E. S. Geller (Ed.), *Applied psychology: Actively caring for people*. Cambridge University Press.

Fournier, A. K., Letson, E. A., Berry, T. D., Laitala, J., Proels, L., & Kavanaugh, K. (2021). The anodyne-agent model: A framework for conceptualizing the animal's role in animal-assisted intervention. *Human-Animal Interaction Bulletin, 9*(1), 55–75.

Geller, E. S. (2018). Seven life lessons from humanistic behaviorism: How to bring the best out of yourself and others. In *Leadership and cultural change* (pp. 137–156). Routledge.

Geller, E. S., & Fournier, A. K. (2019). *Actively caring for your child: How to be a more effective parent*. Cognella.

Kazdin, A. E. (2012). *Behavior modification in applied settings*. Waveland Press.
Macdonald, H. (2014). *H is for hawk*. Grove Press.
Macdonald, H. (2021). *Fox & I: An uncommon friendship*. Grove Press.
Schilthuizen, M. (2018). *The urban naturalist: How to make the city your laboratory*. Picador.
Skinner, B. F. (1938). *The behavior of organisms: An experimental analysis*. D. Appleton-Century Company.
Skinner, B. F. (1948). *Walden two*. Macmillan.
Skinner, B. F. (1953). *Science and human behavior*. Macmillan.
Tracy, S. J. (2020). *Qualitative research methods: Collecting evidence, crafting analysis, communicating impact* (2nd ed.). Wiley.

7

Turning Moments into Measures

Observing Specific Behaviors

Field Story 7: Lying Down on the Job

Ashley was an undergraduate student visiting the ranch as part of her McNair Scholars[1] research. Her goal was to experience equine-assisted learning firsthand and then write a research paper on the process. This was her first time visiting the ranch. She was quite nervous because she had a fear of horses; she had fallen off a horse as a child. We assured her there would be no horseback riding and that she could keep her distance from the horses. She spent some time outside of the pasture, just watching the horses. It was late morning in September; the weather was sunny and mild. While Ashley watched outside the fence, the seven horses were engaging in a variety of low-energy activities. Some were slowly munching on hay, others were standing still looking off into the distance, occasionally one or two would walk slowly from one area of the pasture to another. Ashley noted that the horses seemed quite calm and she was ready to go into the pasture.

She went through the gate and slowly walked up to Cleo, a miniature donkey. She petted Cleo a bit and then Cleo slowly walked away. Ashley stood in place and watched the animals. Soon one of the horses farther away from her laid down on the ground. She stayed where she was and kept watching. Then another horse laid down. And another. And another. Slowly, one by one, over a period

DOI: 10.4324/9781003640257-10

FIGURE 7.1 A unique experience in the pasture.

of about five minutes, all seven of the horses/donkeys in the pasture laid down (see Figure 7.1). Some kept their heads up and some laid their heads on the ground and closed their eyes, appearing to fall asleep. As facilitators of the session, we were amazed because we had never seen anything like that. To have everyone lying down at once is unique. We all just watched, and after a while, slowly, one by one, most of them stood up. One remained on the ground, looking very sleepy. Ashley walked over to us and was ready to process the experience.

This unique situation is related to a question we had about the horses – how often do they lie down and/or sleep during equine-assisted sessions? And is that any different from their sleep behavior outside of sessions? We thought this was an important question because it could tell us about the horses' well-being. A disruption to their typical sleep patterns could indicate a potential cost to the horses. In addition, we were curious whether our assumptions about the horses' experiences of equine-assisted sessions were true. To that point, we hadn't noticed any major changes in the horses during session and non-session time. Gathering some evidence could help us test out our assumptions. So we planned behavioral observations of some specific behavior – the topic of this chapter.

Systematic Observation

Systematic observation is a method of data collection in which specific behaviors are intentionally selected, clearly defined, and recorded in a structured and consistent way. Unlike naturalistic observation, which helps us explore what might be happening, systematic observation is used when we know what we want to look for and want to measure it in a structured way. Principles of systematic observation and behavioral measurement are deeply rooted in applied behavior science (Geller, 2001). Before beginning, we carefully describe the behavior we will be observing by creating an **operational definition** – a clear, observable description that specifies exactly what counts as the behavior and how it will be recorded in a particular situation. Table 7.1 provides the operational definitions we used for recording one specific horse behavior – level of alertness.

> Operational definitions help ensure that observations are consistent, replicable, and focused on what can be seen or heard rather than assumed.

Each time you make systematic observations, whether for research, evaluation, or assessment, you determine the behaviors you will observe and the operational definitions for those behaviors. We are not directing you to use these specific definitions. We give these as examples; you determine your operational definitions based on your SAGA question, your professional experience, and existing resources. We share relevant resources throughout this chapter, including information on several tools you can use to make systematic observations. The process always begins with selecting and defining the target behavior.

TABLE 7.1 Operational definitions and data sheet used in systematic observation

Animal Partner	***Sleepy*** *– Standing still or lying down with eyes closed*	***Alert*** *– Head up, ears relaxed, eyes open and relaxed*	***High Alert*** *– Head up high, ears up, eyes wide, body tense*
Crackerjack	III	II	I
Superman	II	IIIII	I
Tilly	III	IIII	
Cleo	III	II	I
Prince	II	III	I

Define the Target Behavior

The technical term for the grid in Table 7.1 is *ethogram.* An **ethogram** is a list of specific animal behaviors and their definitions. It's from the field of **ethology**, which is the scientific study of animal behavior. Teaming up with an ethologist can be a great way to move your data-driven process forward. You can find ethologists in educational/academic settings and in the private sector. You can also find books and research articles that provide ethograms for your use, by searching for an ethogram for whichever animals you work with. We work mostly with equids, so we have found Sue McDonnell's *A Practical Field Guide to Horse Behavior: The Equid Ethogram* (2003) helpful. It's a book describing and illustrating equine behaviors, including level of alertness.

> When possible, we recommend using operational definitions from existing ethograms.

Sometimes you will want to record a behavior for which you cannot find an existing resource. In that case, create your own based on your experience and preliminary observations. Below is a list of ways to find ethograms relevant to your work:

- Use the search terms "[animal] ethogram"
  - Online
  - Your local library
  - Bookstores
  - Online book sellers
  - Google Scholar

Most ethograms catalog behaviors of a single species. Later, in Chapter 8, we will look at ways to extend this approach to *dyadic* behavior, when observing *humans and animals interacting*.

Determine the Unit of Measurement

Once you know the behavior you need to observe and have defined that behavior, your next decision is which unit of measurement to record. Any behavior can be measured in a number of different ways. The specific type of data you will record is referred to as the **unit of measurement**. For example, when baking a cake, you can measure your flour in cups or

TABLE 7.2 Different ways to measure specific behaviors

Category	*Unit of Measurement*	*Description*
Count	Frequency	Number of times a behavior occurs
Time	Duration	For how long a behavior occurs (seconds, minutes)
	Latency	How long it takes for a behavior to begin (seconds, minutes)
Quality	Intensity	Rate the intensity of a behavior (e.g., 1 = mild, 5 = extreme)
	Description	Record exactly what you observe (e.g., writing, audio, video)

grams. Cups versus grams is the unit of measurement. Table 7.2 describes the major ways you can record behavior:

The column labeled Unit of Measurement lists different ways to measure behavior. Frequency means the number of times a behavior occurs. Duration means we record for how long the behavior occurs, while latency means the amount of time it takes for a behavior to begin occurring. For intensity, we can create a rating scale that fits our context. Description is what it sounds like; we describe what we see in narrative form. Let's apply the different units of measurement to the behavior of touching a rabbit during an episode of animal-assisted occupational therapy.

- Frequency
  - What you observe: the child touched the animal six times
  - What you record: Touch Frequency = 6
- Duration
  - What you observed: the child touched the animal for four minutes during the session
  - What you record: Touch Duration = 4 minutes
- Latency
  - What you observe: the child first touched the animal after 20 minutes
  - What you record: Latency to touch = 20 minutes

- Intensity
  - What you observe: the child touched the animal lightly, barely contacting the fur
  - What you record: Intensity of touch = 1
- Description
  - What you observed: the child held the animal and pet them throughout the session
  - What you record: the child held the animal and pet them throughout the session (what you record is the same as what you observe)

Determine Your Sampling Method

Remember from Chapter 3 that a sample is a bit of data we collect to inform us about a population. In our SAGA method, we gather a sample of data to answer a question we have about the larger group, population, or program. There are a number of ways to gather your sample in systematic observation. For our purposes, the two types of sampling are event sampling and time sampling. Here is a quick description of each, with our touching rabbit example applied:

- Event sampling – record every instance of the behavior
  - Record every time the child touches the animal throughout the session
  - Data: child touches animal 10 times
- Continuous time sampling – continuously record the amount of time the behavior occurs
  - Use a stopwatch to record how much time in a session the child touches the animal
  - Data: child was touching animal 14.32 minutes of the 50-minute session; child was touching animal 28.6% of the time
- Interval Time Sampling – record whether or not the behavior is occurring during a particular time period
  - Every 10 minutes, record whether or not the child is touching the animal
  - Data: child was touching animal during 4 of the 5 10-minute intervals

Which method you use – event or time – depends on the behavior you are observing and your resources. One might assume that recording every instance of a behavior (event sampling) would be the most accurate, but only if it is achievable (the A in a SMART question). Some behaviors happen too frequently or are too quick to catch every instance. For example, we were interested in whether horses do more walking or standing still during equine-assisted sessions, compared to non-session time. A few preliminary observations revealed that horses do a lot of walking and stopping and walking and stopping throughout the session. We realized that recording all of them, and analyzing all of that data, may not be feasible. So, we decided to break a session into 5-minute intervals (interval time sampling). Every five minutes, we recorded whether the horses were walking or standing still. It was a much more reasonable amount of data to collect and interpret.

Feasibility leads to consistency, which increases reliability. We can be more confident in our data – that the sample is an accurate reflection of the whole – when everyone collecting data can do it the same way every time. Data collection that is complicated or cumbersome may be gathered inconsistently. And inaccurate data means we're using incorrect information to make important decisions. So, think about the target behavior, its natural frequency and complexity, and decide whether event or time sampling makes the most sense. As with all of this, you can try out both and see which is best before moving on in your systematic observation process. Once you have determined your sampling method, you're (almost) ready.

Choose Your Recording Method

Once you have chosen and defined the behaviors you want to observe and determined your unit of measurement and sampling method (wow, this is complicated!), you'll need a way of recording your observations. The description of the scene in the field story at the beginning of this chapter is more consistent with naturalistic observation. Recording a description like that is one way of recording behavior. Another, more systematic way, is to use an existing or create a new data collection tool. You can call it an ethogram, a behavior checklist, a data sheet, a whose-y-what's-it, whatever you like. It's your tool, so call it something that makes sense for you. Look again at Table 7.1. Below the operational definitions is a grid where we tallied level of alertness using our operational definitions. This is something we created for our use, based on our naturalistic observations, and personal and professional experience with human–horse interaction. You can copy this for your own use or create something of your own. Perhaps you don't need to record sleepy, alert, and high alert. Maybe you only need to record whether the animals are asleep or awake. It's really up to you to create what you need to gather the evidence to answer your SAGA questions. The key is to use definitions, recording methods, and notations or codes that work for you, and then to train your team so that everyone uses them consistently. If you begin recording and notice that your team is having difficulty consistently recording observations, discuss it and decide if changes need to be made. There are many ways you can define a behavior and gather behavioral observations. The "right" way is the way that allows you to gather the most accurate data most consistently across subjects, situations, and data collectors.

Make Your Systematic Observations

Finally! You are ready to make your observations. Below is a list of steps to take when making systematic observations:

1. Develop your SMART question.
2. Decide on the behavior you want to observe (your target behavior).
3. Create an operational definition of the behavior.
4. Determine the unit of measurement.
5. Decide on your sampling method.
6. Choose your recording method.
7. Test out your method by gathering a small amount of data.
8. Review and reflect, make adjustments as needed.
9. Gather your sample, recording your systematic observations.
10. Reflect.
11. Revise, or gather more data, or move on to data analysis.

Once you begin this process, resist the urge to rush through the early steps. Clear questions and well-defined behaviors make the rest of the process easier and more meaningful. Testing your plan with a small amount of pilot data is especially important; it often reveals practical issues you couldn't anticipate in advance, such as unclear definitions, awkward recording procedures, or timing challenges. Use what you learn from this initial trial to refine your approach before committing to full data collection.

As you gather your observations, take notes about anything that stands out or feels important. After reviewing your data, decide whether you need to revise your plan and collect additional data, continue with the same approach, or move forward to analysis. Once you have the data you need, you're ready for the next step in the SAGA process – analyzing and acting on your evidence, which we cover in Part IV of the book.

Applying the Steps

Let's look at an example from our work, applying each of these steps. Early on in our work on animal-assisted services, we wanted to record the different ways humans interact with animals during animal-assisted services. We created a list of different behaviors that can occur during a session. Figure 7.2 illustrates one of these behaviors – a human spending time near an animal. Below is our process of gathering that data, moving through the steps in systematic observation.

Steps in Systematic Observation

1. Develop a SMART question
   - *What percentage of the time, during an animal-assisted service session, is the human near the animal?*
2. Decide on the behavior(s) you want to observe
   - Human standing near an animal
3. Create operational definitions for the behavior(s)
   - Human standing near an animal = human standing within 4 feet of an animal

4. Determine the unit of measurement
   - Duration in minutes – we counted the number of minutes the human stood near the animal during the session.
5. Decide on your sampling method
   - Time sampling – recorded the number of minutes the human stood near an animal throughout two mock sessions.

FIGURE 7.2 Angela's son Bleu standing near Tilly, a miniature donkey who provides services and helps with SAGA work at the ranch.

6. Create or find a recording device (data sheet, app, etc.)
   - We used a stopwatch to start/stop each time the human stood near an animal and recorded the total time at the end of the session.
7. Test out your definitions and recording device
   - We had two staff record throughout the two mock sessions.
8. Make adjustments as needed
   - Our mock sessions revealed that it is difficult to estimate when the human is 4 feet from an animal; the two raters were inconsistent. They also noted that it was difficult to record time by starting and stopping the stopwatch. Together, these challenges made the data unreliable. We decided to change the operational definition and the sampling method. Our new operational definition was: human standing near an animal = human standing within [human] arm's reach of an animal. Estimating arm's reach is easier and thus more reliable than estimating number of feet. We changed our sampling method from *percentage of time* to *frequency*. The raters would record a hashmark each time they observed the human standing within arm's reach of an animal.
9. Make observations; write notes as needed
   - These changes improved our process. We gathered data during three practice sessions and three actual sessions, with the participant's permission.
10. Review the data and reflect – do you have what you need to answer your question?
    - The data suggested standing near an animal varied, depending on the animal and the human participants. We felt we were gathering the right data, but did not have enough to answer our question.
11. Revise, or gather more data, or move on to data analysis
    - We opted to gather more data to see if patterns would emerge.

As you can see, our process required some adjustments to the initial data collection plan. That is very common, so we always test out our method before gathering too much data.

When You're Not Sure What to Observe

All the information and skills in this chapter assume that you know what to observe and how to observe it. But what if you don't? These are two important and likely situations – (1) not knowing what behavior to observe and (2) identifying an observable behavior you would like to capture but not knowing how to access it.

Unsure Which Behavior to Observe

First, let's address not knowing what behavior to observe. This is actually pretty easy. The main tool here is naturalistic observation. You probably have an inkling of the broader type of behaviors you're curious about. Spend some time making naturalistic behaviors with that in mind. Your observations will naturally lead to the target behavior. Trust the process of watching behaviors occur naturally.

Unsure How to Access the Target Behavior

Perhaps you have a target behavior but are unsure of how to access it. This is when a brainstorm is helpful. In addition to making some naturalistic observations, reflect on your experiences and talk with your team. Share your thoughts and brainstorm as a group on how to capture the behavior. The synergy of multiple people with relevant experience can lead to the answer.

Sometimes we only have access to artifacts of the behavior. For example, maybe we are interested in digestive behavior of our animal partner as a measure of their health and wellness. We could record piles of horse manure in the pasture or clumps in the cat's litter box. Sometimes it's the absence of a behavior that catches our attention, such as when a horse who typically turns toward a person's approach instead remains still with their head oriented away, or when a client who usually reaches out to initiate contact no longer does so. In these cases, what we "observe" is not the behavior itself, but the gap it leaves behind – and those absences can be just as meaningful to document as the behaviors we do see.

Incorporating Both Naturalistic and Systematic Observation

Remember that observing behavior is an excellent way to gather evidence and make decisions about your work, and both naturalistic and systematic observation are useful tools. You can use one or both. We recommend you and your team practice making both naturalistic and systematic observations and see what comes up. Some people have a natural inclination toward one or the other. Our work was initially all systematic observation, but relatively recently we have added in naturalistic observation. We can attest that a combination of both is an excellent way to get a "picture" of the behavior you're interested in, especially when trying to capture the complex behavior of humans and animals interacting with each other. That is a topic we cover in detail in the next chapter.

Try It! Make Systematic Observations

Now that you've seen systematic observation in action, it's time to try it yourself. Return to the step-by-step process outlined earlier in this chapter and apply it to one behavior you're curious about.

- ◆ Start small.
- ◆ Choose a behavior that is easy to observe and define and focus on consistency rather than complexity.
- ◆ As you work through the steps, pay attention to where you feel confident and where you feel uncertain – that's often where the most learning happens. Review the chapter as needed.

There is no single "right" way to do this. Your goal is to create a process that works for your context and allows you to gather accurate data.

Note

1. Working with universities can be a great way to get help with data-driven practices and provide learning opportunities for students. We share more about this in Appendix B.

Bibliography

Altmann, J. (1974). Observational study of behavior: Sampling methods. *Behaviour, 49*, 227–267.

Bakeman, R., & Quera, V. (2011). *Sequential analysis and observational methods for the behavioral sciences*. Cambridge University Press.

Berry, T. D., Mitteer, D. R., & Fournier, A. K. (2015). Examining hand washing rates and durations in public restrooms: A study of gender differences via personal, environmental, and behavioral determinants. *Environment & Behavior*, 47 (8), 923–944. doi:10.1177/00139i6514527590

Crews, J., Braude, S., Stephenson, C., & Clardy, T. (2002). *The ethogram and animal behavior research*. Washington University.

Fournier, A. K., French, M., Letson, E. A., Hanson, J., Berry, T. D., & Cronin, S. (2024). The behavioral cost of care: Changes in maintenance behavior during equine-assisted interventions. *Animals, 14*(4), 536.

Gawande, A. (2011). *The checklist manifesto: How to get things right*. Metropolitan Books.

Geller, E. S. (2001). *The psychology of safety handbook*. CRC Press.

Geller, E. S., Berry, T. D., Ludwig, T. D., Evans, R. E., Gilmore, M. R., & Clarke, S. W. (1990). A conceptual framework for developing and evaluating behavior change interventions for injury control. *Health Education Research, 5*(2), 125–137.

Gut, W., Crump, L., Zinsstag, J., Hattendorf, J., & Hediger, K. (2018). The effect of human interaction on guinea pig behavior in animal-assisted therapy. *Journal of Veterinary Behavior, 25*, 56–64.

Hartmann, D. P. (1977). Considerations in the choice of interobserver reliability estimates. *Journal of Applied Behavior Analysis, 10*(1), 103–116.

Martin, P., & Bateson, P. (2007). *Measuring behaviour: An introductory guide* (3rd ed.). Cambridge University Press.

McDonnell, S. M. (2003). *The equid ethogram: A practical field guide to horse behavior*. Eclipse Press.

McGreevy, P. D. (2004). *Equine behavior: A guide for veterinarians and equine scientists*. Elsevier.

McGreevy, P. D., Starling, M., Branson, N. J., Cobb, M. L., & Calnon, D. (2012). An overview of the dog–human dyad and ethograms within it. *Journal of Veterinary Behavior, 7*(2), 103–117.

Skinner, B. F. (1938). *The behavior of organisms: An experimental analysis*. Appleton-Century.

Skinner, B. F. (1953). *Science and human behavior*. Macmillan.

Skinner, B. F. (1974). *About behaviorism*. Knopf.

8

Capturing the Heart of Our Work

Measuring Human-Animal Interaction

Field Story 8: From Measuring a Moment to Feeling It

Megan was spending the semester as an intern at Eagle Vista Ranch. A psychology major and lifelong animal enthusiast, she was learning about both animal-assisted practice and research. She assisted with several projects focused on observing and recording the many ways participants engaged with the ranch animals. With clipboard in hand, she stood at the edge of the pasture while ranch volunteers conducted a mock session, piloting a new data-collection method. Megan positioned herself carefully – quiet, attentive, trying to blend into the background. The animals had other plans.

Anders, a beige, broad-bodied Norwegian Fjord horse, slowly wandered toward her. A gentle giant, Anders was known for his steady curiosity and his tendency to join whatever was happening in the pasture. He approached Megan with unhurried confidence, lowered his head, and sniffed her clipboard and hand. The excellent researcher that she is, Megan attempted to remain neutral, keeping her eyes on the mock session as she subtly shifted one step backward. Anders followed. He nudged the clipboard, shown in Figure 8.1, his soft nose and slack lower lip rubbing against the papers. Megan eased back another step. Again Anders drifted forward, calmly persistent.

DOI: 10.4324/9781003640257-11

FIGURE 8.1 Megan and Anders exploring human-animal interaction data.

As this quiet negotiation unfolded, Red – an orange tabby who lives and works at the ranch strolled over and began weaving around Megan's legs, his purr loudly announcing his participation. Megan finally broke. She smiled, laughed, and reached up to stroke Anders. He leaned gently into her touch. Red continued his figure-eight pattern around her boots. When Megan knelt down to pet Red, Anders' large head followed, and for several minutes she remained there, surrounded by animals, smiling and fully engaged in the interaction. She had arrived prepared to observe humans and animals interacting. Within minutes, she was living it.

Moments like this are common in animal-assisted settings. Interaction with animals is easy to recognize, easy to feel, and often easy to describe informally. Yet if we want to study, communicate, and build knowledge about engaging with animals, we need ways to move beyond impression and into systematic description. **How do we move from intuition – "we know it when we see it" – to something we can reliably describe, measure, and share?**

The Heart of What We Do

Ever had someone ask you what you do? And when you say animal-assisted activities/learning/counseling/fill-in-the-blank, they say, *"Yeah, but what actually happens? What does your dog (or horse or cat, etc.) do? What do the people in the sessions do?"* This is one of the questions we get often from family, friends, and community members. We usually explain it by sharing an anecdote from our work. We tell a story about a person who had a powerful experience with a horse or dog or cat and then saw themselves or the world differently. Sometimes that is enough to satisfy others' curiosity. Other people want more specific descriptions, especially in our work with horses. People often assume that participants ride horses. When we say that no, there is no riding, they wonder even more – then what do you do? We used to say things like "we hold space for clients to engage with the horses." This would be met with several more questions. It seemed people wanted concrete details – what happens first, second, and third. Do we ride horses, pet horses, or talk to horses? Ultimately, we were describing, and our audience was curious about, human-animal interaction. This is what we think of as the heart of animal-assisted services.

Whether you incorporate animals in education, medical treatments, personal or professional development, or visitation and recreation, people and animals interacting is the centerpiece, the touchstone of the service. Human-animal interaction is what makes your service different from other services. And because it is the heart of your work, it is essential that your data-driven process includes the measurement of human-animal interaction. First let's provide a definition so we are on the same page.

What Is Human-Animal Interaction?

Human-animal interaction is defined broadly as any interaction between humans and animals. At its widest scope, this includes activities such as owning, housing, and caring for animals; animal sheltering and rescue work; and working alongside animals. It also encompasses animals involved in entertainment and sport, as well as interactions embedded in everyday human practices, including eating and wearing animals. For our purposes as animal-assisted service providers and researchers, **we define human-animal interaction as observable interactions between humans and animals (e.g., physical contact, proximity, orientation, and communicative behavior)**. These interactions can be from a human toward an animal (e.g., a human petting, talking to, or watching an animal), from an animal toward a human (e.g., an animal sniffing, licking, or approaching a human), or between a human and animal (e.g., a human and animal playing together or doing training together).

Because human-animal interaction is a key ingredient in animal-assisted services, its accurate and consistent measurement is important for (1) describing to others what happens in your services (you can say things like "our clients spend most of their time petting and talking to the dogs") and (2) explaining the role of the animal in your animal-assisted services (you could say things like "the more clients interact with the horses, the more calm they report feeling"). Describing and explaining are essential when sharing what you do with important stakeholders. The rest of this chapter focuses on measuring human-animal interaction to serve those purposes. We share two tools that we developed and use regularly – the Human-Animal Interaction Scale and the Human-Animal Interaction Ethogram.

The Human-Animal Interaction Scale[1]

The Human-Animal Interaction Scale (HAIS) was developed to provide a practical, behaviorally anchored way of describing and quantifying human-animal interaction across settings. Rather than measuring attitudes, attachment, or beliefs about animals, the HAIS focuses on what humans and animals actually do during interactions. Readers interested in the development and early applications of the scale, including its origins in correctional-facility dog training programs, can find a more detailed account from sources listed in this chapter's bibliography.

The HAIS is a 24-item instrument designed to describe and quantify a human's interactions with a non-human animal. It was designed for systematic observation of human-animal interaction in a wide range of settings, including, but not limited to:

- Animal-assisted services
- Pet keeping
- Animal shelters and rescues
- Veterinary practice
- Animal husbandry
- Research

How It Works

The scale is meant to work as a self report measure – the human interacting reports on their experience – or as an observation record – an observer reports on interactions they see others engage in. After an instance or period of human-animal interaction, the HAIS form is completed by the person interacting (Participant Form) or observing (Observer Form). The same 24 items are used for both forms.

The images in Figure 8.2 show the HAIS being used as an observation record. On the left, you can see how we've used it to make observations of humans interacting with horses. The observer stands apart from the interaction, silently watching and recording interactive behavior. We've used this during research studies and actual sessions. The image on the right shows a student researcher making observations during a mock

FIGURE 8.2 The Human-Animal Interaction Scale being used in the field (left) and laboratory (right).

session. The researcher is watching a student interact with a dog through a two-way mirror in our laboratory. Although you may not have access to a laboratory, you can get creative in finding a way to make unobtrusive (not obvious) observations. And you can practice your skills in mock sessions like we described in Field Story 8.1, where Megan was recording on the HAIS Observer form before Anders turned the clipboard into a connection.

The scale includes behaviors a human can do, such as spend time near an animal, watch an animal, pet an animal, etc. It also includes behaviors an animal can do, like making a friendly sound, sniffing, or licking. Figure 8.3 shows the HAIS form partially completed. You can see the top questions are human behaviors and the bottom questions are animal behaviors. The scale gives you three scores – a human behavior total, an animal behavior total, and a combined total score.

Notice that the scale includes what might be considered positive interactions (e.g., petting, talking) and negative interactions (e.g., declining interaction, aggressive behavior). For the human total, the positive items (1–12) are added, then negative items (13–14) are subtracted. Similarly for the animal total, the positive items (15–20) are added, then the negative items (21–24) are subtracted. Then the two scores are combined to get the total score.

Human-Animal Interaction Scale (HAIS) – Participant Form

Name: ______________________ Date: __________

Which animal(s) did you interact with? ______________________

Instructions: For each **type** of interaction on the left, rate the **amount** of interaction you experienced on the right.

During the session, how much did YOU...	Not At All		A Moderate Amount		A Great Deal
1. Watch the animal(s)	0	1	2	3	4
2. Spend time near the animal(s)	0	1	2	3	4
3. Pet the animal(s)	0	1	2	3	4
4. Talk to the animal(s)	0	1	2	3	4
5. Hug the animal(s)	0	1	2	3	4
6. Play with the animal(s)	0	1	2	3	4
7. Kiss the animal(s)	0	1	2	3	4
8. Groom the animal(s)	0	1	2	3	4
9. Offer food to the animal(s)	0	1	2	3	4
10. Attempt Tricks or Training with the animal(s)	0	1	2	3	4
11. Hold the animal(s)	0	1	2	3	4
12. Take Pictures of or with the animal(s)	0	1	2	3	4
13. Decline or avoid interaction with the animal(s)	0	1	2	3	4
14. Behave aggressively toward the animal(s)	0	1	2	3	4
Human Total					
During the session, how much did THE ANIMAL(S)...	Not At All		Moderate Amount		A Great Deal
15. Initiate friendly interaction with you	0	1	2	3	4
16. Make friendly sounds	0	1	2	3	4
17. Accept food from you	0	1	2	3	4
18. Obey tricks or training	0	1	2	3	4
19. Sniff or smell you	0	1	2	3	4
20. Lick you	0	1	2	3	4
21. Make unfriendly sounds	0	1	2	3	4
22. Behave aggressively toward you	0	1	2	3	4
23. Cause a mess or inconvenience for you	0	1	2	3	4
24. Decline or avoid interaction with you	0	1	2	3	4
Animal Total					
TOTAL					

FIGURE 8.3 The Human-Animal Interaction Scale.

What Can You Do with HAIS Data?

This is a great question. As mentioned earlier, you can use HAIS data to describe your work and to help explain how your animal(s) help people. Let's look at some examples applied to a hypothetical case:

Anthony is an 8-year-old boy beginning counseling that incorporates a therapy dog. Anthony was hesitant about counseling, but when learning his counselor, Dr. Jackson, works with a therapy dog named Buck, he agreed to give it a try. After three sessions, Dr. Jackson felt they were starting to make some progress. She described Anthony as very quiet and reserved during session 1, beginning to warm up during session 2, and finally beginning to connect and disclose during session 3. During session 2 he warmed up quicker and began to interact with Buck while replying to Dr. Jackson's offers of small talk. For the third session, Anthony seemed quite comfortable, chatting right away and beginning to disclose more personal information as the session continued. Buck's behavior changed slightly over these three sessions as well. He was friendly but kept to himself for most of the first session, staying in his dog bed even when called by Anthony and Dr. Jackson. During the second session, he approached Anthony and sniffed his hand before being petted. In the third session, he greeted him as he entered the room and stayed near him throughout the session.

Describing Your Work

At its core, the HAIS gives you a description of the behaviors occurring during human-animal interaction. It can help you describe what happens during your animal-assisted services, quantifying what human participants do and what your animal partner does. Take a look at the line graph in Figure 8.4, showing scores on selected HAIS items across Anthony's three sessions. Notice that *Watch* was high during session 1 and stayed that way for the next two sessions. Conversely, *Near* was lowest during session 1

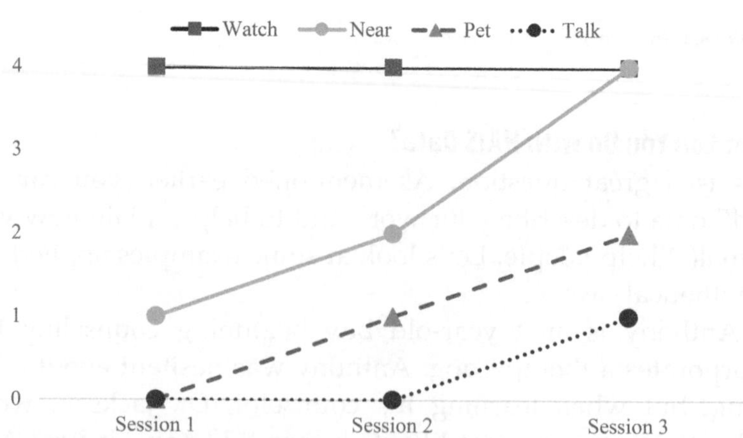

FIGURE 8.4 HAIS human behavior scores of one participant across three sessions.

and increased throughout the next two sessions. The graph also shows that Anthony did a little bit of petting the dog in session 2 and more in session 3. In session 3, he began talking to the dog. Taken together, we get the picture across these three sessions that Anthony is slowly increasing his interaction with the dog. These statements and the graph are not saying whether these interactions are good or bad; there is no right or wrong or correct or incorrect pattern. It is just describing. But we think *just describing* human-animal interaction is actually a pretty big deal. The numbers on the HAIS and graphs like that in Figure 8.4 make the complex process of human-animal interaction a little less mysterious. They help us take an abstract concept – Anthony engaged with the dog increasingly over three sessions – and make it more concrete. This can be helpful for the counselor to gauge progress over time; it can help Anthony's parents better understand what happens during sessions, and it may help argue for more dog-therapy sessions since the data indicate Anthony is warming up to the process.

Once you have completed the HAIS on your animal partner consistently, you can see patterns in their behavior. Each animal may have their own signature interaction patterns within and across sessions. This can be useful in describing your work to others. It could also help in identifying when well-being changes for the animal. If Dr. Jackson saw a big change in Buck's behavior during sessions – for example, changing from consistently interacting with participants to avoiding interaction, a potential sign of exhaustion or a health issue – it would be documented and perhaps identified quicker. We share more about using data to monitor your team's wellness in Chapter 13.

Explaining Your Work

The HAIS can also be used to help explain your work to others by tying outcomes to interactions with animals. The graph in Figure 8.5 is a scatterplot, showing HAIS scores on the horizontal axis (x-axis) and Mood scores on the vertical axis (y-axis). Each dot on the graph represents one person's scores for how much they interacted with animals (HAIS Score) and how they felt emotionally (Mood Score). For example, the dot on the bottom left of

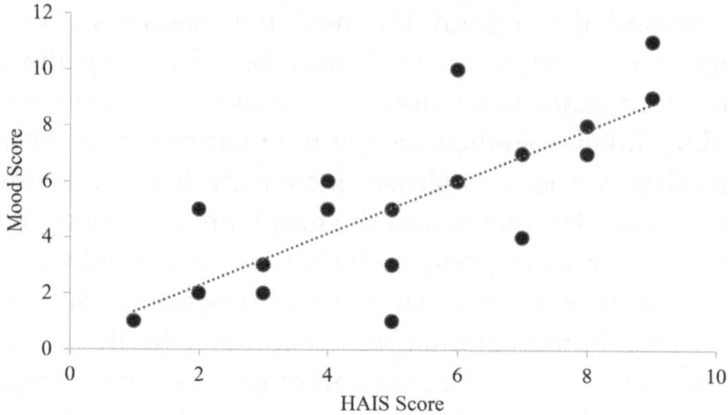

FIGURE 8.5 Chart showing the relationship between human-animal interaction (horizontal axis) and mood (vertical axis).

the graph indicates a reported HAIS score of 1 (very little interaction with animals) and a mood score of 1 (very low or negative mood). In other words, this person reported not interacting very much with animals and feeling pretty low. In contrast, look at the uppermost right dot on the graph. This point represents a relatively high amount of interaction and good mood. The rest of the dots fall between these two endpoints.

The thin line running across the chart is called a fit line, calculated from the data points. This is the straight line that best fits these data points. It helps us see that although the dots are a bit spread out, they do generally fit a pattern. This fit line indicates a positive association between HAIS and Mood scores, such that higher interaction is associated with improved mood.

Applying the HAIS in Your Work

The HAIS was designed for use across a wide range of settings, species, and practitioners. You can use it anytime you would like a number to represent the amount of human-animal interaction, especially if you want to connect human-animal interaction to some other numerical variable. The number on the y-axis of the scatterplot in Figure 8.5, in this case mood, could be replaced with any number of outcome variables – things you think are changing in connection with human-animal interaction. We could have measured specific symptoms like anxiety or depression, specific behaviors like prosocial behavior or aggression, physical health indicators like blood pressure or heart rate, or institutional variables like rule-following or infractions. Gathering and plotting data like this is very helpful in understanding whether engaging with therapy animals is associated with important outcomes.

Pause here and think about your work. If you gathered data and created graphs like these, what variable would be in place of the mood score? What is your outcome that might be associated with HAIS scores? We cover visualizing your data in more detail in Chapter 12. For now, let's cover just a few more details about the HAIS.

HAIS Reliability and Validity

Recall from Chapter 5 the importance of our measurement instruments being valid and reliable. As a reminder, validity means the instrument measures what it is intended to measure. For the HAIS, validity is a question of whether it actually measures human-animal interaction. And reliability means an instrument measures the same way every time, across situations and time. We conducted research to determine the HAIS's reliability and validity. The research involved administering the HAIS, along with comparison measures, to several different groups of people. Psychometric evaluation demonstrated that the HAIS measures behavioral human-animal interaction and does so reliably across time and settings (Fournier et al., 2016). This means you can use it confidently; there is scientific evidence that it is valid and reliable. Since its publication in 2016, HAIS has been translated into several different languages. If you think you might need to use the HAIS in a language other than English, contact us at our website so we can connect you to other translations.

HAIS Limitations

Every measurement instrument or method has limitations. There is no perfect way to measure anything; every measurement is an estimate of an underlying reality. Even your bathroom scale is only estimating your body weight – a fact worth remembering

Understanding and acknowledging limitations is essential when selecting, administering, scoring, interpreting, and communicating findings from any instrument.

the next time the number feels personally offensive. This principle sits at the heart of measurement.

Operational definitions help clarify what is being measured, but they do not eliminate subjectivity. The HAIS is a descriptive tool rather than a diagnostic one, and no single instrument can capture every behavior that may be meaningful in a given context. Refer to this chapter's field story. Anders interacted with Megan by nudging and nuzzling her clipboard. That is a unique behavior and not explicitly listed on the HAIS. However, the animal items *Initiated Interaction* and *Made a Mess/Inconvenience* are meant to capture experiences like that. Differences between participant and observer perceptions and ratings are common and reflect perspective rather than error. Because HAIS items are weighted equally and the 0–4 rating scale is inherently somewhat arbitrary, patterns and trends over time are typically more informative than isolated scores. Thoughtful interpretation preserves the value of the data while guarding against overconfident conclusions.

The two most important things to do with any instrument's limitations are to (1) remain aware of the limitations as you move through the SAGA process, and (2) acknowledge the limitations when sharing your findings. Although it may seem counterintuitive, acknowledging limitations in our measurement can increase our credibility. It indicates you are thinking critically about the work and it is a suggestion of integrity. It shows that you tell the truth even when it can allow others to question your work.

Other Ways of Measuring Human-Animal Interaction

Just as you can *define* human-animal interaction broadly, you can also *measure* it from a range of perspectives. Beyond using the HAIS, there are a few instruments or coding tools for measuring human-animal interaction; some of them are listed in Table 8.1. And beyond that, there are many different but related constructs

TABLE 8.1 Tools for measuring human-animal interaction

Tool	*Species and Context*	*What It Measures*	*Strengths*	*Limitations for Measuring HAI*
OHAIRE Coding System (O'Haire, 2013, 2014)	Primarily dogs; therapy, school, and structured intervention settings	Human social behavior (smiles, eye contact, communication), physical interaction, engagement, and disruptive behavior; minimal animal coding	Well-validated human-behavior coding system; strong reliability; widely used in AAS research	Interaction largely human-centered; animal behavior minimally represented; relational processes inferred
CARing Kids Human–Dog Ethogram (Lee et al., 2022)	Children and dogs in humane education/ AAI contexts	Affiliative, touch, proximity, approach/avoidance, and stress-related behaviors for both humans and dogs	Explicit inclusion of both partners; clear operational definitions	Behaviors coded in parallel; interactional sequences and reciprocity not directly modeled
Human–Dog Stress Task Ethograms (Dowling-Guyer et al., 2024)	Adolescents and therapy dogs in standardized stress-induction tasks	Human approach/avoidance and affiliative cues; dog affiliative, displacement, and stress behaviors	High experimental control; excellent behavioral definitions; strong internal validity	Experimental structure limits generalization; interaction patterns remain implicit
Dog Well-being Behavioral Instrument (e.g., Glenk, 2017; Ng et al., 2014)	Dogs participating in therapy or intervention sessions	Dog stress-related and affiliative behaviors pre-, during, and post-session	Strong welfare emphasis; temporal sensitivity	Animal-only measure; human and relational behaviors absent
Equine Handling/ Groundwork Ethograms (e.g., Fureix et al., 2010; Hausberger et al., 2008; Sankey et al., 2010)	Horses in EAS, riding instruction, and welfare research	Horse stress indicators, affiliative behavior, locomotion, and responses to human cues	Developed within equine science; strong welfare relevance	Primarily horse-focused; human behavior and interactional dynamics limited
Horse–Human Interaction Ethograms in Welfare Research (e.g., Fureix & Hausberger, 2016)	Horses in grooming, feeding, loading, routine care	Human handling behaviors and horse responses (compliance, avoidance, and tension)	Illuminates how human actions influence horse behavior; valuable for welfare assessment	Interaction framed as stimulus–response; reciprocity and mutual regulation not explicitly measured

that you can measure, such as attachment or the human-animal bond. Those tend to be self-report instruments focusing on human experience, which we cover in the next chapter.

Taken together, these tools provide invaluable foundations for understanding human behavior, animal behavior, and welfare in animal-assisted contexts. What they largely share, however, is an *implicit* treatment of interaction. Even when both species are observed, behaviors are typically coded in parallel rather than coordinated, reciprocal processes. Human-animal interaction, as a phenomenon, often emerges only in interpretation – not in the measurement itself. To fill this gap, and to compensate for one of the major limitations of the HAIS – that it records discrete behaviors rather than interactional patterns – we incorporate a second method, one more consistent with systematic observation – Human-Animal Interaction (HAI) Ethograms.

HAI Ethograms

Recall from Chapter 7 that an ethogram is a structured list of operationally defined behaviors used for systematic observation. Many of the tools listed in Table 8.1 focus on the behavior of a single species, such as horses or dogs. These tools are extremely helpful for documenting animal welfare, stress signals, or affiliative behaviors, but they do not always capture the relational dynamics occurring between partners. Because human-animal interaction is central to animal-assisted services, we argue that measurement should explicitly reflect both human and animal behavior – and importantly, the coordination between them.

Although the HAIS moves us closer, by allowing a way to systematically record both the human's and the animal's behavior during a session, it doesn't quite capture the interaction *between* the animal and human. It's as if the HAIS measures two separate streams of behavior, rather than capturing the complex *interaction*. Our naturalistic observations (refer back to Chapter 6) indicated that *approaching someone* (approach) and *responding to being approached by someone* (response) were common interactions occurring during sessions. Building on those observations, we conducted systematic observation (recall from Chapter 7) using

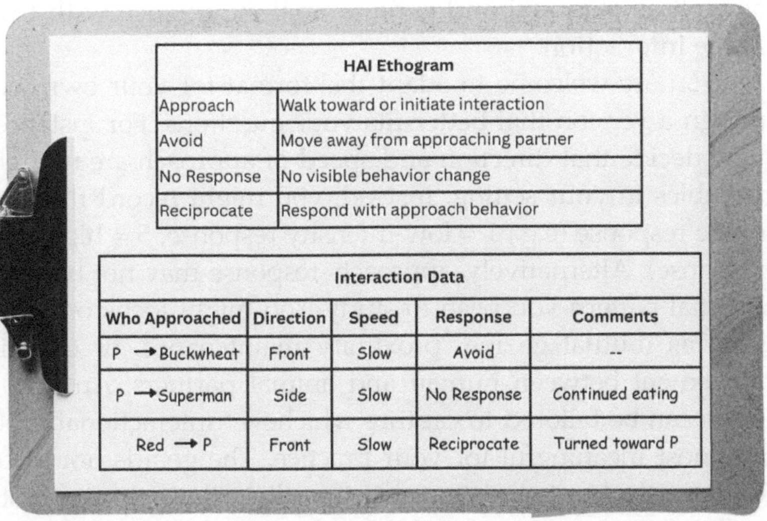

HAI Ethogram	
Approach	Walk toward or initiate interaction
Avoid	Move away from approaching partner
No Response	No visible behavior change
Reciprocate	Respond with approach behavior

Interaction Data				
Who Approached	Direction	Speed	Response	Comments
P → Buckwheat	Front	Slow	Avoid	--
P → Superman	Side	Slow	No Response	Continued eating
Red → P	Front	Slow	Reciprocate	Turned toward P

FIGURE 8.6 HAI Ethogram and data sheet for measuring approach behavior.

what we call an **HAI ethogram** – an ethogram for human-animal interaction. Specifically, the HAI ethogram in Figure 8.6 captures approach-response behavior, providing the operational definition of approach and three potential responses (avoid, no response, reciprocate). Rather than asking, "What did the human do?" or "What did the animal do?" the HAI Ethogram aims to ask, "What did they do together?" Figure 8.6 also shows the data sheet we used to record approach-response sequences during research sessions.

Beginning with the upper left column, we documented who was approaching whom. The arrow indicates the direction of the approach. For example, on the first line, P → Buckwheat indicates that the participant approached Buckwheat. We then recorded the direction of the approach – the participant approached Buckwheat from the front, walking towards him face-to-face. Next, we recorded the speed of the approach as slow. Finally, we recorded Buckwheat's response – Buckwheat avoided the participant by walking away. The remaining entries reflect additional approaches and responses observed during the session. This data sheet was created for our specific research purposes, informed by naturalistic observations as well as personal and professional experience with human–horse interaction.

You are welcome to adapt this format for your own work or design a version that better fits your questions. For instance, you may decide that direction and speed of approach are not relevant variables in your setting. Instead, you might record the intensity of the response (e.g., 1 = low-intensity response, 5 = high-intensity response). Alternatively, approach–response may not be the interactional pattern you wish to study. You might focus on behaviors such as mutual gazing, proximity maintenance, or coordinated movement between human and animal partners. An HAI ethogram can be tailored to capture whichever interactional processes are most meaningful for your practice. The goal is not to copy a tool exactly, but to create a structure that allows you to systematically observe and record the interactions that help answer your questions. HAI ethograms can become a powerful lens for revealing the subtle, dynamic patterns that shape animal-assisted services.

Try It! Measure Human-Animal Interaction

To get started measuring human-animal interaction, access the Human-Animal Interaction Scale in the Digital Resources section of our website [www.bringingsciencetoourstories.com]. We recommend trying out the scale as both a participant and an observer to experience the different perspectives. This exercise can be done with any animal. Try this exercise with different animals, one at a time. That is, engage with one animal, record the experience, then try it with a different animal.

1. Access the Human-Animal Interaction Scale online.
2. Try it as a participant
   - Spend some unstructured time engaging with an animal.
   - After the interaction, record your experience on the scale.
   - Reflect on how this was for you and how this may be useful in your animal-assisted work.

3. Try it as an observer
   - Ask a colleague, friend, or family member to interact with an animal while you observe.
   - After the interaction, complete the Human-Animal Interaction Scale, recording what you saw.
   - Reflect on the experience and think about how the observer form may be helpful for your work.
4. Try it both ways
   - Try using both the participant and observer forms for the same interaction. Ask a friend to interact with an animal while you observe.
   - After the interaction, ask your friend to complete the participant form while you complete the observer form. Share your responses with each other and discuss. Reflect on the strengths and weaknesses of recording human-animal interaction this way.
5. Try these steps with different animals, in different settings, and with different people, and decide if/how you might want to use the scale in your work.

Note

1. You can find an open-access copy of the scale and manual at our website: www.bringingsciencetoourstories.com

Bibliography

Anderson, D. C. (2006). *Assessing the human-animal bond: A compendium of actual measures*. Purdue University Press.

Binfet, J. T., Green, F. L., & Draper, Z. A. (2022). The importance of client–canine contact in canine-assisted interventions: A randomized controlled trial. *Anthrozoös*, *35*(1), 1–22.

De Santis, M., Contalbrigo, L., Borgi, M., Cirulli, F., & Luzi, F. (2018). Evaluation of animal-assisted interventions: A systematic approach to monitoring behavioral outcomes in dog-assisted therapy. *Animals*, *8*(3), 1–14.

De Santis, M., Filugelli, L., Mair, A., Normando, S., Mutinelli, F., & Contalbrigo, L. (2024). How to measure human-dog interaction in dog assisted interventions? A scoping review. *Animals*, *14*(3), 410.

Dowling-Guyer, S., Dabney, K., Robertson, E. A. R., & Mueller, M. K. (2024). Behavioral coding of adolescent and therapy dog interactions during a social stress task. *Veterinary Sciences*, *11*, 644.

Fournier, A. K. (2016). Pen pals: An examination of human-animal interaction as an outlet for healthy masculinity in prison. In *Men and their dogs: A new understanding of man's best friend* (pp. 175–194). Springer International Publishing.

Fournier, A. K., Berry, T. D., & Letson, E. (2016). The human-animal interaction scale: Development and evaluation. *Anthrozoös*, *29*(4), 455–467.

Fournier, A. K., French, M., Letson, E. A., Hanson, J., Berry, T. D., & Cronin, S. (2024). The behavioral cost of care: Changes in maintenance behavior during equine-assisted interventions. *Animals*, *14*(4), 536.

Fournier, A. K., Letson, E. A., & Berry, T. D. (2017). *HAIS: Human-animal interaction scale & manual* (1st ed.). CreateSpace Independent Publishing Platform. ISBN 9781539134411.

Fureix, C., & Hausberger, M. (2016). How horses (*Equus caballus*) see the world: Humans as significant agents. *Animal Cognition*, *19*, 643–654.

Fureix, C., Menguy, H., & Hausberger, M. (2010). Partners with bad temper: Reject or cure? A study of chronic stress in horses. *PLOS One*, *5*(8), e12434.

Glenk, L. M. (2017). Current perspectives on therapy dog welfare in animal-assisted interventions. *Animals*, *7*(2), 1–17.

Hausberger, M., Roche, H., Henry, S., & Visser, E. K. (2008). A review of the human–horse relationship. *Applied Animal Behaviour Science*, *109*, 1–24.

Hosey, G., Melfi, V., & Pankhurst, S. (Eds.). (2023). *The Routledge international handbook of human-animal interactions and anthrozoology*. Routledge.

Lee, C. Y., Ngai, J. T. K., Chau, K. K. Y., Yu, R. W. M., & Wong, P. W. C. (2022). Development of a pilot human–canine ethogram for an animal-assisted education programme in primary schools–A case study. *Applied Animal Behaviour Science*, *255*, 105725.

Ng, Z., Albright, J., Fine, A. H., & Peralta, J. (2014). Our ethical and moral responsibility: Ensuring the welfare of therapy animals. *Applied Animal Behaviour Science*, *159*, 1–10.

O'Haire, M. E. (2013). Animal-assisted intervention for autism spectrum disorder: A systematic literature review. *Journal of Autism and Developmental Disorders*, *43*, 1606–1622.

Rodriguez, K. E., Guérin, N. A., Gabriels, R. L., Serpell, J. A., Schreiner, P. J., & O'haire, M. E. (2018). The state of assessment in human-animal interaction research. *Human-Animal Interaction Bulletin*, *6*, 63–81.
Samet, L., Vaterlaws-Whiteside, H., Upjohn, M., & Casey, R. (2023). Status of instrument development in the field of human-animal interactions and bonds: Ten years on. *Society & Animals*, *32*(1), 74–94.
Sankey, C., Richard-Yris, M. A., Henry, S., Fureix, C., Nassur, F., & Hausberger, M. (2010). Reinforcement as a mediator of the perception of humans by horses (*Equus caballus*). *Animal Cognition*, *13*, 753–764.

9

Honoring Experience

Listening through Self-Report

Field Story 9: Cuddles at Curious Cows and Company

Curious Cows and Company is housed on a family-owned dairy farm in Corcoran, Minnesota, and offers calf-cuddling visits in which guests spend one-on-one time with young calves in a quiet pen, sitting or lying beside them, and interacting at the animal's pace. The business was started by Quinci and Caleb, a brother–sister team interested in connecting with the community by inviting visitors to tour their working dairy farm and spend time with the calves. Over time, Quinci has noticed consistent patterns in both human and calf behavior, particularly with Ducki, a young female calf. Ducki was born on April 1, 2025, alongside a litter of kittens who quickly became her companions. Figure 9.1 shows Ducki with her kitten friends. Described as "born a cuddler," Ducki often rested in the straw while the kittens curled against her stomach, trailing after her when she stood, and waiting for her to lie down again. Noticing Ducki's calm temperament and strong affinity for close contact, Quinci believed she could offer similar comfort to visitors coming to the farm.

For one summer, Ducki participated in up to nine cuddle appointments per week, typically lying down almost immediately upon entering the pen and waiting calmly for visitors to approach. She allowed people of all ages to rest beside her and remained settled

DOI: 10.4324/9781003640257-12

FIGURE 9.1 Ducki sharing her bed with sleeping kitten friends.
Source: Photo provided by Quinci Schmidt

throughout the session, often chewing her cud – a strong indicator of a relaxed cow. Across sessions, Quinci noticed emotional themes in visitors' responses. Some have described the time as grounding during periods of grief or stress, and others as unexpectedly soothing or renewing. Many appear calmer afterward and express gratitude for the quiet, steady nature of the experience. Emotional reactions – including tears – are not uncommon. For many guests, this is also their first close interaction with cows, and that novelty appears meaningful. Taken together, these observations represent patterns noticed over time rather than outcomes measured in a formal study. As with other animal-assisted services, the consistency of both animal behavior and human response invites reflection on what may be happening during these visits – and how those patterns might later be described, explored, or measured more systematically.

Shifts in Internal Experience

In our work, we use the **anodyne–agent model** (Fournier et al., 2021) as a way of thinking about the different roles animals can play in animal-assisted services. Sometimes animals function as *agents* in the intervention process – actively participating in learning, therapy, or behavior change. Other times, animals function as *anodynes*, eliciting short-term changes in emotional or mood state, such as increased calm, comfort, or positive affect. Ducki's role in sessions most closely aligns with an anodyne effect. Her presence does not replace a therapist, teacher, or intervention activity. Instead, interactions with her appear to coincide with shifts in how people feel inside – often quickly and without deliberate effort.

Cases like Ducki's highlight an important measurement question: *How do we capture changes that are primarily internal and subjective?* The outcome of interest may be a person's emotional state – feeling calmer, lighter, less tense, or more at ease. In fact, the *Handbook on Cow Cuddling Therapy* (Sharma & Kaur Dhanoa, 2025) suggests that engaging with cows can have positive effects on several psychological variables – stress, emotion regulation, self-esteem, and empathy. When addressing these internal experiences, behavioral observation alone may be insufficient. This is where **self-report measures** are especially useful. Mood and emotion are, by definition, internal experiences. A self-report score tells you how a person experiences or interprets something, which may or may not match observable behavior. Both are evidence; they answer different questions. While we may observe correlates of these self-reported emotional states – such as posture, facial expression, or verbalizations – the most direct way to understand them is to ask the person experiencing them.

In our work, we have used brief self-report measures of emotion and mood to examine subtle effects associated with human–animal interaction. These tools allow us to document shifts that occur during or immediately following experiences with animals like Ducki. In the remainder of this chapter, we define self-report instruments, discuss when and where they are most appropriate, outline strategies for identifying valid and reliable measures, and review the basics of administering, scoring, and interpreting self-report data.

What Is Self-Report?

A **self-report** instrument is a measurement tool that involves asking an individual about themselves. The respondent (person completing the form) is meant to read each item, reflect on the answer for themselves, and then respond in the format provided. Traditionally, this was done with paper-and-pencil self-reports. Today, they may be completed on paper, on a computer, or on a mobile device. Self-reports are probably the most common method of data collection used in our field and across health and wellness disciplines. A common self-report used is the Rosenberg Self-Esteem Scale. This is an instrument designed to measure an individual's self-esteem, how they feel about themselves. The HAIS can also be used as a self-report measure (refer to Chapter 8).

There are several types of self-report instruments you might use – journals/diaries, logs, interviews, checklists, and questionnaires – described in Table 9.1. You may be familiar with these terms, and their definitions are somewhat self-explanatory. However, they each have their caveats – things to think about when deciding on your self-report method.

Journals or Diaries

Journals or diaries are self-report tools in which individuals record thoughts, feelings, or experiences in their own words over time (Bolger et al., 2003). Unlike interviews or questionnaires,

TABLE 9.1 List of self-report methods and their use, strengths, and limitations

Format	*What It Captures Best*	*Strengths*	*Limitations*	*Best When*
Journals/ Diaries	Meaning, reflection, subjective experience over time	Rich, nuanced data; allows participants to use their own language; good for exploring *how* and *why* change occurs	Time-intensive; variable detail and quality; harder to summarize or compare	You want to understand lived experience, sense-making, or personal meaning related to animal interactions
Logs	Frequency, duration, or occurrence of events	Simple; low burden; good for identifying patterns over time; easy to summarize	Limited insight into emotional or cognitive experience; little context	You want to track exposure, consistency, or patterns (e.g., time spent with animals or number of visits)
Inventories	Traits, symptoms, or broader functioning	Standardized; often reliable and validated; useful for comparison across people or settings	Can be lengthy; may miss short-term or session-level change; less flexible	You need baseline or periodic measurements of constructs like anxiety, stress, or well-being
Checklists	Presence or absence of experiences or states	Very brief; easy to administer; accessible for many populations; consistent across sessions	Limited depth; does not capture intensity or meaning	Time is limited, and you want a quick snapshot of experiences (e.g., emotions felt during a session)

journals allow participants to reflect privately and capture experiences as they unfold, rather than responding to predefined questions. Reflective journal entries are a relatively recent research tool for studying psychotherapy, with studies examining reflections of therapists, and especially clients (e.g., Zacks & Nitsani, 2025). In animal-assisted services, journals are particularly useful for understanding subjective experience, meaning-making, and emotional shifts that may not be easily quantified. Applying this topic to the chapter's field story, calf-cuddling participants could write about how they felt during or after spending time with Ducki, what stood out to them, or how interactions with her influenced their day. Practitioners may also keep reflective journals to document observations, hypotheses, and questions that arise in practice. Journals can be:

- **Open-ended**, with no prompts.
- **Semi-structured**, with brief guiding questions (e.g., "How did you feel during today's session?").
- **Time-limited**, such as writing for five minutes immediately following a session.

Because journal data are qualitative, they are best suited for **exploration, reflection, and pattern recognition**, rather than precise outcome measurement. They are especially helpful when the goal is to understand *how* and *why* change may be occurring.

Logs

Logs are structured self-report tools used to record **when, how often, or how long** something occurs. They focus on frequency, duration, or occurrence rather than meaning or interpretation. In animal-assisted services, logs are commonly used to track:

- Time spent with animals
- Number of visits or sessions
- Types of activities completed
- Occurrence of specific events (e.g., animal present vs. not present)

For example, a participant might complete a simple log noting how many minutes they spent interacting with an animal each day, or a practitioner might record whether an animal was present during a session and for how long. Logs can also be combined with brief self-report ratings (e.g., stress level before and after interaction). Logs are especially useful when:

- You want to examine **patterns over time**
- You are interested in **dose, exposure, or consistency**
- You want a low-burden tool that can be completed quickly

Because logs are relatively structured, they are easier to summarize and analyze than journals, but they capture less depth.

Interviews

Think of an **interview** like a conversation that provides data (Kvale & Brinkmann, 2009). In an interview, you ask questions of the respondent, and the answers to your questions are the data. Interviews can be structured or unstructured. For **structured interviews**, the interviewer asks the respondent a specific list of predetermined questions, stating them specifically as written, in a predetermined order. Structured interviews often have decision-tree-like instructions such that the answer to a question determines the next question (e.g., if the respondent answered No, skip to question #…). The goal with structured interviews is consistency and reduced interviewer bias. Interviews can be in person, online via a platform like Zoom, over the phone, or through a chat platform. Structured interviews are less flexible but promote consistency across practitioners and respondents and are easier to quantify than unstructured interviews. They are useful for screening, measuring outcomes, and providing standardized documentation. An example of a structured interview could be your intake interview. Perhaps you have an intake form that you talk through with your new clients, asking them the same questions every time, in the same order. Here is an example:

1. What are the primary goals you hope to achieve through (name of service)?
2. Do you have any allergies to animals that we should be aware of (animals, grass, or hay)?
3. How comfortable do you feel being around (animal species involved)?
4. What is your previous experience with these animals?
5. How do you typically respond when you feel stressed or overwhelmed?

There are some published structured interviews available for specific purposes. They tend to be designed for diagnosing specific disorders or conditions. For example, the Structured

Interview for PTSD (Davidson et al., 1990) consists of fixed, scripted questions about symptoms of PTSD. It can be helpful in gathering consistent, unbiased evidence for PTSD diagnosis and treatment progress. Aside from diagnostic interviews, you may find structured interviews for gathering personality information. For example, the Structured Interview for the Five-Factor Model (Trull et al., 1998) is a personality assessment. The respondent is asked specifically worded questions, in a particular order, providing data on five major personality domains.

In contrast to structured interviews, **unstructured interviews** feel more like open conversations. The interviewer has a general purpose or goal for the interview and may have a list of topics to cover. But the questions are not pre-written, there is more unscripted back-and-forth conversation, and the interview may take different directions, depending on the interviewee's responses. Unstructured interviews provide rich, narrative, individualized data, and are more difficult to quantify. An example of an unstructured intake interview could be:

- **Initial prompt** – "Tell me what brings you here for [animal]-assisted counseling."
  - **Topics to include**
  - ☐ History of the problem
  - ☐ Severity of the problem
  - ☐ Animal allergies/comfort level
  - ☐ Participant strengths

Now that we have described these two extremes, there is a third option to consider, one that is quite common – the semi-structured interview. A **semi-structured interview** is what it sounds like – something in between structured and unstructured. There is a predetermined list of questions, but the interview is allowed to flow naturally. The interviewer follows the respondent, and there is a genuine back-and-forth dialogue while making sure to get to all the necessary questions before the interview is through. Semi-structured interviews have a specific list of questions to ask, but the order may vary depending on the interviewee's responses. They provide a middle ground.

Semi-structured interviews may be ideal for gathering data on animal-assisted sessions. You can have a list of questions or prompts, but allow openness for the participant to provide a narrative description of what happened. This allows the participant to reveal or develop insight by reflecting on interactions with the animal(s). This is important because human–animal interactions, and their interpretation by the participant, are unique and unpredictable. A process that is flexible and adaptable will be useful.

Checklists

Checklists are self-report tools that ask respondents to indicate whether specific items are present or absent. They are typically simple, brief, and easy to complete. In animal-assisted services, checklists can be used to capture:

- Emotional states experienced during a session (e.g., calm, tense, happy, overwhelmed)
- Perceived benefits of an interaction
- Observed changes following a visit
- Client preferences or comfort levels

For example, a post-session checklist might ask calf-cuddling participants to check all emotions they experienced during a session with Ducki or indicate which aspects of the interaction were helpful. Practitioners may also use checklists to standardize reflection across sessions. Checklists are especially useful when:

- Time is limited
- Participants may have difficulty with lengthy questionnaires
- You want consistency across sessions without a heavy measurement burden

While checklists do not capture intensity or depth as well as rating scales or interviews, they provide a practical way to document experiences systematically.

Inventory, Scale, Survey, or Questionnaire

An **inventory**, also referred to as a scale, survey, or questionnaire, is a self-report instrument consisting of a list of questions the respondent answers. Inventories are generally on paper or on the computer. The respondent reads the question and answers it. While they can be quantitative or qualitative, most inventories are quantitative. The question is formatted so that the respondent provides an answer that can be counted and scored. Questions can take a variety of formats. Below, we share several formats. Next to the format is an example question relevant to measuring stress levels:

- ♦ Closed-ended
  - True/False
    - ☐ *I am feeling stressed right now.* (circle one) True/False
  - Yes/No
    - ☐ *I am feeling stressed right now.* (circle one) Yes/No
  - Likert scale
    - ☐ Circle the number that represents your level of agreement with the statement (1 = strongly disagree, 2 = disagree, 3 = agree, 4 = strongly agree)
      - *I am feeling stressed right now.*
  - Rank order
    - ☐ Put these statements in the order that describes how you are feeling right now, from best (top) to worst (bottom)
    - ☐ *Calm, Relaxed, Stressed, Anxious, Worried*
- ♦ Open-ended
  - *Tell me about your stress level right now.*

Remember our mantra – begin with the end in mind. If you imagine answering your question with a number (e.g., you want to report an average, or you want to determine whether your participants' attitude toward pets is correlated with their progress in animal-assisted service), then you need to gather evidence that gives you numbers. That is more likely with closed-ended questions than open-ended ones. Refer to Chapter 5, where we discussed choosing your data format. Later, in Chapter 11, we will cover how to analyze your data. Even before getting there, we find that people have an idea, whether they realize it or not, of what kind of data they want. Often, people imagine sharing an average score, the highest and lowest scores, and percentages. Sometimes they also want to report on the relationship between variables. All of these require quantitative data – numbers. And as we will see later, the kind of numbers you get leads to different analysis and reporting options.

How Do I Find a Measurement Instrument?

This is a great question and one that led to us writing this book. Practitioners often have the inclination to gather evidence, and many of them have asked us what instruments they should use. In this section, we walk you through the process of finding an existing measurement tool. Here are the basic steps:

1. Return to your SMART question and variable from Chapters 4 and 5.
2. Search online for an existing instrument to measure your variable of interest; possible search terms could be:
    - "Instruments to measure [your variable]"
    - "[your variable] scales"
3. When you find the name of an instrument, do another search on that specific instrument. Look for information on:
    - Purpose
        a. What is it intended to measure?
        b. Who is it intended for?
    - Reliability and Validity
        a. Has it been evaluated?
        b. Who has it been validated for?
    - Logistics
        a. Who can administer and score it? Do you have the credentials?
        b. Length – how many questions does it include and how long does it typically take to complete?
        c. Availability – how do you get it? Is it open access or do you have to purchase it?

4. Follow these steps for each instrument you are considering. Choose the one that is most likely to accurately measure the variable of interest in your population, within the resources and training that you have.

How Do I Know if This Is a Valid and Reliable Instrument?

Whenever you ask yourself this question, we hope you give yourself a big ol' pat on the back. Because this means you are thinking critically about your SAGA work, and that will lead to the best outcomes. You know from Chapter 5 that we should always use measurement instruments that are valid and reliable. But how do we know that? This is really two questions – what information tells us that an instrument is valid and reliable, and how do we find that information?

First, how do we know an instrument's reliability and validity? Remember from Chapter 5 that reliability and validity are determined through research – administering the instrument and comparing it with other measures. Each administration or comparison provides a piece of evidence for or against reliability or validity. You could take a whole college course on this material if you wanted. And you could definitely read an entire book on the topic. We have put some helpful sources in the Bibliography section of this chapter.

For our purposes, we can keep it pretty simple. Table 9.2 shows the kinds of information you will see, what they mean, and what is a good enough score. In most cases, the number (statistic) you will see reported is a correlation, which will be a decimal number between 0 and 1. The higher the number, the stronger the correlation – in other words, the stronger the evidence. In most cases, we are looking for a positive number above 0.60. The table gives the basic description of each, as well as the statistics you will see reported and the threshold. No need to memorize all of this. We suggest bookmarking this page, maybe even taking a picture of it on your phone. Refer back to it when you are reviewing measures and their properties.

Let's look at an example of reliability/validity information you will come across and how to interpret it. Below is a paragraph

TABLE 9.2 Helpful benchmarks for evaluating a self-report's reliability and validity information

Reliability or Validity	*Type of Evidence*	*What's It Testing?*	*Statistic*	*What's Good Enough?*
Reliability *Looking for evidence that your instrument measures the same across situations and time*	Internal consistency	Do all of the items measure the same thing?	Cronbach's alpha (α)	0.70 or higher
	Test–retest reliability	Do you get the same score every time? (assuming nothing changed)	Correlation (r)	0.70 or higher
	Inter-rater reliability	Do the observers agree on what they see?	Percent agreement (%)	The higher the better (>80% preferred)
			Cohen's kappa (k)	0.60 or higher
Validity *Looking for evidence that the instrument measures your specific variable*	Content validity	Do the items represent the whole variable?	Expert review	Items match the variable, not too narrow or repetitive
	Construct validity	Does the scale compare to other tools the way you would expect?	Correlation (r)	Higher than 0.60 for similar variables; 0.30 for different variables
	Criterion validity	Does it relate to a standard or predict important outcomes?	Correlation (r)	Higher than 0.30

Note: These are general recommendations; always consider the context of the instrument's development and your intended use.

on the reliability and validity of a hypothetical scale. Read through the paragraph, referring to Table 9.2 for each term/statistic.

> Reliability and validity data were calculated from several samples, totaling 1,000 adults. The samples included 598 adult college students, 300 adult outpatients at a counseling center, and 102 male inmates of a state correctional

> facility. Internal consistency was determined by calculating Cronbach's alpha for each of the different groups of participants. The reliability coefficient ranged from .73 to .88, with a mean of .85. A subset of participants (n = 400) was subjected to test-retest analysis, taking the scale twice, one week apart. The correlation between the first and second administration was .79. Regarding construct validity, the scale was administered alongside an existing, related scale. The correlation was .36; this lower correlation is consistent with the scale measuring a different variable from human-animal interaction.

Before reading this book, you may have seen a paragraph like this and run in the other direction. We admit we still have that inclination. Content like this is technical and can seem like it was written for someone else. But it wasn't. This information is for you! We hope that you now have what you need to understand it. And if you can't understand it, there are resources to help you. You can ask AI for help ("AI, put this paragraph in plain language for a practitioner wondering if an instrument is valid and reliable"), you can connect with us through our website, or you can connect with a measurement expert in your area. See Appendix C for suggestions on employing AI in SAGA work.

Where Do I Find Reliability and Validity Information?

There are two main places to find information like this (1) the instrument manual or instruction materials and (2) research literature.

Instrument Manual

Some instruments come with a manual that explains everything you need to know about the instrument – how it was developed, how to administer and score it, its psychometrics, and its validation. The HAIS, which we covered in Chapter 8, has a manual with all this information. You can find it on our website. Take a look to get an idea of the different kinds of information a manual includes. Other scales may not have a whole manual, but the document on which you find the items also includes some of this information, including reliability and validity information.

Research Literature

When you have no manual or instruction materials, you can search the research literature. For any published measurement tool, you should be able to search online and find a research article or some reference to its reliability/validity assessment. We use Google Scholar to do our searches. Go to www.scholar.google.com and type in "human-animal interaction scale validation." This should pull up the research article, published in *Anthrozoos* in 2016, that describes the research we did to determine the HAIS's reliability and validity. It will also pull up other related studies. Try a different variable. Search for "companion animal bonding scale validation." This should pull up an article by Poresky and colleagues in 1987. Go ahead and do some searching for scales you have heard of or variables you are interested in.

Once you've found the article, we recommend reading it all the way through. It's going to be quite technical, but it will give you valuable information about the variable you want to measure. The methods and results section will tell you how they tested the instrument and what they found, respectively. If you're having difficulty or just don't have time to slowly read through and digest the article, you can use AI. Upload the article and ask for a synopsis of the instrument's reliability and validity. We recommend saving the article in your files for later referral.

Red Flags

Unfortunately, there are many self-report "measures" and other tools available online that look credible but actually have no scientific backing. Here are some red flags to watch for when searching for reliability/validity information on an instrument:

- The authors describe the instrument as "reliable and valid" without providing evidence

- Descriptions of reliability and validity don't include any findings
- The scale is extremely short, unless it is a well-validated brief version
- Most items don't match the variable of interest
- The instrument was tested on a very small sample (<100)
- There are no citations or peer-reviewed sources
- Description includes buzzwords or sounds like a sales pitch

Use Current Tools and Resources

Notice that our second search in Google Scholar pulled up an article from 1987. At the time of this writing, that article is 38 years old. Is that good or bad? It depends. We should always use the most accurate information we can when examining the evidence of a tool's reliability and validity. Some instruments were validated a while back, and there have been no new data since. In that case, the original study/article/information is what we use. However, other scales are revised over time or evaluated repeatedly. In those cases, it is important to sift through and find out the current status of the instrument.

Is it considered valid and reliable for your intended use? Remember from Chapter 3 that one study only tells you about one sample at one point in time. We cannot pick and choose which studies to cite based on what is convenient. For example, the Rorschach Inkblot test is a famous psychological test. It was developed in 1921 and published with validation information. Since then, it has been evaluated in many studies. Some find evidence for good reliability and validity, but mostly the research shows its properties are questionable. If I plan to use it, I need to read a recent review on the current status of the instrument in the context of my intended use.

Beyond validation studies, we should also use the most up-to-date information when referring to any scientific literature.

Some variables have been studied for a very long time and others are more recent. When reviewing the literature, and there

> Science is a never-ending saga; each study offers insights and leads to another study. There is no endpoint; we are constantly conducting research and gaining knowledge.

are many studies on your topic of interest, we recommend narrowing your review to the last 5–10 years. For a test like the Rorschach, which has been studied for a long time, it's good to cite the original source and then limit your review to more recent studies.

Administering, Scoring, and Interpreting Self-Reports

Using a self-report instrument involves more than handing someone a questionnaire. Some instruments require specific credentials, training, or permissions to use. Pay attention to this when selecting an instrument.

Administering

Administration refers to how and when the measure is given. Small differences – before vs. after a session, in a quiet space vs. a busy barn, verbally vs. written – can influence responses. Consistency matters. Try to administer measures under similar conditions each time and according to the instructions that accompany the instrument.

Scoring

Scoring refers to converting responses into usable data. Some tools require simple summing, while others involve reverse-scored items or software-generated values. Always review scoring instructions carefully and seek help when you need it. We recommend understanding the scoring process *before* deciding on a measure. An instrument can sound like a perfect fit until you reach the scoring stage and discover the procedure is so complicated that you struggle to produce – or even interpret – the final scores. We learned this lesson the hard way.

Interpreting

Interpretation involves understanding what a score actually means. A number is not inherently meaningful until it is compared – to prior scores, normative data, or meaningful benchmarks. Interpretation should remain humble and contextual. Self-report scores reflect perception and experience, not objective truth.

Should I Make My Own Self-Report Instrument?[1]

The short answer is: "no."

Search for a measure of your variable that has been developed, validated, and published. That is your easiest path to accurate data. If you can't find a self-report instrument to measure your variable, it is possible you're gathering evidence on something new. Or your spin on the variable is new. Cool! Good for you! Then it might make sense to create a measurement tool. Appendix D provides steps and tips to help you develop a useful self-report measure. Again, this is a last resort, after you've ruled out the possibility of using an existing instrument. One thing to keep in mind when developing your own self-report questions, and also when reading items on existing instruments, is the cognitive task participants are engaging in with every survey question.

> Don't spend your valuable time creating a self-report instrument if one already exists.

Completing Self-Reports Is Mental Work

Figure 9.2 illustrates Sudman et al.'s model (1996) of the cognitive processes involved in responding to a survey (inventory) item.

Let's walk through this with an example from the Human–Animal Interaction Scale. The scale asks the respondent, after interacting with an animal, to rate their interactions with an animal. The respondent is instructed to rate the amount of

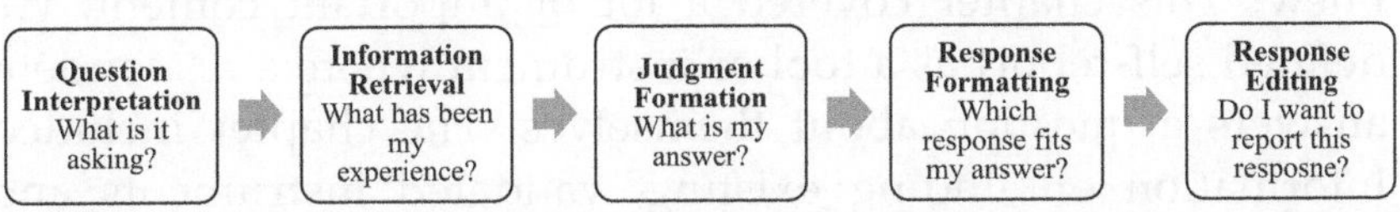

FIGURE 9.2 A model of cognitive processing, showing the mental steps we go through when answering a self-report question.

interaction for each behavior listed. Let's think about just the first item – *Watch the animal(s)*, where the participant rates their experience from 0, meaning *Not At All*, to 4, meaning *A Great Deal*. Upon reading this item, the respondent must interpret what *Watch the animal(s)* means. We define *Watch* as having eyes directed toward the animal while looking at and focusing on the animal. Individuals may interpret this differently. Regardless of interpretation, the next step is information retrieval. They think back to their memory of the experience to remember their interactions with the animal. Next, in judgment formation, they arrive at a tentative judgment about how much they watched the animal. During response formatting, they try to fit their experience of watching to the question format, deciding if their experience fits a 0, 1, 2, 3, or 4. Finally, whichever number they choose, they decide if they want to report that number in the response editing stage. Perhaps they remember their experience as a 1 but think it would look better to report a 3. They decide in this step which to report.

This complicated process all happens very quickly and largely at an unconscious level. Bottom line – it's mental work to answer a survey question, with lots of room for misinterpretation, recall errors, decision-making, and biased reporting (Schwarz, 1999). What does this mean for you when creating an item? Make it as clear, simple, and judgment-free as possible. Test items out amongst your team or with friends and use feedback to improve questions before using them with real participants. Then, acknowledge limitations throughout your SAGA process. Limitations include any obvious issues related to this cognitive processing model, as well as the general limitation of undetermined reliability and validity of a new scale.

In Summary

Phew! This chapter covered a lot of important content. We defined self-report as a tool or instrument where a respondent answers a question about themselves. The chapter included information on finding existing, validated instruments and interpreting technical information on reliability and validity.

Finally, we discussed why NOT to create your own self-report instrument if you can help it. Lastly, the cognitive processing model of answering a survey item was discussed to describe just how much our brains are working when answering what we might think is a simple self-report question. We hope your takeaway from this chapter is that self-report is a useful method for gathering data and you have the skills to find existing measures and determine whether they are trustworthy.

Self-report measures are easy to administer and dangerously easy to misuse. More than any other part of the SAGA process, selecting self-report measures requires sustained critical thinking. We imagine you think carefully and critically about your animal's care and training, and we ask you to use those same skills to select measurement instruments.

They are, after all, going to provide evidence that impacts your animal one way or another.

Try It! Find a Good Self-Report Instrument for Your SAGA

To get started using self-reports, follow these steps to find a measure that fits your question and your context.

1. Identify one clearly defined variable you would like to measure. Refer to Chapter 4, where you developed your SMART question, and Chapter 5, where you chose a variable to measure.
2. Do a general online search to see what self-report options exist for that variable. For example, if you are interested in communication skills, you might search "self-report measures of communication skills."
3. As you browse potential instruments, look for one that:
   - Is designed for the population you work with (e.g., adults, children, specific clinical or educational groups).
   - Is within your scope and expertise to administer, score, and interpret.
   - Is practical and accessible for your participants or clients.

4. If a measure seems like a good fit, look for information on its reliability and validity.
   - Do a general search such as "reliability and validity of [instrument name]."
   - Search Google Scholar or another scholarly database for articles on the measure's development, psychometrics, or validation.
   - When you find this information, refer back to Table 9.2 to see whether the reported values fall within acceptable ranges.
5. Once you have selected an instrument, take it yourself. Complete the questionnaire, then score and interpret it. This step is essential. It helps you experience what your participants will experience, assess how easy or difficult the measure is to score and interpret, and understand the kind of data it produces. All of this will inform whether the instrument is a good fit for your SAGA process.

Note

1. In this section, we are referring to creating your own self-report instrument, which we do not recommend. Creating your own behavioral observation tool, such as an ethogram tailored to your needs, is good practice. Refer to Chapter 7 for guidance when creating observation tools.

Bibliography

Bolger, N., Davis, A., & Rafaeli, E. (2003). Diary methods: Capturing life as it is lived. *Annual Review of Psychology*, *54*, 579–616. https://doi.org/10.1146/annurev.psych.54.101601.145030

Compitus, K., & Bierbower, S. M. (2024). Cow cuddling: Cognitive considerations in bovine-assisted therapy. *Human–Animal Interactions*, 12, 1. https://doi.org/10.1079/hai.2024.0016.

Das, A., Das, T. K., & Das, S. (2025). Cow-cuddling: A two-way and true way towards wellbeing. *APCORE Online Journal*, *1*(1), 149–159.

Davidson, J. R. T., Kudler, H. S., & Smith, R. D. (1990). Assessment and pharmacotherapy of posttraumatic stress disorder. In J. E.L. Giller

(Ed.), *Biological assessment and treatment of posttraumatic stress disorder* (pp. 205-221). Washington, DC: American Psychiatric Press.

DeVellis, R. F. (2016). *Scale development: Theory and applications* (4th ed.). Sage.

Fournier, A. K., Letson, E. A., Berry, T. D., Laitala, J., Proels, L., & Kavanaugh, K. (2021). The anodyne-agent model: A framework for conceptualizing the animal's role in animal-assisted intervention. *Human–Animal Interaction Bulletin, 9*(1), 55–75.

Furr, R. M. (2022). *Psychometrics: An introduction* (4th ed.). Sage.

Kvale, S., & Brinkmann, S. (2009). *InterViews: Learning the craft of qualitative research interviewing* (2nd ed.). Sage.

McGiffin, E. (2022). The laudable cow: Poetics of human/cattle relationships. In E. Bencke & J. Bruhn (Eds.), *Multispecies Storytelling in Intermedial Practices, 77–95*. Punctum Books.

Patton, M. Q. (2015). *Qualitative research & evaluation methods* (4th ed.). Sage.

Poresky, R. H., Hendrix, C., Mosier, J. E., & Samuelson, M. L. (1987). The companion animal bonding scale: Internal reliability and construct validity. *Psychological Reports, 60*(3), 743–746. https://doi.org/10.2466/pr0.1987.60.3.743

Schmied, C., Waiblinger, S., Scharl, T., Leisch, F., & Boivin, X. (2008). Stroking of different body regions by a human: Effects on behaviour and heart rate of dairy cows. *Applied Animal Behaviour Science, 109*(1), 25–38.

Schwarz, N. (1999). Self-reports: How the questions shape the answers. *American Psychologist, 54*(2), 93–105. https://doi.org/10.1037/0003-066X.54.2.93

Sharma, S. (2021). 'Cow cuddling': Psychotherapy to reduce stress and anxiety. *International Journal of Indian Psychology, 9*(1). https://doi.org/10.25215/0901.011.

Sharma, S., & Kaur Dhanoa, S. (2025). *Handbook on cow cuddling therapy*. Literatureslight Publishing House.

Sudman, S., Bradburn, N. M., & Schwarz, N. (1996). *Thinking about answers: The application of cognitive processes to survey methodology*. Jossey-Bass.

Trull, T. J., Widiger, T. A., Useda, J. D., Holcomb, J., Doan, B.-T., Axelrod, S. R., Stern, B. L., & Gershuny, B. S. (1998). A structured interview for the assessment of the Five-Factor Model of Personality. *Psychological*

Assessment, 10(3), 229–240. https://doi.org/10.1037/1040-3590.10.3.229

Zacks, A., & Nitsani, O. (2025). A methodological tool for characterizing the therapeutic acts of animal-assisted therapy. *Human–Animal Interactions*, *13*(1), 0029. https://doi.org/10.1079/hai.2025.0029

Part IV
Act on Your Findings

10

Analyzing and Interpreting Your Data

Field Story 10: From Presence to Pattern

Teddy is a large, long-haired orange tabby who was rescued as a tiny kitten in 2014. Over time, he became an unexpected but consistent presence in animal-assisted services at Eagle Vista Ranch & Wellness Center. Although Teddy's participation in sessions is not formally "planned" in the way therapy dogs or horses often are, he routinely inserts himself into the work – both indoors during office visits and outdoors in the horse pasture (see Figure 10.1). In office settings, Teddy approaches clients on his own, climbing into welcoming laps, leaning against legs, or settling nearby. Teddy's presence is not goal-directed in a traditional therapeutic sense. He does not participate in structured activities or respond to cues meant to advance a treatment plan. Instead, his impact appears to be organic and subtle.

Clients often comment on feeling calmer, lighter, or more relaxed when Teddy is nearby. Some describe his presence as comforting or grounding, noting shifts in mood or emotional state during and immediately following interactions with him. Teddy also moves freely through the horse pasture during equine-assisted sessions, sometimes positioning himself near clients or horses, and other times simply observing from a distance. Even in these less direct moments, clients frequently notice him and reference his presence when reflecting on how the session felt.

DOI: 10.4324/9781003640257-14

FIGURE 10.1 Teddy, a therapy cat who joins equine sessions as he pleases.

Each interaction with Teddy tells a small story. Data analysis is how we begin reading those stories together. By organizing, summarizing, and comparing our observations, we move from isolated impressions toward something more structured: patterns we can describe, examine, and use to guide decisions. This chapter is about learning how to make that shift.

Welcome to Data Analysis[1]

Here it is – the chapter you have been waiting for – data analysis! Or perhaps you've been dreading this chapter. We appreciate that these topics can be intimidating. Even if you enjoy math, which a lot of folks don't, you might see data analysis as more than you can handle. But the truth is, you can totally handle this.

Having anxiety about analyzing data is normal. And your level of *anxiety* with data analysis has no relationship to your actual *ability* to *perform* data analysis.

This chapter covers a five-step process of data analysis:

1. Determine the level of analysis you need
2. Create simple summaries
3. Visualize your data (get the picture)
4. Run statistical tests (only if needed)
5. Interpret patterns

Before we get to these steps, let's ease into the topic by discussing what data analysis is and is not, as well as your role in all of this.

What Data Analysis Really Means

Data analysis means noticing things about your data in a structured way. Refer to this chapter's field case. Over the years of sessions, we have noticed recurring patterns in how clients respond to Teddy. Analysis is the next step – organizing those observations so we can distinguish what feels memorable from what is consistently occurring. In this chapter, we teach you a structured process for noticing things in your data and then combining what you notice with your professional judgment to make the best decisions for your practice. These skills will help you understand your story better before writing the next chapter of your animal-assisted work. Find patterns and decide what to do about those patterns. If you're a bit weary, no worries. Take your time with this chapter, follow us step-by-step, and you will see how awesome analysis can be.

The term data analysis is an abstract concept that may be difficult to connect with or see yourself doing. But data analysis is just a range of activities. Take a look at this list of activities and you'll see they don't sound so scary:

- Sorting
- Organizing
- Counting
- Summarizing
- Comparing

In Teddy's case, this might include summarizing how often he approaches clients or comparing responses across indoor and outdoor sessions. The goal with data analysis is to summarize the data, to take a bunch of numbers or words, and notice both patterns and oddities. Those patterns and oddities are the pieces of information that allow us to answer our SAGA question and tell our story to others. Before beginning data analysis, we need to get the data into a database.

Creating a Database

A **database** is an organized collection of information, or data. Creating a database might sound like a big deal. And it is a big deal in the sense that you need to do this step to make sense of your data and answer your SAGA question. But it's not a big deal in terms of difficulty. Once you know the basics, it's a piece of cake. The basic ingredients are spreadsheets, rows, and columns – that's it!

Spreadsheet

We need a **spreadsheet** (a document arranged in rows and columns) to house our database. We use Microsoft Excel in our practice. You can also use Google Sheets, Apple Numbers, or any number of cloud-based free options. Find spreadsheet software that works for you. It should look something like Table 10.1 – a bunch of rows and columns that you can type into:

TABLE 10.1 Sample spreadsheet showing HAIS scores across five sessions

Client	*Session 1*	*Session 2*	*Session 3*	*Session 4*	*Session 5*
Sue	23	24	22	25	7
Charles	11	10	11	10	3
Carla	13	20	8	20	4
Dana	6	7	5	6	1

Rows and Columns

The hardest part of creating a database is knowing how to set up your rows and columns – figuring out what goes where. In our experience, the best organization is to designate rows (horizontal) as cases and columns (vertical) as the variables you are tracking. Each row is a case or an instance of data you collect. Examples of cases/instances are one session, one interaction, one client, one animal, one day, or one observation period. The key is consistency: every row in the same database must represent the same type of case. Don't mix rows for clients with rows for sessions or interactions. If you want to track different kinds of cases, create separate databases for each. Each column is a variable you are tracking for that case. Examples of column data might be date, session length, HAIS score, weather, or behavior codes. Table 10.1 is a sample database showing four human participants (rows) and their HAIS scores (columns) for each of five sessions with Teddy.

Summarization and Comparison

This database allows you to track scores for multiple people across time. You can use it to look at any individual's scores over time. For example, looking at Sue's row, we can see that their HAIS score is pretty consistent for Sessions 1 through 4 (23, 24, 22, 25). On the other hand, Carla's scores are more variable for the same Sessions (13, 20, 8, 20). Looking at these individuals over time, we can get an idea of their pattern of interaction with the animals. Sue's is consistently moderate; Dana's is consistently low. If we know their pattern, we can monitor for any fluctuations – numbers that are inconsistent with their patterns. This could indicate a change for the participant and something to examine more closely.

Beyond looking at the raw numbers as we have just done, creating a database allows you to summarize and make comparisons of your data. It also allows you to create charts to visualize your data. You could create a similar spreadsheet, but with animal data. At the ranch, we gather HAIS data for individual animals, including Teddy. Just as with human participants, tracking human–animal interaction across time for the animals can help us understand their typical interaction patterns and notice any changes. Now let's get started on the five-step process of data analysis.

Step 1: Determine the Level of Analysis You Need

We always begin with the end in mind, right? In this case, think about what you will do with your analysis results. The answer to that question will determine the type of evidence you need. Yes, there are different levels of analysis; some are more rigorous (credible, defendable to certain audiences) than others. The level you choose depends on your purpose, your comfort level, and your audience. Here is a table to help you decide which level of analysis you need.

Being data-driven does not require complex statistics or large samples. It requires curiosity, structure, and a willingness to let information guide action (Morrow, 2018). Use Table 10.2 as a guide every time you're ready to analyze your data. The level you need can vary from question to question. Notice there are many situations, we would guess even most situations, where descriptive analysis is all you will need. So breathe easy and stress not. Let's move to the next step in data analysis.

Step 2: Create Simple Summaries

Once your data are in a spreadsheet, the next step is to get a sense of the overall picture. Much of your data analysis will consist of summarizing and noticing patterns. These simple summaries help you quickly understand what is typical, what is unusual, and whether anything stands out. Here are some examples of simple summary activities:

- Calculating the participant's average HAIS score across sessions

TABLE 10.2 Tool for determining the level of data analysis you need

Level of Analysis	*Description*	*Purpose*	*Audience*
Level 1 (Descriptive)	Simple summaries, raw scores, visuals (charts, graphs)	Summarizing, detecting patterns, and noticing changes	◆ Self-evaluation and reflective practices ◆ Internal team members ◆ Clients ◆ Boards, committees ◆ General audiences
Level 2 (Statistical)	Statistical tests (correlation, t-test)	Confirming the finding is probably not due to chance	◆ Funders, grant agencies ◆ Insurance, 3rd party payers ◆ Accrediting bodies, certification programs ◆ Schools, administrators ◆ Multi-site teams that need standardized evidence ◆ Skeptical or data-savvy audiences

- Determining which score a participant or animal usually gets
- Determining how much an individual's scores vary from session to session
- Detecting whether the animal's behavior is pretty steady or shows big fluctuations
- Examining whether this week was similar to last week

For example, we might calculate Teddy's average number of client approaches per session or determine the typical duration of his interactions. Simple summaries help us describe (1) what is typical in your data (e.g., Teddy's average number of client approaches per session), and (2) how much your data varies (e.g., what is the highest and lowest number of interactions Teddy has had in a session). The table below provides the name for several simple summaries on what is typical in the data (top three rows) and how the data varies (bottom two rows).

You don't need to calculate these by hand. Any spreadsheet software can give you these numbers. You only need to know where to click, not how the math works. Your job is to ask

TABLE 10.3 Simple summaries to use in data analysis

Question	*Simple Summary*	*Definition*	*Example Question*
What is typical in the data?	**Mean** (Average)	The typical score across sessions or interactions	◆ What is an individual participant's average score across all sessions? ◆ What is the average score for a group of participants? ◆ What is the average number of service hours you provide per week?
	Median (Middle Score)	The middle value when the scores are ordered from lowest to highest. It can help you notice unusual data points (outliers).	◆ What is the middle HAIS score for teen participants? ◆ What is the middle score of the dog's heart rate readings this month? ◆ What is the middle number of barks during the sessions?
	Mode (Most Common Score)	The score that shows up most often	◆ What is the most common HAIS score? ◆ What is the most common animal the client interacts with?
	Frequency	The number of times something shows up in the data	◆ How many participants endorsed each behavior on the HAIS?
	Percentage	The proportion of the whole represented by different categories	◆ What percentage of the session included human–animal interaction?
How much do scores vary?	**Range** (Lowest to Highest Score)	The spread between the lowest and highest numbers	◆ If a participant's hours of sleep per night range from 5 to 10 compared to 7 to 8, that is a big spread and worth noticing.
	Standard deviation – SD (Average difference from the mean)	Small SD means scores are consistent; large SD means scores vary	◆ If one group's HAIS SD is 2 and another group's is 8, the second group is more variable. We might wonder whether they vary in other ways or if there is some reason for the variability.

SMART SAGA questions and use your resources to get these simple summaries. This table may also be helpful when you are reading about other people's data in books and articles. Use it as a reference to recall the terms and their definitions and relevance to your work. You can also use this table when asking for help with data analysis. Perhaps you add someone to your team or consult with someone who analyzes your data for you. Having this understanding and language allows you to ask for what you need (e.g., *"I'd like someone to calculate the mean and standard deviation of HAIS scores for all sessions at the nursing home"*).

Step 3: Visualize Your Data

The next step in the data analysis process is to visualize your data.

This is usually in the form of a chart but can also include infographics. Visualization comes after simple summaries because it helps you move from *"What do the numbers say?"* to *"What patterns are emerging, and what stands out?"* We have been showing you examples of data visualization in the form of charts throughout the book. In Chapter 11, we explore which charts to choose, how to make them, and how to interpret them with confidence.

> Visualization means turning numbers or words into a picture so that you can see patterns, changes, and relationships more clearly.

Step 4: Run Statistical Tests (If Needed)

Often, describing and visualizing your data will give you a clear enough answer. But if you want to examine a difference or relationship more formally – or if your audience requires stronger evidence – Step 4 allows you to run simple statistical tests. These tools help you check whether the patterns you see in your summaries and charts are **statistically meaningful**, meaning they are unlikely to be due to chance. You do not need to calculate anything by hand or memorize formulas. Programs like Jamovi, Excel, and Google Sheets can run these tests for you. Your role is simply to understand what the results mean for your practice.

TABLE 10.4 Simple comparisons to use in data analysis

Simple Comparison	*Common Analysis*	*Definition*	*Example Question*
Are these groups different?	t-Test	Compares averages from two different sets of people, animals, or conditions	Are anxiety scores different for participants working with dogs compared to cats?
Did something change over time?	t-Test, ANOVA, repeated measures	Compares scores from one point in time to another	Did the client's stress score change from session 1 to session 5?
Are these variables related?	Correlation	Shows whether two things move together in a predictable way	Is a change in anxiety over time related to HAIS scores?

If you need Level 2 analysis, or you're learning about a study that used statistical tests, you'll generally be working with three types of questions: (1) *Are two groups different*, (2) *Did something change over time*, or (3) *Are two variables related*. These three questions, described in Table 10.4, form the basis for most statistical tests, and each one aligns with a different kind of SAGA question.

You don't need to know the math behind these comparisons. Work on understanding the concept, creating each type of question relevant to your work, and, for questions you have already asked, identify which type of comparison you're making. Use this table similarly to Table 10.3 as a reference for your SAGA work, when reading about others' studies, and when asking for data analysis help.

Once you've summarized your data and performed any necessary statistical tests, the final step in the analysis process is interpretation. Interpretation is simply asking, "*What does this mean for my SAGA question?*"

Step 5: Interpret Patterns

You've gathered information, explored patterns, and, if needed, checked those patterns with statistical tools. Now you're ready to understand the story your data are telling. Interpretation is the heart of data-driven practice. This is where your skills, experience, and observations all come together. It requires curiosity, reflection, and a willingness to consider context. The fact that you picked up this book and have made it this far means you have all of that.

To interpret your data, go back to your SAGA question – what is the question you were trying to answer with these data that you have gathered? Below are the key things to keep in mind as you make sense of your findings. For readers who would like additional support, accessible guides such as *Statistics for Dummies* (Rumsey, 2016) provide friendly explanations of many concepts introduced here.

Look for Meaningful Patterns

Your SAGA question is probably related to some pattern. Maybe you thought there was a pattern in the way your human participants and animal partners interact, and you gathered data to test that. Or maybe you were hoping that participant scores improved from the first session to the last; that is also a pattern. When looking at these patterns, it's important to know that most data in real-life practice – maybe especially in animal-assisted services – are messy. For example, maybe you imagined the data would change over time in a straight line, and it looks like it's kind of a straight line with a bit of a curve at one end. That's okay. Instead of looking for perfect patterns, ask yourself:

- What seems to be happening overall?
- Are scores mostly moving in one direction? Which direction, and what does that mean?
- Are changes consistent enough to matter?
- Is there a pattern that feels meaningful?

To answer the question that's relevant to your data, look at your simple summaries and charts all together, zoom out to a broad perspective, and see what the overall picture is. Do things seem to be changing or staying the same? Are the numbers for participants or animals similar or do they vary as individuals?

The answers to some of these questions are subjective (e.g., are changes consistent enough to matter?). You will not find a hard and fast rule about what is "consistent enough to matter" or "a pattern that feels meaningful." However, you have tools to help you – your professional training and experience, the manual for any standardized measurement instruments you use, and research on the variables in question. Use your knowledge and resources to draw conclusions about your data. In many cases, interpretation can be as simple as "are the scores moving up over time?" You can answer that by looking at raw scores and charts.

Consider Context

The numbers in your database, the output of your simple summaries and comparisons, and the images in your charts tell part of the story. But that story takes place in a particular context (Shadish et al., 2002). The data that you have are influenced by:

- Individual participants
- Individual animals
- The setting
- The type of service and activity
- Environmental factors (e.g., weather, noise, time of day)

Before we get too excited about data that confirms our predictions or upset about data that disputes them, we should look at context.

> Always think critically about your findings and ask, "*Is there anything else that could explain what I found?*"

A dip in scores might indicate progress slowing down…or it might reflect a windy day, a new horse in the pasture, or a client arriving tired.

Avoid Overinterpreting

It can be tempting to draw big conclusions from a small amount of data. For example, because Teddy's presence often *feels* calming, it would be easy to assume every client experiences him that way. Keep your interpretation grounded by asking yourself:

- Am I going beyond what the data actually show?
- Am I confusing progress with perfection?
- Do I need more data before making a decision?
- Could there be another explanation for this pattern?

You don't need certainty to make a good decision. You're not trying to prove anything or declare hard facts. You're simply making observations based on the data you gathered and offering your best interpretation of what those data mean. Over time, these interpretations become part of your growing toolkit for making thoughtful decisions about your participants, your animals, and your business.

Bring It Back to Your SAGA Question

Interpretation is complete once you can say, *"Based on what I see here in my data, I know the next step is…."* Your interpretation should guide:

- A participant's future sessions
- Adjustments for your animals
- Changes to the environment or activity
- Confirmation of or changes to your data gathering plan
- Future SAGA questions
- Program improvements
- Understanding among your team members
- Communication with stakeholders

You might find that your interpretation becomes even clearer when you can *see* your data. Visualization helps highlight patterns that summaries alone can't show. In the next chapter, we'll explore how to create simple, effective charts that bring your data to life and help you communicate your findings with confidence.

Try It! Analyze and Act on Your SAGA Data

Now it is time to work with the data you have gathered and use it to inform action. You can try this activity with either systematic observation data, self-report data, or both.

1. Gather one small, complete data set.
   This might be:
   - A set of systematic observation records (e.g., tallies, rating scales, coded behaviors), and/or
   - A set of self-report responses (e.g., questionnaire scores, subscale scores, or written responses).
2. Create a database and enter your data
3. Create a simple summary.
   For systematic observations, this might mean:
   - Counting how often each behavior occurred,
   - Calculating averages or percentages, or
   - Laying out ratings in a simple table or chart.
   For self-report data, this might mean:
   - Calculating total or subscale scores,
   - Looking at averages or ranges, or
   - Grouping responses into meaningful categories.
4. Look for patterns.
   Ask yourself:
   - What stands out?
   - What is common or rare?
   - Are there differences across time, situations, individuals, or groups?
   - If you have both observation and self-report data, do they tell a similar story or different ones?
5. Interpret the patterns in relation to your SAGA question. Return to the question you began with. What do these data suggest about it? What tentative conclusions can you draw?
6. Acknowledge any limitations in your process.
7. Decide on one action. Based on what you see, identify one concrete next step. This might be:
   - A change to your intervention or program,
   - A modification in how animals, clients, or staff are supported,

- A new question to investigate, or
- A decision about what to keep doing because it appears to be working.

8. Document your analysis and decision. Write a brief data story – what you measured, what you found, and what you plan to do in response. This completes the SAGA cycle by explicitly linking evidence to action.

Note

1. The approach to data analysis presented here draws from established principles in behavioral science, descriptive statistics, and data visualization (Field, 2018; Gravetter & Wallnau, 2021; Kazdin, 2011), adapted specifically for animal-assisted practice.

Bibliography

Few, S. (2012). *Show me the numbers: Designing tables and graphs to enlighten*. Analytics Press.

Field, A. (2018). *Discovering statistics using IBM SPSS statistics* (5th ed.). Sage.

Gravetter, F. J., & Wallnau, L. B. (2021). *Statistics for the behavioral sciences* (11th ed.). Cengage.

Kahneman, D. (2011). *Thinking, fast and slow*. Farrar, Straus and Giroux.

Kazdin, A. E. (2011). *Single-case research designs: Methods for clinical and applied settings* (2nd ed.). Oxford University Press.

Morrow, J. (2018). *Be data driven: How organizations can harness the power of data*. Lioncrest Publishing.

Rumsey, D. J. (2016). *Statistics for dummies* (2nd ed.). John Wiley & Sons.

Salkind, N. J. (2017). *Statistics for people who (think they) hate statistics*. Sage.

Shadish, W. R., Cook, T. D., & Campbell, D. T. (2002). *Experimental and quasi-experimental designs for generalized causal inference*. Houghton Mifflin.

Sorensen, H. (2019). *Data analysis for dummies*. Wiley.

Tracy, S. J. (2020). *Qualitative research methods: Collecting evidence, crafting analysis, communicating impact* (2nd ed.). Wiley.

11

Sharing Your Data Story

Reporting Findings with Purpose

Field Story 11: Working with Wynter

Lori is an experienced therapy-dog handler who has been involved in animal-assisted visits for many years and has raised English Springer Spaniels for nearly fifty years. Over that time, she has worked with multiple dogs in therapy settings and has a well-developed sense of when a dog is ready for work and how individual dogs differ in their responses to it.

Lori's dog Wynter, pictured in Figure 11.1, is a four-year-old English Springer Spaniel who participates in animal-assisted visits in hospitals, schools, senior living communities, and a cancer center. Lori describes Wynter as an active sport dog outside of visits – animated, energetic, and highly engaged with her environment. When Lori puts Wynter's therapy harness on, however, she notices a consistent and reliable shift in Wynter's behavior. Wynter slows down, settles more quickly, and appears focused on her work. Most of Lori's previous therapy dogs did not begin visiting until they were closer to two years old or older. Wynter began therapy visits at approximately eighteen months of age. From the start, Lori noticed that Wynter was able to remain still for extended periods and showed a strong tendency to seek close physical contact with people, often leaning in, settling her body against them, or resting her head near their chest or shoulder.

DOI: 10.4324/9781003640257-15

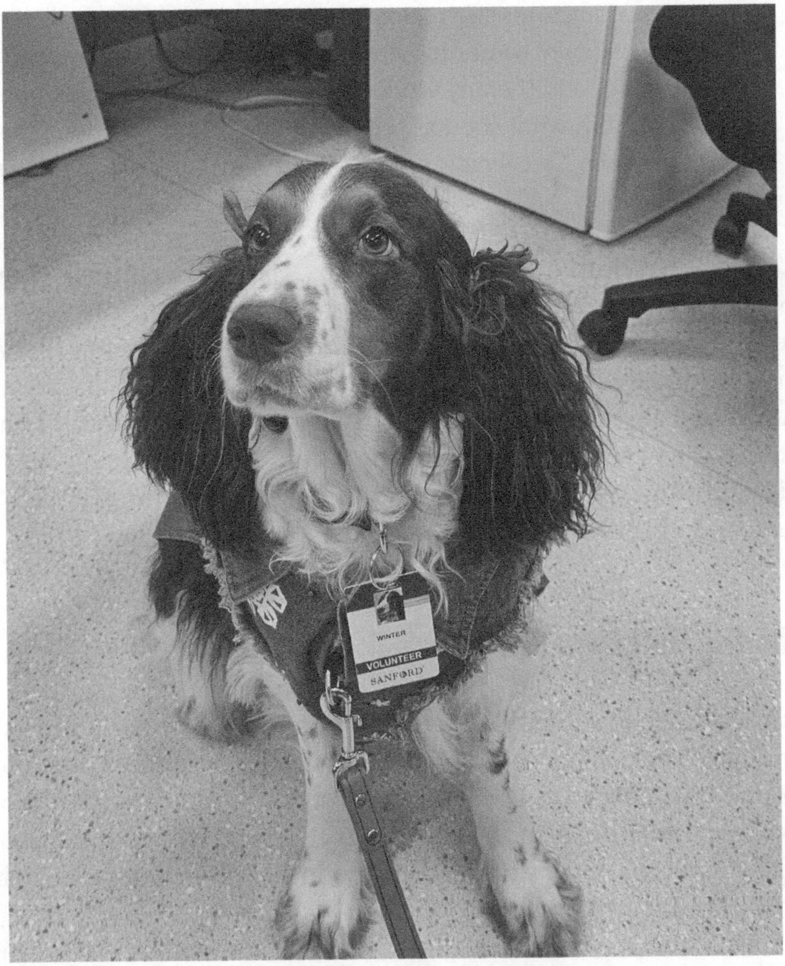

FIGURE 11.1 Wynter the therapy dog at work.
Source: Photo provided by Lori Brama

During visits in high-stress settings such as the emergency department and the cancer infusion center, Wynter frequently climbs onto a bed or chair when invited and settles into sustained physical contact. Lori has observed people visibly relax during these interactions – posture softens, breathing appears to slow, and emotions sometimes surface. Some individuals close their eyes while holding her; others cry or smile quietly. Over time, Lori has also noticed that Wynter occasionally remains with particular individuals longer than expected. When Lori attempts to cue her to move on,

Wynter sometimes resists, maintaining physical contact until the interaction naturally comes to an end. Based on decades of experience with dogs and therapy work, Lori experiences these moments as different from what she has seen with other dogs and describes Wynter as having a calming presence that draws people in during periods of stress.

Notice what Lori's account contains. There is context (Lori's experience and Wynter's work), a complication (a discrepancy between expectation and observation), and plot points (behavioral shifts with the therapy harness, sustained stillness, and variations across settings and individuals). Even without charts or numerical scores, Lori is sharing a data story – noticing details, highlighting patterns, and communicating meaning based on repeated observations.

Sharing Your Data Story

You've asked a SMART question, gathered your evidence, and analyzed what you found. Now comes one of the most important parts of the SAGA process – sharing the story. Evidence becomes more meaningful when we help someone else see the pattern, understand the insight, or make a decision with more confidence.

This chapter is about that moment. It's about how to take the numbers, charts, observations, and context you have collected through the SAGA process and shape them into a clear message. We'll focus on choosing visuals that illuminate rather than distract, writing summaries that get to the point, and tailoring your data story to the people who will use it. Whether you're talking with a client's parent, meeting with a ranch partner, presenting to your board, or writing a short report, your goal is the same – share your work in a way that is accurate, ethical, and useful. There are many books and online tutorials on creating charts within various computer programs. Here, we focus on the core skills that help your data come alive.

Who Is Your Audience?

The first step in sharing your data story is getting really clear about who your audience is and what you want to communicate to them. Sometimes the audience is you or your team, using the data to make decisions. Yay! We are so excited you're doing data-driven work. In that case, think about you and your team's learning style and the kinds of decisions you'll make from the data. Of course, this should be connected to your SAGA question.

We're guessing you'll also need to communicate your work to outside audiences – community members, funders, clients/participants, etc. Each time you share your work, **think about who that audience is and what you're hoping they get from your data story**. Knowing your audience helps you include the appropriate level of detail, how much background information to provide before getting into the data findings, and whether words or pictures or both are preferred. That should set the foundation for your data storytelling.

Choosing an Effective Way to Share Your SAGA Findings

There are a variety of ways to share your SAGA findings with your audience. Here is a list and description of the main ones:

- **Quick verbal summary** – A brief, conversational explanation of what the data show. This is the format you'll use most often – sharing a pattern you noticed, a change in a client's progress, or a welfare observation about an animal. Keep it simple: one sentence about your SMART question, one sentence about what the data show, one sentence about what it means, and one about what you'll do next.
- **Written note or short report** – A few paragraphs that document your findings. This might be a case note, a progress update for a parent or caregiver, or a summary for your records. Use clear titles, one chart if needed, and a short explanation of what the data mean in plain

language. This format supports ethical documentation while staying to the point.

- **Single chart** – A clean, well-designed visual that makes one idea instantly clear. A single chart works well when you want to highlight a pattern – change over time, comparison across sessions, or a relationship between scores. The chart should stand on its own with a title that makes a statement (not just labels the axes). Once you have a chart like this, you can paste it into any of the formats for your different purposes.
- **One-page infographic** – A visual summary that combines one or two charts with short text, icons, or key numbers. Infographics are great for busy audiences – administrators, funders, and partners – who will skim rather than read. They emphasize clarity, story, and the "so what?" more than detail.
- **Team or board update** – A structured overview for colleagues or board members. This format typically includes a few charts, brief explanations, and a recommendation or next step. The goal is to support group decision-making – staffing, scheduling, program adjustments, or animal-care changes – without overwhelming the team.
- **Grant application** – A formal, concise use of data to demonstrate need, effectiveness, or impact. Grant applications often require one or two strong charts and a short narrative explaining results. The emphasis is on clarity, credibility, and linking your findings to the goals of the funder. Accuracy and transparency matter more than showing "perfect" results.
- **Public presentation** – A slide-based presentation for community groups, volunteers, schools, or partners. These focus on storytelling and clarity – large visuals, minimal text, and examples that make the data relatable. The goal is to connect emotionally while also communicating something accurate and useful.
- **Business brochure** – A high-level, client-facing overview that uses data sparingly and visually. This might include one or two "impact" numbers or a simple graphic ("95%

of participants reported feeling calmer after sessions"). The purpose is to introduce your services, not to provide a full analysis. Keep the tone welcoming and the data easy to understand.

Bringing Your Data to Life with Visuals

We introduced the topic of data visualization in Chapter 10, as Step 3 in the five-step process of data analysis – (1) determine the level of analysis needed, (2) create simple summaries, (3) **visualize your data**, (4) run statistical tests (if needed), and (5) interpret patterns.

Data visualization is turning your data into a picture, creating one or more images to illustrate your data. This is important because, as we know, a picture can tell a thousand words. Images in the form of charts and infographics are pictures that help tell a data story. Data visualization serves at least two important functions – it is part of the data analysis process, and it is a vehicle for communicating our data story to others.

Visualize during Data Analysis

Visualizing your data during data analysis is a good practice because you might notice something when the data are illustrated that is not so obvious in a table format, such as a database. Even a simple summary like a mean (average) can miss an important aspect of your data. Look back at the database in Table 10.1, showing HAIS scores for four participants across five animal-assisted sessions. From the raw data, we can calculate the mean, or average, HAIS score for each participant:

- Sue: 23 + 24 + 22 + 25 + 7 = 101 ÷ 5 = **20.2**
- Charles: 11 + 10 + 11 + 10 + 3 = 45 ÷ 5 = **9**
- Carla: 13 + 20 + 8 + 20 + 4 = 65 ÷ 5 = **13**
- Dana: 6 + 7 + 5 + 6 + 1 = 25 ÷ 5 = **5**

These means (in bold) tell us clearly that Sue's HAIS scores, on average, are the highest, then Carla, then Charles, then Dana.

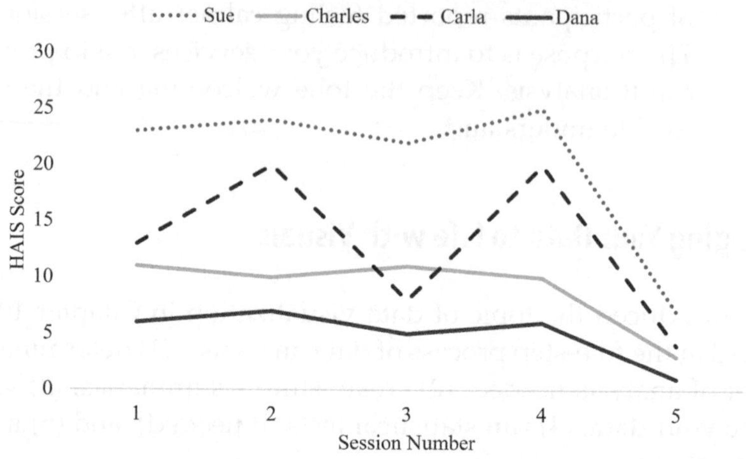

FIGURE 11.2 Chart illustrating multiple clients' scores across sessions.

And while that is interesting, there may be more to this data story that is missed when calculating the mean. To be more thorough, we should see the data illustrated in a chart. To that end, we created a line graph from the same database, pictured in Figure 11.2.

This picture of the data really brings the numbers in the database to life. Looking at the graph, you can see even more clearly the differences in scores. Yes, we can see who scored highest to lowest, but we can also see how the scores change from session to session. We can see how Carla's scores change quite a bit while Charles's scores change less. Most noticeable in the line graph, compared to the database of raw scores, are the lower HAIS scores during Session 5. Everyone's scores went down. If I were looking at these data, I would be curious about what happened before or during Session 5. It could be any number of things, no need to list them all here. The point is, we may have missed this big change in scores if we hadn't plotted the data in this chart.

The Language of Data Visualization

In this book, you'll see several ways to picture your data. The terms *chart* and *graph* are sometimes used interchangeably, but chart is a broader term. To keep things simple, we use **charts** when speaking about data visualizations in general, and we use the common names for specific displays – line graph, bar chart, scatterplot, etc.

You'll also see the term **infographic**, which refers to an image that combines data with visual elements to tell a story.

Charts – Not as Fancy as You Might Think

Charts are a tool that may seem like they are reserved for academics or data analysts working for big companies. They can seem kind of fancy and untenable. And historically, they were reserved for scientists. But thanks to modern technology, charts are useful tools that anyone can make. That being said, making *accurate* charts so an audience can *understand* the point you are trying to make – that is a skill. And after working through this chapter, you will have that skill. So let's get started! Table 11.1 lists several different types of charts.

Rather than look fancy, the purpose of a chart is to help you tell your data story.

This is not an exhaustive list. In fact, it's quite brief, but it's everything you'll need to share your findings. Even though you can find more types of charts, ones that look pretty fancy, we recommend sticking to these tried-and-true charts. More fancy can actually be more confusing – for you and your audience – so stick with the classics. These are all charts that your audience(s) have probably seen before and they will likely understand the basics of how to read them.

A good chart should serve one of the following functions:

- ◆ Make patterns more visible
- ◆ Help you see change over time
- ◆ Reveal differences between groups or contexts
- ◆ Highlight inconsistency or variability
- ◆ Get your attention about something important
- ◆ Help you communicate with others

Table 11.1 includes information on the type of data required and the situation in which to use each graph. We categorized the type of data as categorical or continuous. Remember that categorical data are data that can be put into one of several

TABLE 11.1 Go-to charts for illustrating your data

	Name	*Type of Data*	*Best Use*
	Line Graph	Continuous	Change over time
	Bar Chart	Categorical	Group comparisons
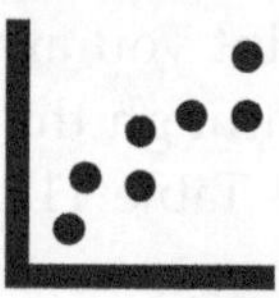	Scatterplot	Continuous	Relationship between 2 variables
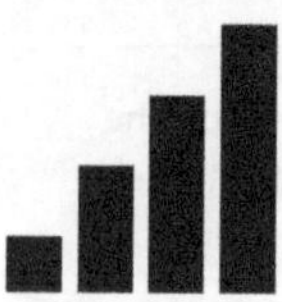	Histogram	Continuous	Frequency of each score in a group of scores

distinct categories. For example, eye color is typically treated as a categorical variable. Respondents might tell you their eyes are brown or blue or green, etc. Species is another categorical variable; animal-assisted services can include horses or dogs or cats, etc. Continuous data, on the other hand, consists of data points with continuous numbers between them. Length in inches is a good example of continuous data. Length of time, number of sessions, and scores on a test are all continuous variables that we might record in animal-assisted services. Choosing your charts based on the type of data you have is key. Software programs generally do not tell you which chart to make or tell you when you've chosen a chart that is inappropriate for your data. Selecting the best chart for your data is the first skill in data visualization.

There are wonderful resources on data visualization if you would like to dig deeper into this topic. Two favorites that we leaned on while writing this chapter are *Effective Data Storytelling* by Brent Dykes (2019) and *Storytelling with Data* by Cole Nussbaumer

Knaflic (2015). These books both provide great information and visual examples of ways to tell a story through data visualization. And they provide the information in the context of storytelling, which is wonderfully consistent with the SAGA process.

Principles of Clear Visualization

Once you choose a chart, the next step is making it clear, accurate, and easy for your audience to understand. The goal of a chart is never to "decorate" your data. Its job is simple – **help your audience see the point you want to make**. A good chart removes friction; a confusing chart adds it. Below are practical principles – small decisions that make a big difference – so your visuals support your data story rather than get in the way of it.

- **Use axes that tell the truth.** Changing the scale of your chart changes the message it communicates. In most chart-making programs, you can change the scale of the axes. For example, we could list HAIS scores from 0 to 10 versus 0 to 50. The smaller the scale, the larger the effect will seem – the bigger the bar in a bar chart, bin in a histogram, or hill/valley in a line graph. We should use the scale that best depicts the data, that tells the honest story.
- **Use titles that communicate the message**. Rather than a chart title that is stilted and archaic like "Attendance Across the Semester," use a title that says something, like "Attendance Dipped During the Colder Months". Both titles could be applied to the same chart, but the second one provides the overall message – that attendance went down.
- **Use color with intention**. Color in a chart is a powerful tool, so we should use it thoughtfully. Use specific colors or color patterns for a reason, and use a combination of color and black and white or grayscale to differentiate information. If everything is in color, nothing stands out.
  - Highlight only the data you want your audience to notice.

  - Keep everything else in neutral tones (gray works well).
  - Use consistent colors across charts – blue for clients, green for animals, etc.
  - Avoid bright, clashing, or purely decorative colors.
- **Simplify by removing clutter.** Much like your office desk or your refrigerator, clutter in charts makes it difficult to find what's important. Remove anything that is not essential to tell your story accurately. You can usually improve your graph by getting rid of gridlines, shading, and shadows. Use font style and size consistently; changing fonts within a chart can be confusing or irritating. Avoid adding 3-D images or icons unless you think they will help draw attention or make a point.
- **Highlight the main insight.** One highlight color or a bolded line is far more effective than many. Use emphasis to guide the reader's eye by circling a meaningful spike, bolding one bar, or using a single contrasting color to show progress or concern.
- **Less is more.** Avoid adding extra items like 3-D font, extra images, or icons. Stick with flat, simple visuals that tell a clear story.
- **Don't let the software tell the story.** Whichever software you use will have default settings, and those settings may or may not work for you. Don't assume the computer knows best and that whatever chart it spits out should fly. Look at each aspect, with your intended message and audience in mind. Give yourself the confidence and permission to change layout, colors, text, scaling, highlights, deletes, etc. You know your audience and your data better than the software does.

Sharing Your Data Story – Finding the Message

Now you're ready to share your data story. You know your audience, you chose an appropriate format, and you created clear visuals that support your point. The last step is putting everything together into a message that others can understand and use. This is where your SAGA process truly takes shape.

If this feels a little like telling a story, that's because it is. Data storytelling follows the same rhythm as any narrative arc – rising tension, insight, and resolution. Let's return briefly to the narrative arc from Chapter 2 and use it as a guide for communicating your findings. Whether you are giving a quick verbal summary, a formal slide presentation, or anything in between, you can apply these ingredients to tell your data story.

1. **Context – What your audience needs to know**
   - Background information about the participant, program, or animals
2. **Complication – Your SAGA question**
   - "We wanted to know ______."
3. **Plot Points – What you did and how**
   - "We observed the horses' eating behavior during sessions."
   - "We tracked HAIS scores across six sessions."
   - "We compared attendance in our reading program at school versus the library."
4. **Climax – Your data**
   - "Our sample included 20 data points across 3 weeks."
5. **Point of Insight – Your findings**
   - "As the chart shows, the horses ate 20% more during sessions."
   - "HAIS scores increased steadily from start to finish."
   - "Attendance was higher at school (76%) than at the library (53%)."
6. **Resolution & Integration – What it means and what comes next**
   - "We decided to encourage more movement after sessions."
   - "We will monitor other groups to see if a similar pattern emerges."
   - "We will tailor our marketing to library patrons."

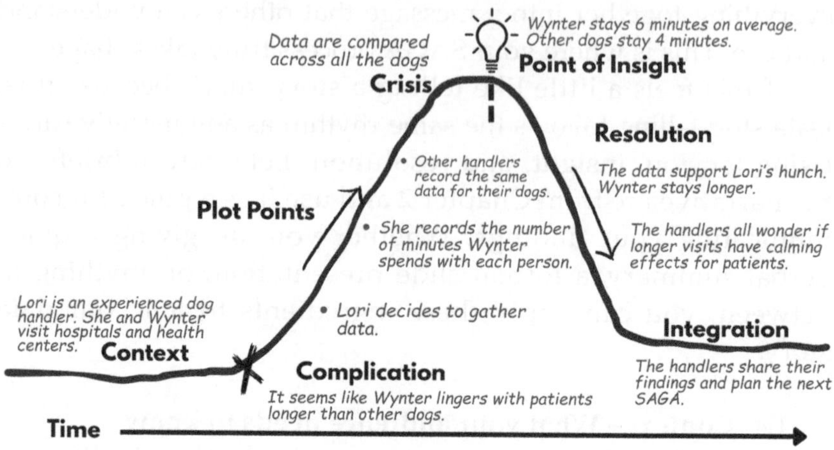

FIGURE 11.3 A hypothetical data story mapped onto the story arc.

To make this more concrete, Figure 11.3 provides an example of how the practitioner in Field Case 11 might map a data story onto the story arc.

We include the story arc here as a conceptual tool – something to help you see how your SAGA process follows the shape of a story. You do **not** need to draw arcs or create images in your reports. The arc simply fuels your confidence in communicating your findings clearly and meaningfully. For practical use, you can simplify the whole arc into a clean, repeatable structure:

A Data Story Has a Beginning, Middle, and End

Beginning

- "We wanted to know ____."

Middle

- "We looked at ____."
- "We found ____."

End

- "This suggests ____."
- "Our next step is ____."

These five sentences can become your elevator speech, a paragraph in a brochure, a summary in a progress note, or the opening script for a presentation. They are a simple, flexible way to tell a clear, honest, useful data story.

Common Mistakes

For detailed instruction on creating effective visuals, especially if you like to nerd out on charts and figures, we highly recommend you check out Nussbaumer Knaflic's *Storytelling with Data*. In the meantime, here is a quick list of things to avoid when sharing your data story with any audience.

Avoid:

- Too many charts – typically 1–2 is enough
- Complicated charts when simple ones work – fancy can be confusing
- Raw data – highlighting a few numbers works; showing all numbers is overwhelming and blurs your message
- Colors that confuse or overwhelm
- Visuals that overdramatize change

Example Data Story

Now we provide three hypothetical data stories as examples of how to share your data story with others.

Example 1: Client Progress across Sessions

Beginning – What we wanted to know. We wanted to understand how Mila's anxiety shifted across her first six equine-assisted psychotherapy sessions. Mila often described feeling "on edge," and we were curious whether her self-reported anxiety scores reflected any changes over time.

Middle – The data we collected and what it showed. We collected her anxiety rating at the beginning and end of each session. A simple line chart shows a clear pattern: her starting anxiety was fairly high in the first two sessions but declined steadily in sessions 3 through 6. Ending anxiety followed the same trend, with the largest drop occurring during sessions that involved grooming and slow-paced groundwork.

End – What it means and what we will do next. This pattern suggests that activities emphasizing rhythm, touch, and pacing may help regulate Mila's anxiety. For her next phase of treatment, we plan to extend the groundwork portion of each session and track her responses again over the next month.

Example 2: Animal Partner Stress Indicators

Beginning – What we wanted to know. We wanted to monitor Cleo, our donkey partner, to see whether group sessions contributed to increased stress. Staff had noticed more ear-pinning behavior and a reluctance to approach during larger groups, and we wanted to look more systematically at her welfare data.

Middle – The data we collected and what it showed. We reviewed five weeks of observational logs that documented stress-indicator behaviors (ear pinning, tail swish frequency, and stepping away). Cleo showed low-stress behavior during individual or two-person sessions but noticeably higher stress during groups of four or more participants. This trend was consistent across all five weeks.

End – What it means and what we will do next. This finding suggests that Cleo may be better suited for smaller groups or individual work. We plan to shift her schedule accordingly and reassess her stress indicators after four weeks. This adjustment supports her welfare and helps ensure that she remains a willing, comfortable partner in our services.

Example 3: Program-Level Decision-Making

Beginning – What we wanted to know. As our equine-assisted coaching program has grown, we wanted to understand seasonal attendance trends to help us plan staffing and scheduling for the upcoming year. Staff noticed some periods felt especially busy, and we wanted to see the pattern clearly.

Middle – What the data showed. We analyzed the past 12 months of attendance and plotted monthly totals in a simple bar chart. The pattern was clear: attendance peaked in May–July, dipped sharply in November–January, and remained steady the rest of the year. A quick comparison to last year's numbers showed the same seasonal pattern.

End – What it means and what we'll do next. This suggests that our busiest months reliably land in late spring and summer. We will schedule additional staff for those periods and adjust outreach efforts in the winter months, when fewer participants typically enroll. Having this data-driven view of attendance helps us plan staffing, manage waitlists, and budget more confidently.

The Takeaway – Share a Clear, Honest, Useful Data Story

Your job in sharing your data story is to communicate and clarify, not to impress or entertain. The data are not the story – they are the characters. Your words and visuals bring those characters to life in a way that others can understand. When you share your data story clearly and honestly, you support better outcomes for your human participants, provide better care for your animal partners, and strengthen your program or business. This chapter offers the core principles, and when you need more support, you can draw on books, websites, or AI tools or connect with data-minded colleagues. No matter who your audience is or what your data reveals, you've got everything you need to tell a meaningful, trustworthy data story.

Try It: Share Your SAGA Data Story

After completing the data analysis steps in Chapter 10, you should have SAGA findings to share. Follow these steps to get started sharing your data story.

1. Decide on the audience. Who will you share these findings with? What information do they need and what level of detail will best communicate your message?

2. Create a presentation or report to share your findings
    - Presentation with 3–5 slides when giving a more formal oral presentation; written report when your audience will be reading your findings. Both formats should include:
        - ☐ The major parts of the narrative arc
        - ☐ 1–2 simple, clear charts to illustrate your data
        - ☐ A clear bottom-line statement and next steps (for you and for your audience)
3. Share your presentation or report with a trusted friend or teammate, asking for feedback on:
    - What is the main message that came through?
    - What questions came up?
    - Are the visuals easy to read and understand?
    - Is the level of detail appropriate?
    - Is anything missing or should anything be removed?

Bibliography

Blastland, M., & Dilnot, A. (2009). *The tiger that isn't: Seeing through a world of numbers*. Basic Books.

Cairo, A. (2016). *The truthful art: Data, charts, and maps for communication*. New Riders.

Duarte, N. (2012). *HBR guide to persuasive presentations*. Harvard Business Review Press.

Dykes, B. (2019). *Effective data storytelling*. Wiley.

Gigerenzer, G. (2002). *Calculated risks: How to know when numbers deceive you*. Simon & Schuster.

Knaflic, C. N. (2015). *Storytelling with data: A data visualization guide for business professionals*. Wiley.

Tufte, E. R. (2001). *The visual display of quantitative information* (2nd ed.). Graphics Press.

12

Ethical Data Practices

Responsibility to Humans, Animals, and Stories

Field Case 12: When a Species Difference Becomes a Welfare Signal

This case occurred during a series of experiential learning sessions at Eagle Vista Ranch. We were gathering data to compare the sessions and look for species differences in how participants and animals engaged with each other. Each session was recorded for later review. The data collection involved Montana, a Paint horse, and Bronco, a yellow Labrador; we shared their approach–response patterns in Chapter 6 when introducing naturalistic observation. Those same recordings also offered information relevant to ethics. During the live sessions, most of our attention was on maintaining safety and gathering reliable data. We noticed that during the horse sessions Montana, pictured in Figure 12.1, appeared to approach participants by walking from the window, past them, to the door, then back again to the window. In contrast, the dog approached by walking directly up to participants and interacting. In the moment, we interpreted Montana's behavior through the lens of our SAGA question: *"The horse is doing something the dog did not."*

DOI: 10.4324/9781003640257-16

FIGURE 12.1 Montana – friend, family member, co-facilitator, and research partner – choosing the pasture.

It wasn't until later – when we reviewed the recordings – that a clearer pattern emerged. On video, Montana repeatedly walked from the window to the arena door and back again. He passed near the participants, but he seemed more oriented to the window (looking out toward his herd mates) and the door (his route back to them) than to the people. What had looked at the time like a quiet approach toward participants appeared, in retrospect, as sustained pacing linked to being separated from his herd. Seeing the full pattern led us to a difficult ethical question: During data collection, whose needs were being served?

Because we were focused on comparing horse and dog sessions, we initially coded Montana's pacing as a species difference. Only when we stepped back – watching the recording – did we recognize that the difference also carried meaning for his welfare. Looking back, we understood that Montana, a herd-living prey animal, had been separated from his social group. His pacing was, in one sense, a valid behavioral difference between species – and in another sense, a signal that participation in that situation may not have been in his best interest. That layer of meaning was not fully apparent to us in the moment. This experience changed the questions we ask during sessions. Rather than focusing only on what animals are doing in relation to the activity or the client, we began asking: What are the animals communicating to us about their welfare while they are working?

That shift eventually led to our work on the behavioral cost of care – paying closer attention to maintenance behaviors and other subtle indicators of effort and strain. Montana reminded us that working with data introduces ethical tensions of its own, and that the same values that guide our work with people – respect, care, and doing no harm – must also guide how we gather, interpret, and respond to the data we collect in our SAGA process.

Ethics

This chapter addresses the **ethics** – right and wrong, good and bad, harmful or not harmful – of your SAGA work. Every step of the SAGA process has an ethical dimension – sharing a story, asking a question, gathering evidence, and acting on the findings. Each piece of the puzzle includes choices you make that should be guided by ethics.

> Ethics is not a barrier; it is a form of care for your human participants, animal partners, your program, and yourself.

Those of you who are teachers, counselors, psychologists, and other professionals have ethics codes that provide guidance within your scope of practice. The material in this chapter will be familiar and complement those codes, tailored to the SAGA process.

Data is powerful. We use data to make important decisions; sharing data can influence how others think, feel, and behave; and sharing your animal-assisted story with data will increase your perceived credibility with some audiences. For these reasons, it is especially important to learn and follow SAGA-specific ethics. This chapter introduces ethical principles grounded in the SAGA framework, practical standards for the most common data situations, a simple tool for working through ethical dilemmas, and several short case examples to illustrate how these ideas apply in real practice.

Remember that data is not just numbers; it is information. And your SAGA process might include gathering information in the form of numbers, words, images, videos, sketches, etc. The principles we discuss in this chapter apply to all those types of data.

Ethical Principles

Ethical principles are aspirational goals, broad ways of doing the work that can be applied to a variety of contexts. Ethical principles do not typically give you a quick, easy, here's what to do answer. Instead, they provide a broad goal to guide you. This is important because animal-assisted work is very broad. It can include many different venues and, unlike other helping professions, it can impact humans, animals, and the setting or environment. It would be impossible to create a neat and tidy list of specific rules to follow. So instead, we are guided by these broad ways of thinking and being. We aspire to do these things in all of our activities.

These principles should be consistent with any ethical codes you already adhere to, practice standards of the field, and legal statutes for licensure. If our suggestions conflict with your training or legal requirements, seek consultation to resolve the conflict. This chapter is informed by the following resources, as well as our experience in providing, researching, and teaching animal-assisted services.

- American Psychological Association Code of Ethics
- American Evaluation Association Guiding Principles
- Health and Human Subjects research standards
- Institutional Care and Use Committee standards
- The One Welfare framework

Figure 12.2 shows five ethical principles of data-driven animal practices. Think of the ethical principles as a compass, guiding all your data-driven work.

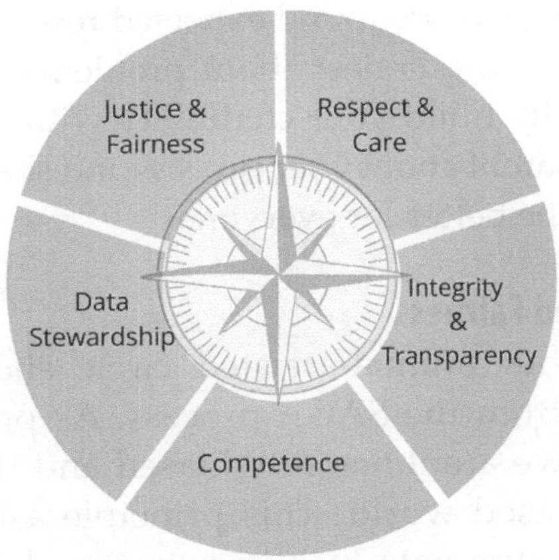

FIGURE 12.2 Ethical principles of data-driven work, like a compass showing the way.

Show Respect and Care for Humans and Animals

This principle is key to most ethical codes. No matter what animal-assisted service you provide, your intention is to help people. You probably already have this on your mind in terms of facilitating human-animal interactions that are beneficial to human participants and are not harmful to your animal partner(s). The principle also applies to data-driven practices. For each SAGA step, we should be mindful of doing good and doing no harm – for humans, animals, stakeholders, and the field.

Practice with Integrity and Transparency

We should strive for accuracy and honesty throughout the SAGA process. This means we tell anecdotes honestly; we ask questions and gather data that ensures the greatest accuracy, we analyze our data for accuracy, and we are honest about our findings. The SAGA process will not necessarily be in plain sight for all to see. You, or a dedicated team member, will be gathering and analyzing data individually. Generally, there is no one looking over your shoulder while you calculate means or create charts. It will be up to you and your team to do these things honestly. This principle includes not making up fake data or cherry-picking the findings that you want or need. It also includes acknowledging errors or limitations in the data process. The irony of this principle is that sometimes we can feel a pull to breach this principle to look good (e.g., say we found expected results when we actually didn't), but being honest about problems, errors, or inefficacies can actually build your credibility with audiences. So be open and transparent about your process and share your findings honestly. It will be better for everyone.

Uphold Justice and Fairness

Everyone in your animal-assisted circle should contribute to and benefit from the SAGA process. As professionals, we recognize that we are inherently biased and that we live and practice in a biased world. This principle asks us to do the best we can to eliminate bias in our data-driven work and, whenever possible, employ our data-driven work to uphold justice and improve equity. Consider accessibility throughout your SAGA process so that any data collection materials you use are accessible. For example, relying on written self-report measures may eliminate participants with reading disabilities or people whose primary language is different from the language of the measure.

Work within Your Competencies

We should always work within our scope of practice and competence. Moving through the material in this book, you are developing skills in asking good questions, gathering simple data, creating simple summaries and comparisons, and sharing your data story. There may be times that you need help with these activities or situations where your SAGA process calls for activities outside of your skillset. It's important that we are honest with ourselves on what our competencies and limitations are and ask for help when we need it.

Be a Good Steward of Data

This principle applies to data storage and use. As with other records, data you gather for your SAGA process must be kept secure. This typically means that electronic software is housed in secure, password protected files on locked password-protected computers and hard-copy data are stored in a locked file cabinet within a locked office. The nature of animal-assisted work may mean that you work from a variety of locations (e.g., bringing your dog to visit schools and hospitals). In that case, you'll need to develop a system to securely transport data from the service site(s) to your professional workspace. Think about who on your team should have access to your data and develop policies and procedures to maintain the security of your data. And finally, as good data stewards, we destroy data when we are no longer using it and it has surpassed any legal requirements to keep it. Data that you gather should be under the same rules as other data you have in your professional records. For example, licensed psychologists and counselors follow state law requirements on when to destroy records. Any data you collect on clients should follow the same rules. Data on your animal partners should be maintained as long as the animal is living/working with you and for at least three years beyond that.

Practice Standards

Table 12.1 provides a description of each ethical principle and examples of specific practice standards.

Ethical Principles Applied to SAGA

Next, let's apply the ethical principles and standards to specific steps of the SAGA method.

Share a Story

- Be mindful of whose story it is; do you have permission to tell it?
- Protect confidentiality in anecdotes
- Tell stories honestly

Ask a Question

- Only collect data you need; don't burden people or animals collecting data you won't use

TABLE 12.1 Ethical principles and practice standards for working with data

Principle	*Description*	*Practice Standard*
Respect and Care (for humans and animals)	Honor the dignity, autonomy, comfort, and welfare of everyone involved. Above all, do good and do no harm.	♦ Collect only data you need. ♦ Use non-invasive, low-burden methods. ♦ Seek consent from both humans and animals to gather and share data. ♦ Protect confidentiality and privacy. ♦ Use respectful, non-stigmatizing language. ♦ Ensure data collection supports both human outcomes and animal well-being.
Integrity and Transparency	Share data truthfully and communicate clearly about what you collected, how, and why.	♦ No cherry-picking data. ♦ Avoid misleading charts or exaggerated claims. ♦ Acknowledge limitations. ♦ Explain data procedures to participants. ♦ Use tentative language ("suggests" vs. "proves").
Justice and Fairness	Treat humans and animals equitably, and avoid bias in what and how you measure	♦ Apply measurement procedures consistently. ♦ Be mindful of cultural and contextual factors. ♦ Avoid interpretations that reinforce stereotypes. ♦ Consider equity when using findings to make decisions.
Competence	Collect and interpret data within your training and seek guidance when needed.	♦ Use tools you understand. ♦ Avoid advanced statistics beyond your expertise. ♦ Consult colleagues or experts when uncertain. ♦ Do not rely on technology or methods you cannot explain.
Data Stewardship	Protect data throughout its lifecycle – from collection to destruction.	♦ Story data securely (passwords, locked files). ♦ Limit access to those who need it. ♦ De-identify data whenever possible. ♦ Retain according to best practices (3–5 years; longer for clinical/welfare records). ♦ Destroy securely when retention ends.

- Remember who the main character of your SAGA is (individual client or animal? Your program?)
- Ask questions relevant to humans *and* animals
- Ask questions relevant to diverse groups

Gather Evidence

- Request and respect consent to gather data
- Use the least-intrusive measurement methods
- Ensure animals are comfortable when gathering animal data
- Ensure safe storage of data
- Keep data de-identified when possible

Act on your findings

- Avoid biased interpretations
- Consider welfare implications
- Consider equity implications
- Don't exaggerate findings or overdeliver
- Get permission from participants if sharing aggregate data outside your organization
- Only share aggregated (grouped) data outside of your organization

Similar to other parts of the book, this is not an exhaustive list of ethical standards or issues you might face. These are the main ones we imagine coming up each time you undergo a new SAGA process. When you have a situation for which a rule is not provided here, lean on the principles and seek consultation.

Managing Data Responsibly

"If it's not documented, it didn't happen." Most of us have heard some version of this phrase, and in animal-assisted services it often rings true. Records matter. Your records should include not only what you did, but also your SAGA process: your question, how you gathered data, what you found, and how (and where)

you shared your results. In Chapter 10, we discussed creating databases to store raw data. In addition to those databases, we recommend keeping brief written notes or memos that document your thinking and decision-making along the way. One simple approach is to create a dedicated SAGA folder that includes both your raw data and short notes describing the process.

Ethical data practice means managing data across its full life cycle – collection, storage, sharing, retention, and eventual destruction. You do not need to be a data-security expert to manage data ethically. You do need to be intentional.

Obtain Informed Consent before Gathering Data

Before gathering data from human participants, include clear language in your consent document that explains how data will be collected and why. If you plan to use data outside of your organization, such as on a website, in brochures, or in presentations, include a separate consent option for sharing de-identified, aggregate results. Consent should be specific, informed, and voluntary.

Protect Identifiable Client Data

Identifying information for human participants receiving health services should not be shared outside of your organization. This includes marketing materials, grant applications, public presentations, websites, and social media. Identifying information includes names or initials, dates of birth, contact information, photos or videos, and detailed case descriptions that could reasonably allow someone to recognize the individual.

Animals Deserve Protection

Identifying information for animal partners may include names, photos or videos, detailed behavioral descriptions, and references to specific caretakers or program locations. Because animals have limited agency, ethical data storytelling requires protecting their dignity and avoiding portrayals that could stigmatize them or indirectly identify the humans connected to their story. When in doubt, aggregate data, use pseudonyms, and remove unnecessary details.

Store Data Safely

Data should be protected while you have it. Use password protection for digital files, secure or encrypted storage when available, and locked cabinets for paper records. Avoid storing sensitive data on shared devices or personal accounts and apply stronger protections to data that would cause harm if accidentally disclosed.

Limit Access to Data

Only individuals who need the data for collection, analysis, or decision-making should have access. Clarify roles within your team, avoid casual sharing of spreadsheets or charts, and be especially cautious when sending data via email, cloud platforms, or messaging apps. Access should be purposeful, not convenient.

Keep Data Only as Long as Necessary

In the absence of specific legal, professional, or institutional requirements, a general best practice is to retain practice-based or program evaluation data for 3–5 years. Clinical records may require longer retention depending on jurisdiction. Animal welfare data may be retained for as long as the animal is actively working, plus additional time to support continuity and review.

Destroy Data Securely When It Is No Longer Needed

Once the retention period ends, ethical practice includes permanently destroying data in a way that protects confidentiality. Shred paper records, securely delete digital files (including backups when possible), and avoid keeping unofficial "extra" copies on personal devices.

Common Ethical Pitfalls in Data Storytelling

Here is a quick list of common mistakes made when sharing data findings with others. Keep this list with you and check it each time you are preparing a summary of your results to share with others. Look at it again when you think you're ready to hit the "send" button on a report or share your findings in a presentation.

- Misleading charts
- Overstated claims
- Calling assessment or evaluation "research"
- Claiming proof or statistical significance without appropriate analysis
- Sharing identifiable information
- Using data to persuade rather than inform

Case Examples

Example 1: Gathering Unnecessary Data beyond the Practitioner's Competence

Marty is a licensed clinical social worker who incorporates her pet cat, Tabby, into her clinical practice. For several years, Marty and Tabby have worked together successfully. During sessions, clients may talk to Tabby, play with her, or gently pet her while working with Marty on therapeutic goals. Recently, Marty began gathering basic data about her practice. She recorded client attendance on days when Tabby was present compared to days when Tabby was not in the office. These data were easy to collect, non-intrusive, and aligned with Marty's professional training. While attending a conference, Marty noticed a sale on heart rate monitors and became curious about whether Tabby's heart rate changed during sessions. Without prior training in measuring or interpreting feline heart rate, Marty purchased a monitor designed to be worn on a collar. She began placing the collar on Tabby during sessions. Almost immediately, Tabby showed signs of discomfort. She scratched at the collar repeatedly and appeared distracted and unsettled throughout sessions. Although Marty found the idea of physiological data interesting, she was unsure how to interpret the heart rate readings and had not considered whether this information was necessary to support client outcomes or Tabby's welfare.

This situation raises important ethical questions about competence, respect for animal participants, and the purpose of data collection. While Marty's curiosity is understandable, the data collection exceeded her training, caused observable distress to Tabby, and did not clearly serve a therapeutic or welfare-related purpose. Here is how each of the ethical principles of data-driven work apply to this case:

- **Respect and Care for All Participants** – Tabby showed clear signs of discomfort by repeatedly scratching at the collar. Ethical practice requires attending to animal assent and discontinuing data collection when it causes distress, even if physical harm is unlikely.
- **Integrity and Transparency** – Marty did not have a clear plan for how the heart rate data would be interpreted or used. Ethical data collection requires clarity about purpose and meaning before data are gathered.
- **Justice and Fairness** – The physiological data placed an added burden on Tabby without clear benefit. Ethical practice requires ensuring that data collection does not disproportionately affect one participant – human or animal – without justification. Furthermore, Tabby's reaction to the collar may disrupt the session, in which case the practitioner's curiosity is negatively affecting the therapeutic process.
- **Competence** – Measuring and interpreting feline heart rate fell outside Marty's training. Ethical practice requires working within one's scope of competence or seeking appropriate consultation before using specialized tools.
- **Stewardship of Data** – Marty had not considered how the heart rate data would be stored, protected, or used. Ethical stewardship begins before data collection and includes deciding whether the data is necessary at all.

Possible Ethical Resolution

Marty could remove the collar immediately, discontinue physiological data collection, and return to non-invasive measures aligned with her training and Tabby's comfort. If physiological data remain of interest, consultation with a veterinarian or animal behavior professional would be an ethical next step.

Key Takeaway

Ethical data practice is not about avoiding curiosity – it is about channeling curiosity responsibly. When data collection begins to compromise welfare, exceed competence, or lose clear purpose, it is time to pause, reflect, and realign with ethical principles.

Case Example 2: A Misleading Chart and an Overstated Marketing Claim

Riverbend Ranch offers an equine-assisted learning program for adolescents. Over the past year, the team collected brief self-report ratings of stress at the beginning and end of each session. When reviewing the data, the program director noticed that average stress scores tended to be lower at the end of sessions. To share this finding with potential funders, the director created a bar chart comparing average "before" and "after" stress scores. To make the change more visible, the y-axis was truncated so that the bars appeared dramatically different in height. The chart was included on the ranch's website alongside the statement, *"Research proves our program significantly reduces stress in participants."* When a colleague reviewed the materials, they questioned whether the chart exaggerated the size of the change and whether the wording of the claim accurately reflected the data process and results. The data did indicate a modest decrease in stress ratings, but the program had not conducted statistical analyses, and the sample size was small. Furthermore, the results are from program evaluation, not research and we rarely if ever use the word "proven." This situation prompted the team to reconsider how they were visually presenting their data, how they referred to their data process, and how confidently they were describing their outcomes to the public.

Ethical Reflection: Applying the Five Principles

- **Respect and Care for All Participants**
  Visuals and claims shape expectations. A misleading chart and claims of proof risk giving families, participants,

and funders an inaccurate understanding of what the program can realistically offer.

- **Integrity and Transparency**
  Truncating the y-axis exaggerated the apparent size of the change in stress scores. Referring to practice-based data as "research" and stating that the program had *proven* effectiveness further overstated what the data showed. Ethical data storytelling requires visuals and language that accurately reflect both the size of observed patterns and the level of certainty supported by the data.
- **Justice and Fairness**
  Overstated charts and claims may influence decisions about enrollment, funding, or referrals in ways that are not fully informed. Ethical communication allows audiences to evaluate programs based on honest representations rather than persuasive visual or statistical framing.
- **Competence**
  Claims about statistical significance and proof require appropriate study design, analysis, and expertise. When formal statistical testing has not been conducted – or when the data were collected for program monitoring rather than research – conclusions should remain descriptive and cautious.
- **Stewardship of Data**
  Once shared publicly, charts and claims may be reused, cited, or taken out of context. Ethical stewardship includes careful chart construction, accurate labeling of data as practice-based (not research), and language that prevents misinterpretation beyond the original purpose of the data.

Possible Ethical Response

The team could revise the chart to include a full y-axis and revised the language to clearly describe the data as practice-based program evaluation, replacing claims of proof or statistical significance with language such as, *"Our practice-based evaluation showed that participants reported modest reductions in stress by the end of sessions."* This approach preserves credibility while still communicating meaningful outcomes.

Key Takeaway

Ethical data storytelling requires alignment between what the data are, how they are shown, and what is claimed. When charts, labels, and language match the strength of the evidence, trust is protected – and **trust matters more than dramatic results**.

Simple Ethical Decision-Making Tool

At the start of any SAGA process, and throughout the process once you are off and running, ask yourself these questions. After a while, they will become second nature.

- Why am I collecting or sharing this data?
- Is it necessary?
- Does it benefit humans and/or animals?
- Could it cause harm or misunderstanding?
- Am I competent to collect and interpret it?
- Is the way I'm presenting it accurate?
- Can I store and share it responsibly?

You've Got This

This chapter has covered key ethical considerations related to gathering, using, storing, and sharing data. As with other aspects of your animal-assisted work, ethical principles can guide you at every step of the SAGA process. When we talk about ethics, it's easy for the conversation to feel full of rules – rights and wrongs, shoulds and shouldn'ts – and that can create pressure to be perfect. Ethics can even spark fear about "getting it wrong." But ethics is not about perfection. It's about being thoughtful, intentional, and reflective. You already apply ethical principles in your work with humans and animals every day. Here, we're simply asking you to extend that same way of thinking to the decisions you make about data.

The reasons we gather data – to understand a process, evaluate outcomes, or inform decisions – can sometimes pull us toward trying to prove something or persuade others. Remember that ethical data practice is about seeking and sharing information, not winning an argument. Ethical practices build trust and credibility over time. Resist the urge to exaggerate findings, cherry-pick only the "good" results, or make claims that go beyond what your data support.

As with other ethical decisions, when in doubt, pause, reflect, and consult. You have the tools, the principles, and the judgment you need to move through the SAGA process ethically and confidently. And yes – you've got this.

Try It! Check Your SAGA Ethics

These steps help you apply the ethics of data-driven work from this chapter. There are two parts: (1) laying a foundation for ethical practice before you begin any SAGA work, and (2) working through ethical issues that arise during a specific SAGA process. Appendix F has an additional tool – an Ethics Checklist – you can use for this activity and throughout your SAGA journey.

When You Are Just Beginning SAGA Work

1. **Create an ethical data plan.** Outline what data you will collect, why you are collecting it, who will have access, where it will be stored, how long it will be kept, and how it will be protected.
2. **Create or revise your consent language.** Update participant consent documents to include clear language about data gathered for assessment or program evaluation. (See this book's Digital Resources for an example.)
3. **Create a process for ethical dilemmas.** Build a simple, repeatable plan you can use when dilemmas occur, including:
   - **Access to relevant ethics codes** (for your profession and setting)
   - **A consultation list** (team members, mentors, trusted colleagues)

- **A documentation habit** (how you will record the dilemma, what you considered, what you decided, and why)

When Working through a Specific SAGA Process

1. **Name the ethical issue.** What is coming up right now in this SAGA?
2. **Identify which principle is in play.** Which ethical principle(s) is involved: **respect and care, integrity and transparency, competence, data stewardship, justice and fairness**? In many cases, more than one principle can provide guidance.
3. **Review relevant ethics codes and policies.** Look at the codes, laws, and workplace policies that apply.
4. **Consult.** Talk it through with your team and trusted colleagues or mentors.
5. **Act and document.** Make the best decision you can with the information you have and then write down your reasoning and steps taken.
6. **Review and reflect.** Afterward, debrief what happened. What went well? What would you do differently next time? What needs to be changed in your procedures to prevent similar dilemmas?

Bibliography

American Evaluation Association. (2018). *Guiding principles for evaluators.* https://www.eval.org/About/Guiding-Principles

American Psychological Association. (2017). *Ethical principles of psychologists and code of conduct* (2002, amended June 1, 2010, and January 1, 2017). https://www.apa.org/ethics/code

Blesch, K. (2023). *Animal-assisted therapy with dogs: Basics, animal ethics, and practice of therapeutic work*. Springer.

Colonius, T. J., & Earley, R. W. (2013). One welfare: A call to develop a broader framework of thought and action. *Journal of the American Veterinary Medical Association, 242*(3), 309–310. https://doi.org/10.2460/javma.242.3.309

Corey, G., Corey, M. S., & Callanan, P. (2015). *Issues and ethics in the helping professions* (10th ed.). Cengage Learning.

Denecke, K., & Krieck, M. (2023). Ethical challenges in data-driven health research: Data collection, processing, and sharing. *Frontiers in Digital Health*, *5*, 112345.

Ekholm Fry, N. (2021). Welfare considerations for horses in therapy and education services. In J. M. Peralta & A. H. Fine (Eds.), *The welfare of animals in animal-assisted interventions: Foundations and best practice methods* (pp. 219–242). Springer.

Fiesler, C., Garrett, N., & Beard, N. (2020). What researchers should know about ethics and the data lifecycle. *Journal of Empirical Research on Human Research Ethics*, *15*(1–2), 3–19.

Fine, A. H., & Chastain Griffin, T. (2022). Protecting animal welfare in animal-assisted intervention: Our ethical obligation. *Seminars in Speech and Language*, *43*(1), 8–23. https://doi.org/10.1055/s-0041-1742099

Floridi, L., & Taddeo, M. (2016). What is data ethics? *Philosophical Transactions of the Royal Society A*, *374*(2083), 20160360. https://doi.org/10.1098/rsta.2016.0360

Fournier, A. K., Berry, T. D., Letson, E. A., Laitala, J., Proels, L., & Kavanagh, K. (2021). The anodyne-agent model: A framework for understanding animal-assisted intervention. *Human–Animal Interactions*, *9*(1), 55–75.

Fournier, A. K., French, M., Letson, E. A., Hanson, J., Berry, T. D., & Cronin, S. (2024). The behavioral cost of care: Changes in maintenance behavior during equine-assisted interventions. *Animals*, *14*(4), 536.

Kitchener, K. S. (1984). Intuition, critical evaluation, and ethical principles: The foundation for ethical decisions in counselling psychology. *The Counseling Psychologist*, *12*(3), 43–55.

Ng, Z. Y., & Fine, A. H. (2021). A trajectory approach to supporting therapy animal welfare in retirement and beyond. In J. M. Peralta & A. H. Fine (Eds.), *The welfare of animals in animal-assisted interventions: Foundations and best practice methods* (pp. 243–263). Springer.

Office for Human Research Protections. (2018). *Federal policy for the protection of human subjects (45 CFR 46)*. U.S. Department of Health & Human Services. https://www.hhs.gov/ohrp/regulations-and-policy/regulations/45-cfr-46/index.html

Office of Laboratory Animal Welfare. (2015). *Public health service policy on humane care and use of laboratory animals*. U.S. Department of

Health & Human Services. https://olaw.nih.gov/policies-laws/phs-policy.htm

Peralta, J. M., & Fine, A. H. (Eds.). (2021). *The welfare of animals in animal-assisted interventions: Foundations and best practice methods*. Springer.

Tracy, S. J. (2020). *Qualitative research methods: Collecting evidence, crafting analysis, communicating impact* (2nd ed.). Wiley.

Winkle, M., Gibson, T., & Bergold, L. (2020). *Dog welfare, well-being, and behavior: Considerations for animal-assisted interventions. Frontiers in Veterinary Science.*

Zook, M., Barocas, S., Boyd, D., Crawford, K., Keller, E., Gangadharan, S. P., … & Wilson, M. W. (2017). *Ten principles for ethical data practice: Recommended guidelines for ethical data collection, analysis, and sharing*. University of Minnesota Press.

13

Your Wellness Saga

Wellness Data on the Animal-Handler Team

Field Case 13: Kicked by Compassion Fatigue

In March 2020, during what should have been an unremarkable evening routine, I (Liz) was grooming our horses in the pasture. They had finished their grain, and the setting was familiar and calm – an environment I had long associated with regulation, grounding, and restoration. Without warning, I felt a sudden, intense, bolting pain in my right hip. Within seconds, I was on the ground, disoriented and thinking, *what just happened?*

Standing behind me was Superman (pictured in Figure 13.1), a lanky retired off-the-track Thoroughbred, gazing down with quiet attentiveness. Moments earlier, I had been brushing Montana, a striking black-and-white Paint horse. There had been no stumble, no obvious warning – just an abrupt collapse. As I lay there trying to determine whether I could move or had lost consciousness, I realized that Superman had kicked me. It was completely unexpected from a horse who had been part of our family for decades.

Frightened and shaken, I crawled under the fence into the barnyard, acutely aware of how vulnerable I was. I was fortunate to have my phone and was able to call for help. The emotional response surprised me as much as the physical one: shock,

DOI: 10.4324/9781003640257-17

FIGURE 13.1 Superman Can. Superman, an off-the-track Thoroughbred, raced prior to retiring to Eagle Vista Ranch. Left: Superman demonstrates his athleticism during a 4-H competition, ridden by Liz's son Donny. Right: Liz shares a quiet moment with Superman, who has become a model of resilience and a reminder to practice self-care. Photos by Jennifer Laitala.

embarrassment, and fear surfaced all at once. Within a few minutes, the panic subsided and it became clear that I would likely recover. At the time, I minimized the incident medically – an attitude that, in hindsight, mirrors the way that many helping professionals downplay their own physical and emotional distress while continuing to care for others. Recovery took months of physical therapy and other treatments, and while function gradually returned, what lingered longer than pain was a profound question: *How did this happen?*

I replayed the scene again and again, trying to understand how such a trusted, predictable horse could have kicked me. There was no evidence of aggression, fear, or startle in Superman. What slowly became clearer was not something about *him*, but about *me*. At that point in my life I was chronically overextended – physically tired, emotionally taxed, and moving through familiar routines on autopilot. I had been preoccupied, rushing through the end of the day, less attuned than usual to subtle shifts in space and positioning. In hindsight, I suspect I placed myself in a vulnerable spot without fully registering it. My body was present in the pasture, but my attention was only partially there.

With distance and reflection, I came to recognize that I had been living with burnout and compassion fatigue. Research tells us that chronic stress and emotional labor are not just psychological experiences; they are embodied. They affect attention, reaction time, situational awareness, and risk perception. In my case, the kick was not a random act of a dangerous horse, but a moment in which my depleted nervous system failed to protect me. That incident became a turning point. Over the years since, I have reduced my caseload, strengthened boundaries, and tended more intentionally to rest and connection, both human and animal. The experience reinforced something I now believe deeply: animals do not only support healing in others. They can also act as sentinels for those of us who work beside them, revealing strain and imbalance before we are ready to acknowledge it ourselves. In listening to that painful message – the literal kick in the pants that I needed – I began the work of restoring not just physical function but a fuller sense of wholeness, which has increased safety and wellness for everyone.

Your Wellness Saga

Now that we have covered all the steps of the SAGA process, we share guidance and suggestions for the SAGA process on a specific set of variables – those related to wellness of the practitioner-animal team. Ultimately, this is your *Wellness Saga* – the data story of your team's wellness. This could be the most overlooked set of variables when folks think of data-driven work, but they are the most important. Because if we don't take care of ourselves and our team, we really can't do our best work helping others. And in fact, a team member that is exhausted or unwell can even cause harm to themselves or others. Therefore, in this chapter, we suggest specific variables you can measure related to your wellness and introduce a method for monitoring your team's wellbeing.

First, we briefly define key concepts and set the stage for why team wellness deserves its own SAGA process. In this chapter, we focus on burnout as a work-related condition that can affect both practitioners and their animal partners. Related concepts such as compassion fatigue, resilience, and self-care are also relevant, but our goal is not to define, diagnose, or treat these experiences. Instead, we focus on how *data* can help practitioners notice strain, make ethical decisions, and support the well-being of the animal-handler team. While reading the next section, think about (1) which of these factors influences your team's wellness and (2) what related variables you could measure in your SAGA process.

Team Wellness Matters

Team wellness in animal-assisted work reflects our ongoing capacity to engage, recover, and participate ethically and sustainably. One important indicator of declining wellness is **burnout**, a work-related syndrome that can develop when the emotional demands of work consistently exceed the resources available to meet them. Burnout may show up as exhaustion, reduced effectiveness, or feeling disconnected from work that once felt meaningful. Some research suggests that working alongside companion animals may support wellness by grounding practitioners and providing emotional nourishment. Many animal-assisted practitioners describe drawing meaning, connection, and motivation from their relationships with animal partners, experiences that can buffer against strain. At the same time, while animal-assisted work is often deeply meaningful, the nature of this work can also place unique demands on practitioners' wellness. We explore some of those demands shortly.

But first, it is important to recognize that wellness is not only a human concern. Animal partners can also experience strain, fatigue, or reduced capacity over time. The concept of animal welfare helps us attend to these issues. Animal welfare is a broad term used across many human–animal contexts, including animal husbandry, sport, entertainment, and companion animal care. In animal-assisted services, we define **animal welfare** as an animal's capacity to cope, recover, and participate without harm, while also living a good life that allows for agency and the expression of natural behaviors. From this perspective, monitoring team wellness means attending to the well-being of both human practitioners and animal partners, as well as how they function together over time. Next, we turn to some of the ways animal-assisted work, despite its many benefits, can place unique demands on the wellness of the team.

We Carry Heavy Loads

Research suggests that animal-assisted services are often sought by individuals with severe trauma, chronic stress, or severe and persistent mental or physical health conditions. Because animals can provide comfort and connection during difficult times, practitioners who incorporate animals into their work may find themselves carrying emotionally heavy caseloads. Regularly bringing a therapy dog into settings such as hospitals, nursing homes, or cancer centers can be emotionally taxing over time. In our experience at the ranch, many clients and community members seek animal-assisted services precisely because their needs are complex, long-standing, or not fully met by other approaches. Some are looking for something different after other services have failed; others are drawn to the unique form of connection animals offer or need animals in addition to mainstream supports.

> While this work can be profoundly rewarding, it also places sustained emotional demands on practitioners and their animal partners.

We Wear Many Hats

Part of the difficulty can be the multiple caregiving roles the animal handler must play, caring for their animal and the animal-assisted service recipient, and perhaps staff members and the facility they are working in. Each of these roles can be emotionally draining and serving them simultaneously is taxing. In addition, animal-assisted services sometimes happen in public spaces, like hospitals or libraries, where an animal-handler team can excite anyone in proximity, not just the direct recipient of services. While these extra interactions can be rewarding, they can also add to the cumulative weight of the work – for human and animal team members.

The Weight of the Work Can Break the Bond

Beyond the personal distress it causes, exhaustion and burnout are problematic for the animal-handler team and for the people we serve. Burnout can strain relationships, including the relationship between a practitioner and their animal partner(s).

When we are depleted, our ability to attune to our partners is reduced, communication can suffer, and safety may be compromised. Burnout can also affect judgment and decision-making, increasing the risk of poor performance and unintended negative outcomes. For these reasons, monitoring team wellness is not only a matter of self-care – it is an ethical issue. Doing good and doing no harm requires attention to the well-being of both human and animal members of the team. The SAGA process offers a way to monitor wellness and respond early, allowing us to care for the team before burnout causes harm.

Burnout Sneaks Up on Us

One more good reason to gather data on the team's wellness is that burnout does not happen suddenly and loudly. It grows slowly and quietly until we reach a breaking point. And that breaking point can be a breakdown, which can have severe consequences for us, our team, and those we serve. Gathering regular data to monitor our wellbeing can help us detect early signs of burnout so that we can address it before it becomes a crisis.

Team Wellness Is Observable

When gathering data on our team's wellness, it's important to remember that the animal-handler team is interdependent. Each needs the other and they have a reciprocal influence on one another. Ironically, although the strength of our work depends on this reciprocity between humans and animals, we can forget that our wellness affects our animal partners and vice versa. This can show up in a couple of ways – we feel unwell or exhausted, but we push through without thinking about how it might be affecting our animal partner and/or we notice a wellness issue for our animal partner and attend to it without considering the effect of the situation on us. In a somewhat extreme case, we can have a practitioner having to make an end-of-life decision about an ill animal partner and not really acknowledge the effect on their own wellness until grieving the loss at a later time.

This reciprocal nature of the work is important for the SAGA process because it can help us identify variables to measure. We must remember to gather data on both human practitioners and animal partners. In addition, **some of the most informative data live in the space *between* the human and animal** – the interaction, the relationship, and the shared task environment. Practitioners often notice changes in how a partnership feels before they can name exactly why – something seems off in the interaction, the timing, the handling, or the ease of working together. Research on human–animal interaction and animal welfare supports this intuition, showing that patterns of engagement, responsiveness, regulation, and consent are meaningful for both human and animal well-being. Rather than focusing only on the practitioner or the animal in isolation, paying attention to these "in-between" variables helps capture how the team is functioning as a unit. Table 13.1 lists different kinds of variables that measure this in-between-ness. We are not assigning or prescribing you to measure these variables. The table is to give you an idea of what we mean by saying that you should measure the space between and to spark ideas relevant to your own practitioner-animal team.

Note that each category includes an example of "Red-flag behavior." These are observable actions that compromise safety or indicate an individual's capacity has been exceeded in that moment. Red-flag behaviors are not moral failures, temperament flaws, or training problems; they are important data points that help practitioners make protective decisions for the animal-handler team. When red-flag behaviors occur, the appropriate response is not to push through, but to pause, prioritize health and safety, and attend to the underlying needs contributing to the behavior. The table offers examples of the kinds of variables that can help make team wellness observable.

The categories in the table are consistent with published work on dyadic interaction/co-construction, synchrony and co-regulation, equipment-mediated communication, and therapy-animal welfare monitoring. This chapter's bibliography section

TABLE 13.1 Potential variables for measuring the relationship and space between animal and handler

Category	*Description*	*Examples*
Behavioral Interaction Variables	Observable patterns of engagement and responsiveness between the human and animal during an interaction. These variables capture *how* the partners relate in real time.	◆ Initiation of contact (human, animal, or mutual) ◆ Responsiveness to cues or signals ◆ Mutual orientation (toward or away) ◆ Reciprocity in approach–response sequences ◆ **Red-flag behavior:** repeated refusal to engage combined with escalating avoidance or threat behaviors (e.g., charging, snapping, or bolting when approached)
Handling and Equipment-Mediated Variables	Information transmitted through physical connection or equipment that reflects communication, tension, and coordination between partners.	◆ Amount of leash or lead-rope tension (slack, light, constant) ◆ Frequency of corrections or adjustments ◆ Smooth vs. abrupt handling movements ◆ Directionality of movement changes ◆ **Red-flag behavior:** sudden, forceful resistance through equipment (e.g., rearing, pulling someone off balance, or explosive pressure against the leash or lead)
Shared Regulation Variables	Patterns that reflect co-regulation – how the human and animal influence one another's arousal, pace, and recovery during or after activity.	◆ Ability to settle together after activity ◆ Matching pace or rhythm ◆ Recovery following stress or excitement ◆ Escalation or de-escalation loops ◆ **Red-flag behavior:** rapid escalation without recovery, where arousal increases for both partners and cannot be safely brought down
Emotional Tone of the Interaction	The observable quality or "feel" of the interaction, reflected in posture, movement, and pacing rather than inferred internal states.	◆ Calm vs. hurried handling ◆ Presence vs. distraction ◆ Ease vs. tension in movement ◆ Playful vs. task-focused engagement ◆ **Red-flag behavior:** persistent tension or irritability that disrupts communication and increases risk (e.g., rushed handling paired with animal agitation)

(*Continued*)

TABLE 13.1 (Continued)

Category	*Description*	*Examples*
Boundary and Consent Signals	How willingness, hesitation, or refusal is expressed by the animal and how those signals are noticed and responded to by the human partner.	◆ Animal avoidance or approach behaviors ◆ Human response to subtle refusals ◆ Respect for pauses or breaks ◆ Adjustment following resistance or hesitation ◆ **Red-flag behavior:** clear loss of consent or safety (e.g., repeated kicking, biting, backing into a person, or striking behaviors)
Downtime and Recovery Variables	Patterns in how the human–animal team interacts outside of formal sessions, which can reveal cumulative strain, burnout, or changes in the relationship.	◆ Willingness to engage during non-work time ◆ Changes in proximity-seeking or avoidance outside sessions ◆ Ease of handling during routine care ◆ Quality of shared rest or recovery periods ◆ **Red-flag behavior:** marked withdrawal or reactivity during routine care that represents a clear change from baseline

includes relevant citations for digging deeper into these technical terms and concepts. Note the last category in the table – downtime and recovery variables. Changes in the animal-handler relationship may appear first during downtime rather than during formal sessions, making these moments especially important for noticing early signs of strain. Any of these can be incorporated into your Wellness Saga. Next, we share *our* system of monitoring team wellness.

Team Wellness Can Be Tracked – The Stoplight Method

The **stoplight method** is a simple, familiar way to monitor wellness and readiness across the animal-handler team. Using a traffic light metaphor, wellness indicators are rated as **green**, **yellow**, or **red** to guide day-to-day participation decisions. While not a new idea, the stoplight framework offers a shared, low-burden system for translating observations into clear, ethical action.

Green Zone. Being in the green zone means the individual is *good to go*. There are no significant wellness concerns, and participation in services can proceed as usual.

Yellow Zone. The yellow zone means *proceed with caution*. Yellow indicates that participation is still possible, but with increased awareness, monitoring, and intentional support. In the yellow zone, there are emerging or moderate wellness concerns that do not yet warrant stopping work altogether, but do call for adjustments, boundary-setting, and renewed attention to balance and recovery.

Red Zone. The red zone means *stop*. Red indicates substantial wellness concerns, and the individual should not participate in services at that time. Red zone situations call for attention and support – this may involve rest and recovery, adjustments to workload, or, when appropriate, further assessment or care. While many wellness indicators emerge gradually, some red-flag behaviors signal elevated risk and may warrant an immediate red zone decision. Each program can determine its own protocol for responding to red-flag behaviors and making red zone decisions. Table 13.2 provides possible indicators of the green, yellow, and red zones for both humans and animals.

We suggest you use this table as a template but tailor it for your team. Individual practitioners could have their own list of indicators – how they know when they are becoming exhausted and need a break – as well as indicators for different animals. Animals will have species-specific indicators as well as personal behavior patterns. There is no one-size-fits-all model to tell you what to do. And this book is not a guidebook on how to do animal-assisted work. We share the stoplight method and these tables to offer ideas on variables you can record related to your team's wellness. The response column provides possible responses. The responses shown here are intentionally broad. The specific actions taken in response to yellow or red zone indicators will vary by role, setting, species, and available supports. **Importantly, these responses are not just actions – they are data**. Tracking wellness indicators before and after

TABLE 13.2 Behavioral wellness indicators for humans or animals in the green, yellow, or red zones

Zone	*Human Indicators*	*Animal Indicators*	*Decision Guidance*
Green – *Good to Go*	◆ Feeling engaged and present ◆ Adequate physical and emotional energy ◆ Clear communication and attunement with animal partner(s) ◆ Able to respond flexibly to challenges and surprises	◆ Typical engagement and responsiveness ◆ Stable maintenance behaviors (eating, resting, movement) ◆ Willing participation in interactions ◆ Normal recovery following sessions	Proceed as planned. Continue current routines and supports, keep monitoring wellness indicators to establish and maintain a clear baseline.
Yellow – *Proceed with Caution*	◆ Fatigue or emotional stretch ◆ Reduced patience, focus, or emotional bandwidth ◆ Increased effort required to stay regulated ◆ Awareness that balance, recovery, or boundaries are slipping	◆ Subtle avoidance or reduced engagement ◆ Slower recovery following sessions ◆ Mild stress behaviors or hesitation ◆ Increased need for support, adjustment, or recovery time	Adjust pace, expectations, or supports. Reduce intensity, modify tasks, increase recovery opportunities, and monitor closely to see whether the adjustment supports a return to Green.
Red – *Stop*	◆ Emotional exhaustion or overwhelm ◆ Illness, injury, or inability to focus ◆ Strong irritability, dread, or emotional detachment ◆ Feeling unable to show up ethically or safely	◆ Clear stress or threat behaviors ◆ Pain, illness, or lameness ◆ Loss of consent or safety (e.g., repeated kicking, biting, bolting, backing into people) ◆ Failure to recover between sessions	Pause participation. Prioritize rest, recovery, or care before returning to work. Use this as information to reassess workload, supports, and readiness over time.

adjustments helps practitioners learn which responses support recovery and sustainability for the animal-handler team. And finally, remember that stoplight ratings should be revisited regularly and never used as permanent labels.

It's about Wellness, Not Evaluation

We share the stoplight method as a framework for thinking about wellness and measuring variables relevant to the team's needs – not as a tool for evaluation or diagnosis. This is a shared system that applies to both humans and animal partners, designed to support care rather than assess performance. It helps guide moment-to-moment decisions based on current capacity, not long-term labels or judgments about competence. Just as physical and emotional states change over time, so can stoplight ratings; an individual may be in the green zone one day and yellow or red the next.

As experienced practitioners, we often sense when something is not quite right. The stoplight method helps translate that professional intuition into action. Recording specific indicators – such as those described in Table 13.2 – provides concrete evidence to support these decisions. Tracking stoplight ratings over time can also reveal patterns, helping teams notice early signs of cumulative strain and intervene before burnout or welfare concerns escalate. In this way, the stoplight method allows us to adjust course before a small drift becomes a collision.

Structured Wellness Assessments

In many programs, informal wellness check-ins, shared reflection, and ordinary conversations about how the work feels may be enough to support the human–animal team. In other settings, practitioners may find it useful to occasionally use a structured self-assessment to notice patterns in stress, resilience, or professional strain over time. When a formal tool is used, it works best when it is chosen thoughtfully and held with care for purpose, privacy, and the well-being of the practitioner.

One example from the broader helping-profession literature is the self-assessment instrument in Skovholt and Trotter-Mathison's *The Resilient Practitioner* (2024), which invites reflection on areas such as emotional depletion, recovery practices, meaning in work, and sources of support. Another widely used option is the *Professional Quality of Life Scale (ProQOL)* (Stamm, 2010), which helps practitioners reflect on both the rewards of caring work and the strains of burnout or secondary traumatic stress. Some programs also use tools such as *the Compassion Satisfaction and Fatigue Self-Test for Helpers* (Figley & Stamm, 1996), a reflective screening measure developed within trauma-care fields to help practitioners recognize emerging patterns of compassion fatigue and resilience in their caregiving work. In some organizations, system-level wellness conversations may draw on the *Maslach Burnout Inventory* (Maslach et al., 1996), a long-standing instrument used across human-service settings to describe patterns of exhaustion and reduced sense of accomplishment, with the greatest benefit occurring when results guide supportive and organizational responses rather than being directed toward the individual.

A Note on Supportive Use

Structured wellness tools are most supportive when they are used with consent and curiosity, and when the information they generate remains under the practitioner's control. If a self-assessment suggests that someone is feeling stretched or distressed, the response is best oriented toward care – supervision or consultation, space for recovery, or attention to systemic contributors – rather than criticism or individual blame.

Try It! Start Your *Wellness Saga*

This chapter has made the case for and offered tools to support gathering data on the wellness of the animal-assisted practitioner–animal team. Wellness matters for everyone, and animal-assisted providers – both human and animal – may face unique challenges inherent in this work. These can include emotionally heavy or complex caseloads, the strain of wearing multiple roles, and the additional energy and expectations directed toward animals. For these reasons, gathering data on team wellness is not optional – it is essential. And there is no time like the present to get started. Here are some simple steps to begin your Wellness Saga:

1. **Share the foundation.** Have everyone on your team – or a representative subgroup – read this chapter and make notes about ideas that stand out.
2. **Define the team.** Identify who will be included in your wellness tracking. (Hint: this usually means *everyone* – animal partners, practitioners, support staff, and volunteers.)
3. **Talk it through.** Hold a group discussion about team wellness, questions you have, and concerns you've noticed. Review Tables 13.1 and 13.2 and reflect on how they map onto your experiences so far.
4. **Ask good questions.** Develop two SMART wellness questions – one focused on human teammates and one on animal partners.
5. **Plan your data gathering.** Decide what you will record, when and how often, and for how long. Then gather your data.
6. **Analyze your data.** Refer back to Chapter 10 for guidance on making sense of your data.
7. **Respond with intention.** Act on what you learn, using the tools from Chapter 11 to guide thoughtful decisions.
8. **Repeat and refine.** Continue the process with additional wellness questions as new needs or patterns emerge.
9. **Document the journey.** Create a Wellness Saga folder to store your data, reflections, decisions, and outcomes.

We're excited for you to move from knowing that wellness matters – and making good decisions based on experience and intuition – to gathering data that supports even better decisions. Believe it or not, caring *is* data – and working with data *is* caring.

Bibliography

Bargigli, G., et al. (2025). Evidence of physiological co-modulation during human–animal interaction: A systematic review. arXiv.2510.10559

Binfet, J. T., & Tardif-Williams, C. Y. (2025). *Optimizing therapy dog-handler team welfare: A guide for researchers and practitioners*. Routledge.

Brown, R. (2023). *Break free from burnout: Essential strategies for everyday stress to create calm amid the chaos*. Independently published.

Cronin, S., Allen, T., Hou, J. M., & Walker, L. (2023). Therapist resilience in an ever-changing world: A systematic review. *Journal of Prevention and Health Promotion*, *4*(1), 60–86.

De Santis, M. et al. (2024). How to measure human–dog interaction in dog-assisted interventions: A scoping review. *Animals*, *14*(3), 410.

Figley, C. R., & Stamm, B. H. (1996). *Psychometric review of the compassion satisfaction and fatigue self-test for helpers*. National Center for PTSD.

Fine, A. H., & Griffin, T. C. (2022). Protecting animal welfare in animal-assisted intervention: Our ethical obligation. *Seminars in Speech and Language*, *43*(1), 8–23.

Fournier, A. K., French, M., Letson, E. A., Hanson, J., Berry, T. D., & Cronin, S. (2024). The behavioral cost of care: Changes in maintenance behavior during equine-assisted interventions. *Animals*, *14*(4), 536.

Fournier, A. K., & Mustful, B. (2019). Compassion fatigue: Presenting issues and practical applications for animal-caring professionals. In *Clinician's guide to treating companion animal issues* (pp. 511–534). Academic Press.

French, M., & Fournier, A. K. (2023). Striking a balance between welfare and therapeutic progress in equine-assisted services. In L. R. Kogan (Ed.), *Animal-assisted interventions: Recognizing and mitigating potential welfare challenges*. CABI International. https://doi.org/10.1079/9781800622616.0009

Glenk, L. M. (2021). *Therapy dog welfare revisited: A review of the literature*. PMC.

Hosey, G., & Melfi, V. (2014). Human–animal interactions, relationships and bonds: A review and analysis of the literature. *International Journal of Comparative Psychology*, *27*(1).

Kogan, L. R. (Ed.). (2023). *Animal-assisted interventions: Recognizing and mitigating potential welfare challenges*. CABI.

Kogstad, N., Christiansen, S. E., Ulberg, R., & Fiskum, C. (2025). Therapists' reasons for including horses into psychotherapy: A qualitative study. *BMC Complementary Medicine and Therapies*, *26*, 20. https://doi.org/10.1186/s12906-025-05185-2.

Leconstant, C., & Spitz, E. (2022). Integrative model of human–animal interactions: A on health-one welfare systemic approach to studying HAI. *Frontiers in Veterinary Science*, *9*, 656833.

Letson, E. A., & Hanson, J. R. (2023). Acknowledging and mitigating professional compassion fatigue: Personal reflections on animal-assisted work. In L. R. Kogan (Ed.), *Animal-assisted interventions: Recognizing and mitigating potential welfare challenges* (chapter 11). CABI. https://doi.org/10.1079/9781800622616.0011

Maslach, C., Jackson, S. E., & Leiter, M. P. (1996). *Maslach burnout inventory manual* (3rd ed.). Consulting Psychologists Press.

Pasiuk, E. L., Schroeder, K., & Stellato, A. C. (2025). Working alliances in counselling and psychotherapy incorporating horse interactions. *Counselling and Psychotherapy Research*, *25*(2), e70025.

Rodriguez, K. E., et al. (2018). *The state of assessment in human–animal interaction*. CABI Digital Library.

Ru, S. (2025). Exploring human–animal interactions beyond academic research. *Animal Welfare*, *34*, e52.

Rudd, C., Pasiuk, E., Anderson, N., Hall, N., Foster, R., & Schroeder, K. (2024). A preliminary assessment of equine affect in equine-assisted services. *Anthrozoös*, *37*(3), 501–518.

Skovholt, T. M., & Trotter-Mathison, M. (2024). *The resilient practitioner: Burnout and compassion fatigue prevention and self-care strategies for the helping professions* (4th ed.). Routledge.

Stamm, B. H. (2010). *The professional quality of life scale: Compassion satisfaction, burnout & compassion fatigue/secondary trauma scales* (version 5). ProQOL.org.

14

Practice-Based Evidence in Animal-Assisted Services

From Individual Sagas to Shared Data Stories

The Story So Far

In this last chapter we begin by going back to some key truths. Humans are natural storytellers. Whether we realize it or not, we engage with story, as tellers or listeners, throughout our lives. Another key truth is that humans have been living and working with other animals for a very long time. Together, these histories have shaped a rich experiential understanding of working with animals in healing contexts and sharing those experiences through story. Healing with animals in the Western medicine sense – what we've been calling animal-assisted services – is a more recent development. Even more recently, empirical research methods have been added to other longstanding ways of understanding these practices. In essence, our field's evidence story is still being written.

Recall from Chapter 2 that *evidence* is information that helps us know if a belief or proposition is true or valid. We distinguished between *anecdotal evidence* – based on personal accounts or

DOI: 10.4324/9781003640257-18

anecdotes – and *empirical evidence* – based on direct observation or measurement. Throughout the book we have argued that both are necessary and we're hoping to impart knowledge and skills so that you can use both to guide your work and share it with others. We've shared with you the SAGA process for sharing a story (anecdote); then supporting the story by asking a question, gathering and analyzing data (empirical evidence); then closing the loop by responding to the data and ethically sharing your findings when appropriate.

This alone – you as practitioner employing the SAGA process to guide your work – is important. It matters for your clients, your animal partners, and the wellness of your team and your organization or business. **But it's bigger than that.** The field of animal-assisted services needs your help growing the bigger evidence story of our field. Not by joining a study, but by contributing your SAGA data stories as a special type of evidence.

From Evidence-Based Practice to Practice-Based Evidence

Perhaps you are familiar with the term **evidence-based practice**. This refers to approaches informed by the best available research evidence. A method or treatment becomes evidence-based by being systematically studied, replicated across settings, and evaluated. This term is sometimes seen alongside a related term – **practice-based evidence** – which starts from a different place. Instead of asking whether a method works under controlled research conditions, practice-based evidence relies on real-world practice (like your animal-assisted work) to build the evidence base for a treatment or method. It is built from careful observation, documentation, and reflection of practitioners working in everyday settings with real people, animals, and constraints.

Both types of evidence – scientific and practice-based – are important. They complement one another. And as a practitioner, you have an important role in contributing to the practice-based evidence on animal-assisted services. In other words, the work you are doing, elevated by the SAGA process, is exactly what our field needs to keep moving forward. You don't need to be a researcher. You are already generating evidence through careful practice. Keep reading this chapter to learn how your data-driven work can become part of the field's larger data story.

A Capstone SAGA Example

To see how individual SAGA work can move beyond one practitioner and contribute to the field's larger evidence story, we walk through a complete example below. In the first part, we take you through an example of one full SAGA process. Use this as a model for any of your SAGA work. Like all SAGA work, this example begins with a small story and ends with insights that could matter far beyond one setting.

Share a Story: Practitioner's Anecdote

Luna is a rabbit who participates in animal-assisted sessions with children in a school-based counseling program. The practitioner notices something unexpected. While many children appear relaxed and engaged when interacting with Luna, a subset of children – particularly those who are highly anxious or sensory-sensitive – seem to respond differently to her than they do to dogs. With Luna, these children seem to:

- ◆ Approach more slowly but stay engaged longer
- ◆ Use softer voices and gentler movements
- ◆ Show fewer signs of overwhelm or withdrawal

These observations show up repeatedly, across weeks and across different children. The practitioner begins to wonder whether this is more than coincidence. At this stage, the story is compelling, but still just a story.

Ask a Question

Rather than jumping to conclusions ("Rabbits are better for anxious kids"), the practitioner pauses and asks a more careful question: *For children with high anxiety or sensory sensitivity, does interaction with a small prey animal like a rabbit result in different engagement or regulation patterns than interaction with a dog?* This question is specific, observable, and grounded in practice. It does not require a lab, a grant, or a large sample – just thoughtful, planned observation.

Gather Evidence: Simple, Focused Data

The practitioner begins gathering modest, practice-friendly data during animal-assisted sessions already occurring in the program, comparing sessions involving Luna with sessions involving Buddy, a therapy dog. Three variables are tracked consistently across sessions:

- Duration of child engagement (in minutes)
- Child arousal (rated on 5-point scale, 1 = very dysregulated, 5 = calm and engaged)
- Animal arousal (rated on 5-point scale, 1 = very dysregulated, 5 = calm and engaged)

Nothing about this data is complex. What matters is that the observations are *systematic* and *repeatable*. Over time, the practitioner accumulates data points, and a small dataset begins to form, pictured in Table 14.1.

Analyze the Data: Simple Comparisons to Identify Patterns

The practitioner begins analysis by looking for patterns over time. To do this, they create a simple line graph like the one in

TABLE 14.1 Database of engagement and arousal across sessions

	Engagement (min)	*Child Arousal*	*Animal Arousal*
Clover	12	4	4
Clove	14	4	4
Clove	15	5	5
Max	6	2	3
Max	7	3	3

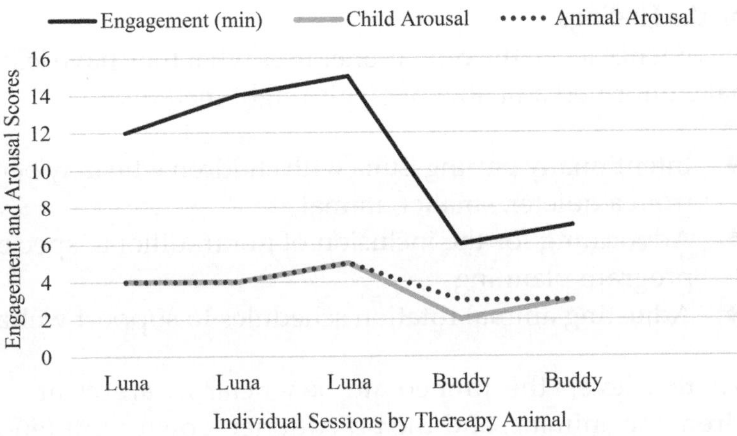

FIGURE 14.1 Line graph illustrating engagement and arousal across sessions.

Figure 14.1. The x-axis indicates five consecutive sessions, three with Luna and then two with Buddy. The y-axis shows engagement and arousal numbers. The three lines are for the three variables that were tracked.

Looking at the graph, we see:

- ◆ The children showed longer sustained engagement with Luna than with Buddy
- ◆ Child arousal ratings improved
- ◆ Luna's arousal ratings remained steady, suggesting good welfare fit

Importantly, the practitioner notes that higher child engagement does not coincide with lower animal arousal – a potential welfare concern that does not appear in these data. The practitioner is careful not to overclaim. This is not evidence that rabbits are universally "better," nor that dogs are "too much." Instead, the analysis highlights *fit*: between animal characteristics, child needs, and context. The graph makes visible something that was previously only felt. It's empirical evidence supporting the anecdote.

Act on the Findings

At the practice level, the practitioner uses what they have learned to make informed adjustments. This might include:

- Intentionally pairing Luna with children who may benefit from a quieter, smaller animal
- Advocating for the inclusion of nontraditional species in program planning
- Adjusting animal rotation schedules to support welfare

At this level, the immediate beneficiaries are clear – the children, the animals, and the practitioner's own confidence in their decisions. This is where SAGA most obviously strengthens practice – and that alone is valuable. But SAGA is not meant to stop there.

When Individual SAGAs Connect: Shared Inquiry

The next layer, known as shared inquiry, emerges when practitioners begin to share questions, data plans, and emerging patterns with others – at trainings, conferences, supervision meetings, or informal practitioner networks.

In these conversations, practitioners are careful to frame what they are seeing as *patterns within context*, not proof. They ask questions such as: *Have you noticed something similar?* or *What does this look like in your setting?* As colleagues engage with the same underlying questions, individual SAGAs begin to connect. Some practitioners may work with rabbits, others with reptiles, fish, or different species altogether. The specific animal matters less than the shared inquiry.

Across conversations and settings, practice-based evidence begins to form – not as a single definitive answer, but as a growing body of observations that point in similar directions or raise curiosity. At this stage, evidence remains contextual. It is tied to particular populations, environments, and animals. But it is no longer isolated. This is the middle ground between anecdote and large-scale research – **shared inquiry grounded in practice**. Crucially, shared practice-based evidence does not compete with research. It prepares the field for it – by clarifying which questions matter most, which variables are worth measuring, and where more formal studies may be most informative.

Toward a Practitioner–Science Evidence Base

As shared inquiry accumulates and patterns become clearer, the field reaches a turning point. Questions that once lived only in individual practice now have enough collective weight to warrant deeper investigation. This is where the **practitioner–science evidence base** begins to take shape. In a practitioner–science evidence base:

- Practice generates meaningful questions
- SAGA processes generate early evidence and refine variables
- Research studies test, extend, and challenge those patterns
- Findings return to practice, shaping the next generation of SAGAs

This is not a linear path, but a feedback loop. Research does not replace practice-based evidence; it builds on it. Likewise, practitioner SAGAs do not end once research exists. They continue to adapt findings to real-world contexts and identify new questions that research alone cannot answer.

Just as importantly, this approach makes limitations visible. Patterns that appear strong in one context may weaken in another. Outcomes that look promising may carry costs – for animals, clients, or systems – that deserve careful attention. Acknowledging limitations is not a weakness of this approach. It is one of its ethical strengths. By positioning practitioners as contributors to the evidence base – not merely consumers of research – the field gains greater relevance, ecological validity, and sustained attention to animal welfare in context. This is how animal-assisted services matures as a field: not by waiting for perfect evidence, but by **building evidence together**, responsibly and transparently.

A Next Chapter for the Field

One promising next step for advancing practice-based evidence in animal-assisted services would be 1) increasing data-driven (i.e., SAGA) work by individual practitioners and programs and 2) connecting SAGA practitioners to facilitate shared inquiry. You are already working on the first part by working through this book and beginning SAGA work of your own. The second part – shared inquiry – can happen informally or formally. Informally, you can share your SAGA data stories with other practitioners and encourage them to take up the work. For our part, we plan to provide a more formal structure for SAGA practitioners to connect via SAGA learning circles. These are learning communities in which practitioners share their questions, data plans, and emerging patterns. These communities will allow practitioners to compare how questions are being asked, what variables are being tracked, and what patterns are beginning to emerge – while preserving context, ethical boundaries, and practitioner autonomy. In this way, collective learning can develop organically, laying the conceptual and relational groundwork for a future practitioner–science evidence base.

Your Next Chapter

Throughout this book, we have shown how stories and science can work together – how anecdotes spark curiosity, how data sharpen understanding, and how informed action strengthens practice. Every SAGA you conduct contributes to more than your own learning.

> When shared thoughtfully, your work becomes part of the field's evolving evidence story.

In Appendix G we've included some tips to make SAGA work feasible, by getting help and making it a regular part of work you already do. You do not need a grant, a lab, or a research team to guide your work with data. You need curiosity, care, and a commitment to learning from your work. In animal-assisted services, knowledge can grow through evolving data stories shaped by practitioner SAGA work and formal research together – forming a practitioner–science evidence base. This book has given you tools to take part in that process.

To support that next step, we have created online resources to accompany this book, including tools, examples, and opportunities to connect with others engaged in SAGA work. Participation is optional and flexible; you are welcome to engage at whatever level fits your context and goals.

What you choose to do with these tools – what questions you ask, what data you gather, and how you act on what you learn – will shape not only your practice, but the future story of the field.

Try It! Continue the SAGA by Joining the Larger Story

This final chapter marks a shift – from using SAGA in your own setting to becoming part of a larger community of practitioners who are collectively building practice-based evidence. Evidence grows when stories, questions, and data are shared, examined, and connected across programs, species, and contexts. The goal is no longer just "What did I learn in my practice?" but "What are we learning as a field?" Use the steps below to take your first intentional step from private SAGA work to shared, cumulative knowledge.

1. **Locate your SAGA in the bigger picture.** Reflect on your work and identify one question, pattern, or outcome that feels larger than your own program. What are you seeing repeatedly? What do you wish the field understood better about clients, animals, teams, or programs? Briefly describe how your current or recent SAGA process connects to this broader question.
2. **Prepare one SAGA cycle for sharing.** Choose one SAGA you have completed (or are currently working through) and summarize it in a way that someone outside your organization could understand and build on. In a page or less, describe:
   - The story that prompted your question.
   - The question you asked.

- The key variables and how you measured them.
- What you found and how it informed your decisions. This is not a formal research paper; it is a clear, transparent practice-based evidence snapshot.

3. **Step into the SAGA community.** Practice-based evidence is a collective effort. Visit this book's companion website www.bringingsciencetoourstories.com to access:
   - Downloadable digital resources (templates, observation tools, consent language, data-story examples, and practice-evidence briefs).
   - Information about SAGA learning circles, where practitioners work through real cases and data together.
   - Workshops and trainings focused on specific SAGA skills.
   - Opportunities to participate in collaborative projects and research partnerships.
4. Write down:
   - One resource you will download and use in the next month.
   - One community activity you are interested in (learning circle, workshop, collaboration).
   - One concrete action you will take in the next 30 days to move your SAGA work from "mine" to "ours."

By completing this step, you are no longer just applying evidence – you are helping to create it. This is how individual stories become shared knowledge, and how a field grows through the steady, thoughtful contributions of practitioners who measure, reflect, and learn together. The field's SAGA is still being written. You are already part of it. Your next chapter begins wherever you decide to look more closely.

Bibliography

Barkham, M., Hardy, G. E., & Mellor-Clark, J. (2010). *Developing and delivering practice-based evidence: A guide for the psychological therapies*. Wiley-Blackwell.

Bohart, A. C., & Tallman, K. (2010). *Clients: The neglected common factor in psychotherapy*. American Psychological Association.

Fine, A. H. (Ed.). (2019). *Handbook on animal-assisted therapy: Foundations and guidelines for animal-assisted interventions* (5th ed.). Academic Press.

Fournier, A. K. (2019). Studying animal-assisted intervention through citizen science. In *Animal-assisted intervention: Thinking empirically* (pp. 95–118). Springer International Publishing.

Glasgow, R. E., Lichtenstein, E., & Marcus, A. C. (2003). Why don't we see more translation of health promotion research to practice? *American Journal of Public Health, 93*(8), 1261–1267. https://doi.org/10.2105/AJPH.93.8.1261

Green, L. W. (2006). Public health asks of systems science: To advance our evidence-based practice, can you help us get more practice-based evidence? *American Journal of Public Health, 96*(3), 406–409. https://doi.org/10.2105/AJPH.2005.066035

Horn, S. D., & Gassaway, J. (2007). Practice-based evidence. *Medical Care, 45*(10 Suppl 2), S50–S57.

Kazdin, A. E. (2008). Evidence-based treatment and practice: New opportunities to bridge clinical research and practice. *American Psychologist, 63*(3), 146–159. https://doi.org/10.1037/0003-066X.63.3.146

Kazdin, A. E. (2017). Strategies to improve the evidence base of animal-assisted interventions. *Applied Developmental Science, 21*(2), 150–164.

Kuhn, T. S. (2012). *The structure of scientific revolutions* (4th ed.). University of Chicago Press.

Lewis, C. C., Boyd, M., & Puspitasari, A. (2019). Implementing measurement-based care in behavioral health: A review. *JAMA Psychiatry, 76*(3), 324–335. https://doi.org/10.1001/jamapsychiatry.2018.3329

Miller, S. D., Hubble, M. A., Chow, D. L., & Seidel, J. A. (2015). Beyond measures and monitoring: Realizing the potential of feedback-informed treatment. *Psychotherapy, 52*(4), 449–457. https://doi.org/10.1037/pst0000039

Reason, P., & Bradbury, H. (Eds.). (2008). *The SAGE handbook of action research: Participative inquiry and practice*. SAGE.

Riley, W. T., Glasgow, R. E., Etheredge, L., & Abernethy, A. P. (2013). Rapid, responsive, relevant research. *Health Affairs, 32*(7), 1201–1208. https://doi.org/10.1377/hlthaff.2013.0625

Serpell, J. A., McCune, S., Gee, N. R., & Griffin, J. A. (2017). Current challenges to research on animal-assisted interventions. *Applied Developmental Science, 21*(3), 223–233.

Shirk, J. L., Ballard, H. L., Wilderman, C. C., Phillips, T., Wiggins, A., Jordan, R., … Bonney, R. (2012). Public participation in scientific research. *Ecology and Society, 17*(2), 29. https://doi.org/10.5751/ES-04705-170229

Wenger, E., McDermott, R., & Snyder, W. M. (2002). *Cultivating communities of practice*. Harvard Business School Press.

Appendix A

Using Published Research to Strengthen Your Stories

Practitioners often ask, *"How do I show others that there is research on the work I do?"* This appendix is designed to answer that question. You do not need to become a researcher or statistician to use published research well. Instead, the goal is to learn how to **find**, **understand**, and **use** research in ways that strengthen the stories you already tell about your work. This appendix focuses on three practical skills:

1. Finding relevant published research
2. Reading and digesting research (research literacy)
3. Summarizing and discussing research alongside anecdotes

Finding Published Research Onllne

Published research can feel inaccessible, especially when articles are written for academic audiences or hidden behind paywalls. Fortunately, many useful resources are available with minimal effort and no special credentials.

Where to Look

- **Google Scholar** (scholar.google.com)
  A user-friendly starting point for locating peer-reviewed[1] articles. Begin with clear, specific search terms such as: *equine-assisted therapy outcomes, human–animal interaction stress, or therapy animal welfare.*

- **University and Public Libraries**
  Many public libraries and universities provide free access to academic databases. Librarians are trained to help locate research and are often happy to assist practitioners.
- **Professional Organizations**
  Organizations in animal-assisted services, psychology, education, health, or veterinary fields often share summaries, white papers, or links to relevant studies.
- **Open-Access Journals**
  Some journals make their articles freely available. Look for links labeled *Open Access, Full Text,* or *PDF*. Some open-access journals relevant to our work are *Human–Animal Interactions, Anthrozoos,* and *Animals*.

Practical Search Tips

- Start broad, then refine your search
- Use quotation marks for exact phrases
- Add terms like *review, systematic review,* or *meta-analysis* when you want a summary of multiple studies

Reading and Digesting Research: A Practitioner's Approach

You do **not** need to read research articles word-for-word or understand every statistic. Think of research reading as a strategic skill rather than a comprehensive task.

A Practical Reading Order

1. **Abstract** – The overview – what was studied and what did they find? Read this to determine if the article is what you're looking for and if you actually want to read it.
2. **Introduction (first few paragraphs)** – What questions were the authors trying to answer?
3. **Methods (optional)** – Useful if you want to understand *how* the study was conducted, but you don't have to remember every detail. Notice who participated in the study, what materials or measures were used, and what the overall design of the study was.

4. **Results and Discussion** – What did they find and what does it mean?

   On an initial read, it is reasonable to skim or skip detailed statistical sections.
5. **References** – Always skim the references. You might find another article, chapter, or book relevant to your work.

Guiding Questions to Ask

- What was the main purpose of this study?
- Who (or what) was studied, and in what context?
- What were the key findings?
- How does this connect to what I observe in my own practice?
- What were the study's limitations?
- What questions remain unanswered?

Think of this as a conversation with the researchers rather than an exam you need to pass.

Using Research to Support – Not Replace – Stories

The purpose of published research in practice-based work is not to overshadow lived experience but to **contextualize and strengthen it.**

Translating Research into Plain Language

When referring to published research, rather than repeating technical phrasing, focus on meaning.

Rather than:

> A randomized controlled trial demonstrated statistically significant reductions in cortisol…

You might say:

> Research suggests that interactions with animals can be associated with reduced stress in humans.

Clarity and understanding matter more than using impressive language.

Blending Research with Anecdotes

A simple and effective structure is:

1. **Story first** – Share the anecdote or field observation
2. **Research connection** – Briefly reference published findings
3. **Reflection** – Note alignment, questions, or limitations

For example:

> I often see clients visibly relax during grooming sessions. This aligns with research suggesting that human–animal interaction may be associated with indicators of stress reduction.

This approach allows research to **support** your story without overwhelming your audience.

Every Study Has Limits

An essential part of using research responsibly is recognizing that **all studies have limitations**. Every research project reflects choices, constraints, and trade-offs. This does not make research unhelpful – it simply means that findings are always **imperfect**.

Common limitations include:

- ♦ Small or highly specific samples
- ♦ Short observation periods
- ♦ Measures that capture only part of a complex experience
- ♦ Settings that differ from real-world practice

Rather than dismissing research because of its limits, practitioners can ask:

- ♦ *What does this study help us understand?*
- ♦ *Where might these findings apply, and where might they not?*

- *How does this fit with other evidence and with my own observations?*

Seeing research as **one piece of a larger evidence story** allows you to use it thoughtfully and ethically.

Research as an Ongoing Conversation

Published research does not deliver final answers. It contributes to an evolving conversation shaped by multiple studies, settings, and perspectives. Practitioner stories, systematic observation, and lived experience are part of that conversation. When used alongside anecdotes, research helps move the field from isolated stories toward shared, evidence-informed understanding – strengthening both individual practice and the collective story of animal-assisted services.

Note

1. Peer-reviewed means the article was reviewed by experts in the field and deemed worthy of publishing. You can be more confident in findings reported in peer-reviewed journal articles than in some other sources (e.g., blog posts, magazine articles).

Appendix B

Collaborating with Universities and Students

Many of the most meaningful advances in practice-based evidence emerge when practitioners and universities work together. Partnerships between programs, students, faculty, and researchers create spaces where learning flows in both directions: you gain support, structure, and fresh perspectives, while students and universities gain authentic, applied learning experiences grounded in real-world practice. If you are curious about inviting learners or academic partners into your work, this appendix offers ways to think about collaboration as mutually beneficial, ethically grounded, and aligned with your SAGA process.

Interns and Student Placements

Inviting interns into your program can strengthen both learning and practice – and there is no single way to structure an internship. Internships may be formal (for academic credit) or informal (not tied to university course requirements). Each option has benefits and constraints, and you may find that different seasons of your program are better suited to one or the other.

Formal, for-credit internships are coordinated through a university. They typically require:

- a set number of hours across a semester or term
- documented supervision or mentoring time

- learning objectives or competency areas
- mid-term or final evaluations

These arrangements are highly structured and often pair well with practice-based measurement because students have consistent engagement across time and may be required to do a project – perfect for getting some help with a SAGA process. They may also require more administrative effort, supervision, planning, and adherence to university calendars and policies.

Informal, non-credit internships or volunteer placements are more flexible. They may involve:

- shorter term or project-based participation
- fewer administrative requirements
- evolving roles based on program needs
- collaborative rather than evaluative supervision

These arrangements can be easier to tailor to your setting and schedule, though they may have less continuity or fewer built-in accountability structures. Both models can be valuable in different ways. Formal placements often create a steady rhythm for reflective learning and SAGA-aligned evidence gathering. Informal internships allow room for creativity, pilot projects, and exploratory collaboration. If you are thinking about hosting an intern, you can find books, articles, and websites with information and helpful guides. When thoughtfully structured, interns can support observation, documentation, and small SAGA projects while gaining meaningful, mentored professional experience.

Connecting with Researchers and Faculty

Collaborating with university researchers can help you move from anecdotal impressions toward structured inquiry without feeling alone in the process. Faculty members may partner with you as thought collaborators, research partners, or guides for student projects that align with your program's goals. You might connect with faculty through:

- psychology, counseling, social work, education, or animal science departments
- professional conferences, workshops, or guest speaking opportunities
- your animal-assisted certifying organization
- regional practitioner–university networks
- alumni or community engagement programs

Researchers may assist with study design, ethics processes, or analysis – but you remain the expert in your setting, with your animals and with your clients. Strong collaborations treat practitioner knowledge as essential, not secondary. Over time, these relationships may grow into ongoing projects, shared presentations or publications, and a sense that your program is contributing to the broader evidence story of the field.

University Libraries as Resources

You do not need to be a university employee to benefit from academic library resources. Many university libraries offer community access options, research consultations, or librarian support for literature searches. Libraries may help you.

- locate peer-reviewed articles related to your practice
- access books on measurement, observation, or program evaluation
- explore emerging research on human–animal interaction
- learn strategies for storing and organizing references

Some libraries provide guest access or on-site use of databases. Others collaborate with community practitioners through faculty sponsorship or community engagement initiatives. Librarians are often skilled at translating academic systems into approachable pathways and can help you find scholarship that informs – rather than overwhelms – your practice.

Data Analysis Support and Collaboration

If you are gathering simple practice-based data, university partners can help you make sense of it in accessible, useful ways. This collaboration may involve:

- A faculty mentor
- A graduate student assistant
- A research methods or statistics course project
- A capstone or thesis student

You might bring a small dataset – even something as simple as observation tallies or pre/post ratings – and ask for help summarizing trends.

Students and faculty can support you by:

- Cleaning and organizing spreadsheets
- Calculating descriptive summaries
- Creating graphs or tables
- Helping translate findings into plain-language summaries

You, in turn, offer a meaningful applied learning opportunity grounded in authentic practice.

When analysis is collaborative rather than extractive, the process becomes reflective, practical, and directly connected to program decisions.

Class Projects and Course-Based Partnerships

Some of the most natural university–practice collaborations develop through course assignments or group projects. Faculty may invite students to engage with real-world practice questions as part of their coursework. Possible course-based collaborations include:

- Students piloting simple observation or documentation tools
- Groups helping refine SAGA-aligned guiding questions
- Small literature reviews to support a program need
- Development of templates, forms, or data-collection sheets
- Structured reflections on human–animal interaction processes

These partnerships work best when the scope is small, expectations are realistic, and the project remains useful – not burdensome – for your program. Students gain authentic applied learning, and you gain thoughtfully developed materials grounded in academic mentorship.

Outreach Email Template for Faculty or Researchers

Subject: Community collaboration opportunity in [animal-assisted] practice

Hello [Name],

I'm writing from [your program/organization name]. We provide [brief description of services/setting], and we are interested in exploring a possible collaboration with your department or students.

We are especially curious about ways to connect practice and learning through small, applied projects such as internships, class-based projects, observation or documentation support, or assistance with simple data summaries. Our goals for collaboration include:

- supporting student learning in an authentic practice setting

- strengthening our ability to reflect on and document our work
- developing mutually beneficial, ethically grounded partnerships

If this aligns with your interests, I would be happy to discuss it further at your convenience.

Thank you for considering,

[Your name]

[Program/organization]

[Contact information]

Appendix C

Using Artificial Intelligence to Support the SAGA Process

As we write this, artificial intelligence (AI) tools and usage are expanding exponentially. We are all just beginning to use AI tools and discover their potential. For that reason, we thought it wise to suggest ways AI may help, serving as a practical companion in your SAGA process. AI tools do not replace your professional judgment, your expertise with clients, or your knowledge of your animals. Instead, they can lessen administrative load, support reflection, and help you transform stories and observations into meaningful information that guides practice. The following sections offer ways you could use AI thoughtfully and ethically at each phase of the SAGA process.

Share a Story

You already carry rich experiences from your sessions – stories that are meaningful, memorable, and full of subtle details. AI tools can help you capture and organize those stories, so they are easier to revisit, reflect on, and learn from. You might use AI to:

- Turn brief session notes into fuller narrative reflections
- Organize journal entries or de-identified case notes into themes
- Summarize written reflections after several similar sessions
- Identify patterns across your anecdotes
- Revise storytelling for length or to better fit the narrative arc

For example, you may paste several of your own short reflections from different sessions and ask the AI tool to identify what seems to repeat – perhaps clients often seek quiet connection, horses frequently choose approaches from a particular distance, or participants describe similar feelings after groundwork activities. Seeing those themes written can help bring implicit patterns into clearer view.

You may also ask AI to help you describe a story in more behavioral, objective language while preserving its meaning. This can be useful when preparing case material for supervision, program documentation, or communication with stakeholders. AI becomes a gentle editing partner – not rewriting your experience but helping you express it more clearly. You might create a log of anecdotes from your work and ask AI to help you decide which story best fits which audiences/purposes.

Ask a Good Question

Once a meaningful story begins to take shape, AI can help you refine it into a focused question that is measurable and useful for decision-making. You might use AI to:

- Reshape broad reflections into clearer guiding questions
- Compare several possible wordings of the same idea
- Think through which version of your question is most feasible in your setting
- Check whether the question aligns with your goals or values
- Help you find previous research on your topic of interest
- Help translate a research article into plain language you can understand and share with stakeholders

For instance, if you notice that clients seem calmer after grooming, you might ask AI to help you explore different ways to frame that question, such as:

- "How often do clients show calm body posture during grooming?"

- "Does reported stress level decrease from before to after a period of grooming?"

You still decide which question matters most – AI simply helps you find appropriate language, explore alternatives, and consider what would realistically fit your work. The goal is not perfection, but clarity that supports meaningful measurement.

Gather Evidence

When you are ready to collect information, AI can help you create simple tools to support observation and documentation. You might use AI to:

- find existing measurement tools you'd like to use
- find out if an existing measure is valid, reliable, and appropriate for your intended use
- draft basic observation sheets or checklists
- create a repeatable template for session tracking
- turn a measurement idea into a practical data form
- refine wording so items are clearer and easier to use

For example, you may describe the behavior you hope to observe – such as "participant initiates interaction with the horse." AI can help you turn that into a small table with labeled columns, definitions, and space for notes that you can edit to match your program.

You can also ask AI to help clarify vague categories. If you start with something broad like "positive interaction," you might ask for suggestions of more concrete indicators (e.g., approach behavior, verbal engagement, participant-initiated touch). In this phase, AI is a formatting and thinking tool – not a data generator. You collect the real-world information; AI simply helps you prepare an organized way to capture it.

Analyze and Act

Once you have gathered data, AI can support you in summarizing patterns and preparing reflections that guide next steps. You might use AI to:

- generate plain-language summaries of de-identified small datasets
- describe basic trends across time or sessions
- prepare short narrative interpretations for reports or grants
- draft reflections that you later review with your team

For example, you may enter a small table of session counts and ask AI to describe what it notices – increases, decreases, or stability. You can then compare that interpretation with your own understanding and experience. You may also ask AI to turn numbers into a brief narrative paragraph you can share with colleagues, supervisors, or stakeholders. You remain the meaning-maker; AI helps give shape to the story your data are already telling.

Ethical Use of AI in Practice-Based Measurement

When using AI as part of your SAGA process, it is helpful to keep a few guiding principles in mind:

- Do not enter identifying or private client information.
- Avoid sharing sensitive program or business details.
- Treat AI output as a draft, not a final authority.
- Ground interpretations in your knowledge, experience, and observations.
- Remember that you – not the tool – are the practitioner.

AI is most valuable when you use it as a ***reflective thinking partner*** rather than a decision-maker.

Summary

Used thoughtfully, AI can lighten administrative tasks, support reflective practice, and help you turn anecdotes and observations into clear, usable information. It cannot replace your expertise, your ethics, or your relationship with clients and animals – but it may sit beside you, helping you throughout the SAGA process.

Appendix D

When You Must Create Your Own Measure: Practical Tips for Practitioners

Start with a Clear Purpose

Before writing any items, answer:

- *What decision will this scale help me make?*
- *What behavior, experience, or change am I trying to understand?*

Define the Variable in Plain Language

Write a 1–2 sentence definition of what you are trying to measure. If you can't define it clearly, you can't measure it clearly.

Generate More Items Than You Need

Brainstorm freely. Write 10–12 possible items, even if you plan to use 3–6. This helps you avoid narrow or biased coverage of the concept.

Use Simple, Concrete Language

Avoid jargon. double-barreled questions ("calm and confident"), and vague terms ("better," "more," "connected"). Prioritize items that reflect **observable behaviors** whenever possible.

Choose One Response Format and Use It Consistently

Good options include:

- frequency ("never" to "always")
- intensity ("not at all" to "very much")
- agreement ("strongly disagree" to "strongly agree")

Keep it the **same** for all items to reduce confusion.

Keep Items Short and Focused on One Idea

One sentence, one thought, one behavior or one feeling.

Ask 2–3 Other Practitioners to Review the Items

This is an informal **validity** check. Ask them:

- Do the items match the definition?
- Is anything missing or repetitive?
- Are any words confusing or ambiguous?

Revise based on their feedback.

Pilot Test with a Very Small Group First

Work with 3–5 colleagues. Ask:

- Was anything confusing?
- Were response options clear?
- Did any items feel irrelevant or redundant?

Score It Simply and Consistently

No complex weighting. Each item scored in the same direction (e.g. higher rating always indicates greater agreement/amount).

Check for Basic Consistency

You don't need fancy statistics. Just look for:

- Items that don't vary
- Items that behave oddly
- Scores that contradict each other
- Patterns that don't make sense
- If an item isn't useful or doesn't match the others, drop it.

Document Everything

Write down your definition, item descriptions, revisions, and what you learned when testing it. This becomes the "mini manual" for your measurement tool.

Use It Sparingly, Locally, and Honestly

Self-created scales should:

- be decision-support tools
- be short-term tools
- be used within your team or program
- not be for publication or comparison across sites
- acknowledge the tool's limitations, including the lack of data on reliability/validity

Appendix E

Talking about Evidence Clearly, Carefully, and Credibly

Stories and data are powerful. When combined, they can inform decisions, influence policy, shape funding, and affect how animal-assisted services are understood by the public. With that influence comes responsibility. This appendix focuses on **how** to talk about research and data in ways that are accurate, ethical, and credible.

Why Tentative Language Matters

Tentative language is not about being vague or noncommittal. It is about **accuracy**.

Published research and SAGA data stories describe patterns, relationships, and probabilities – not guarantees. If we use overly definitive language, we may unintentionally overstate what the evidence actually supports. This can erode trust over time, especially with stakeholders who are familiar with research-based decision-making.

Using careful language:

- Reflects the true nature of the evidence
- Protects your professional credibility
- Respects the complexity of human–animal interactions and measurement
- Leaves room for learning, adaptation, and growth

Confidence and tentativeness are not opposites. In evidence-informed practice, they coexist.

From Certainty to Accuracy: Choosing Words Carefully

Some phrases are common in everyday conversation but risky when describing evidence.

Language to Avoid

- "This proves that…"
- "Research shows that this works."
- "This always leads to…"
- "The data says…"

More Accurate Alternatives

- "Research suggests…"
- "Studies have found associations between…"
- "The evidence indicates…"
- "This finding is consistent with…"
- "There is growing evidence that…"

Talking about Findings without Overclaiming

One helpful habit is to separate **what was observed** from **what it might mean.**

For example:

- *Observation*: "Participants showed lower heart rate during sessions."
- *Interpretation*: "This may reflect increased regulation or relaxation."

This distinction allows you to:

- Share findings clearly
- Acknowledge interpretation without presenting it as fact
- Invite dialogue rather than debate

Communicating about Data: Practical Tips

Match the Message to the Audience

What you say to a funder, a client, a colleague, or a conference audience may differ. Adjust your language, not the meaning of the message.

Ask yourself:

- What does this audience need to understand?
- What level of detail supports clarity rather than confusion?

Focus on Patterns, Not Single Data Points

Individual numbers matter less than trends and patterns over time.

Instead of:

Stress dropped by 12% in this session....

Try:

Across sessions, we observed a general pattern of reduced stress indicators.

Avoid Absolutes

Words like *always, never,* and *guarantees* rarely reflect what data actually show. Replace them with language that reflects variability and context.

Acknowledge What You Don't Know

Stating uncertainty is not a weakness – it is a hallmark of ethical practice.

Examples:

- "This raises questions about..."
- "We do not yet know whether..."
- "More information would help clarify..."

Using Tentative Language with Stories

Stories are often told with confidence – and that confidence is part of what makes them compelling. Tentative language does not dilute a story; it **frames it responsibly**.

For example:

> This story reflects *one client's* experience and aligns with research suggesting that animal-assisted interactions *may* support emotional regulation.

This approach:

- Honors the story
- Respects the evidence
- Avoids claiming universality

When Stakeholders Want Certainty

Practitioners are sometimes pressured to provide clear answers to complex questions:

- *Does this work?*
- *Is it effective?*
- *Is it safe?*

A useful response framework is:

- What we know
- What we are still learning
- What we are doing to learn more

This keeps communication transparent and grounded.

Consistency and Transparency Help Build Credibility

Over time, credibility is built not by bold claims, but by consistent, careful communication. Practitioners who speak accurately about evidence – acknowledging both strengths and limitations – are more likely to be trusted by clients, collaborators, and decision makers.

Tentative language is not about hesitation. It is about **respect for complexity**, **honesty about evidence**, and **confidence in ongoing learning**.

A Closing Reminder

Science does not tell a single story. It offers many small, carefully constructed ones. Your role as a practitioner is to blend stories, data, and judgment in ways that are ethical, transparent, and useful. When you speak about evidence carefully, you strengthen not only your message but also the field as a whole.

Wording to Avoid	*More Accurate Alternatives*
This proves that…	This suggests that…
Research shows that this works.	Research suggests this may be effective.
The data says…	The data indicate…
This always leads to…	This is often associated with…
This guarantees…	This may increase the likelihood of…
This causes…	This is linked to…
The evidence is clear.	The available evidence suggests…
This works for everyone.	This appears to work for some individuals.
Studies prove…	Studies have found…
This definitely shows…	This provides support for…
There is no doubt that…	There is growing evidence that…
This eliminates stress.	This may be associated with reduced stress.
Animals heal people.	Animals may support aspects of human well-being.

Appendix F

Ethics Checklist for SAGA Work

Use this checklist anytime you are planning to gather, analyze, or share data related to your animal-assisted work. You do not need to answer "yes" to every question for a decision to be ethical – but unanswered questions should prompt pause, reflection, or consultation.

Purpose and Necessity

- Have I clearly defined *why* I am collecting or sharing this data?
- Does this data directly support a SAGA question, client outcome, animal welfare, or program decision?
- Am I collecting only the data I truly need (not just what is interesting or easy to gather)?

Respect and Care for All Participants (Human and Animal)

- Have human participants been informed about what data are collected and why?
- Do participants have the option to decline data collection without negative consequences?
- Have I considered animal-assent or dissent (behavioral signs of comfort or discomfort)?
- Does data collection minimize burden, intrusion, or stress for both humans and animals?

Integrity and Transparency

- Are my charts, tables, and summaries accurate and not visually misleading?
- Does my language match the strength of the evidence (e.g., "suggests" vs. "proves")?
- Am I accurately describing the work as assessment, program evaluation, or research?
- Have I disclosed important limitations (small samples, missing data, lack of statistics)?

Justice and Fairness

- Are data collected and interpreted consistently across participants or animals?
- Have I considered whether my interpretations could unintentionally reinforce bias or stereotypes?
- Could this data presentation unfairly advantage or disadvantage a person, an animal, or a program?

Competence

- Am I trained to collect and interpret the type of evidence I am using?
- Do I understand what the numbers, charts, or statistics actually mean?
- If using advanced tools or analyses, have I consulted someone with appropriate expertise?
- Am I avoiding claims (e.g., statistical significance, proof) that exceed my methods or training?

Stewardship of Data

- Is identifiable data stored securely (passwords, locked files, limited access)?
- Is access restricted to only those who need the data?
- Do I have a plan for how long data will be retained (typically 3–5 years unless otherwise required)?
- Do I know when and how the data will be securely destroyed?

Sharing and Storytelling

- Have I removed or protected identifiable human and animal information?
- Am I aggregating data or using pseudonyms when sharing externally?
- Could someone reasonably recognize a participant or an animal from what I am sharing?
- Does this data story inform rather than persuade or exaggerate?

Final Pause

- If I were a participant (human or animal), would this feel respectful?
- If this were shared publicly, would I be comfortable explaining and defending my choices?
- Have I paused, reflected, and consulted if something feels uncertain?

Remember

Ethical data practice is not about perfection. It is about being thoughtful, intentional, and responsive. When in doubt, pause, reflect, and seek consultation.

Appendix G

Making SAGA Feasible

SAGA is meant to support your work – not overwhelm it. At first glance, it may seem like you have to create complicated systems or add burdensome tasks to your work. That is not the intention. SAGA will be sustainable when it is woven into what you are already doing, shared across people and partnerships, and approached as a gradual, evolving practice rather than a big project.

This section offers practical strategies for making SAGA realistic in busy programs.

1. **Start small, then grow slowly.** You do not need to measure everything at once. You can begin with one story, one question, one variable, one simple observation.
2. **Share the work – you don't have to do SAGA alone.** SAGA is more feasible when the work is distributed across your team. You might invite
   a. Interns to help make observations
   b. Volunteers or staff to support documentation
   c. Student or faculty partners to help with data analysis
3. **Leverage partnerships to lighten the load.** Some SAGA tasks naturally align with university and student strengths. You could partner with research methods or statistics students to analyze data, faculty partners to help develop good questions and plan data gathering, librarians to gather relevant literature, and practicum students for structured projects.
4. **Let AI *support* thinking, not replace it.** AI tools can save you time and help you think through different parts of the SAGA process. You might use AI to turn session notes

into story descriptions, reword an empirical question or data story, generate an observation form, or create plain-language summaries of datasets.

5. **Fold SAGA into routines you already have.** SAGA will be more sustainable if it lives within your existing practices. This might include adding 5 minutes of SAGA reflection time at the end of each practice day, revising regular documentation practices to include SAGA observations, and reviewing data summaries during regular team meetings.
6. **Permit yourself to make mistakes.** You will inevitably ask a less-than-helpful question and gather data that are difficult or impossible to interpret. That's ok because you'll learn how to do it better next time. SAGA is a process. Data-driven practice is not a quick story that you get "right" and "prove" something. It's in the name – Saga – a long, epic tale. It is an ongoing process of getting more and more clear on the outcomes of your animal-assisted work and how those outcomes come about.

Glossary

Analysis The process of organizing and examining data to identify patterns, relationships, or meaningful insights.

Anecdote A short account of a real experience that illustrates a point or captures a meaningful moment.

Anecdotal Evidence Information based on personal stories or experiences rather than systematic measurement.

Animal-Assisted Services Professional services in which practitioners intentionally incorporate animals to benefit people.

Anthrozooethogram A structured list of clearly defined behaviors used to observe and record human-animal interactions.

Assessment A structured process of gathering information to understand functioning, progress, or needs.

Bar Graph A visual display that uses rectangular bars to compare quantities across categories.

Behavior Any observable action or response of a human or animal in a particular context.

Bias A systematic tendency to interpret or measure information in a way that skews results.

Burnout A work-related pattern of emotional exhaustion, reduced effectiveness, and detachment that develops when demands consistently exceed available resources.

Citizen Science A collaborative research approach in which members of the public contribute to data collection or analysis.

Compassion Fatigue Emotional and physical strain that can occur when caring for others who are experiencing trauma, stress, or suffering.

Compassion Satisfaction The sense of meaning, fulfillment, or reward that comes from helping others.

Confirmation Bias The tendency to notice and interpret information in ways that confirm what we already believe.

Construct An abstract concept, such as stress or engagement, that cannot be observed directly but can be measured through related indicators.

Covert Behavior Internal experiences, such as thoughts or feelings, that cannot be directly observed by others.

Correlation A statistical relationship indicating how strongly two variables change together, without implying that one causes the other.

Data Pieces of information collected to answer a question or support decision-making.

Data Collection (Gathering) The process of intentionally recording information to answer a specific question.

Data-Driven Guided by systematically gathered information rather than assumptions or impressions alone.

Data Stewardship The ethical responsibility to collect, store, use, and share data in ways that protect confidentiality and prevent misuse.

Data Visualization The presentation of data in visual form, such as charts or graphs, to make patterns easier to see and understand.

Empirical Evidence Information obtained through direct observation, measurement, or systematic investigation.

Empirical Question A question that can be answered through observation or measurement rather than opinion or assumption.

Equine Relating to horses, donkeys, mules, zebras, and other members of the equid family.

Equine-Assisted Services Professional services in which practitioners intentionally incorporate horses and other equines to benefit people.

Equine-Assisted Story Transformation (EAST) A theory proposing that embodied, body–mind interactions with horses help clients explore and revise personal narratives as part of therapeutic change.

Ethogram A list of clearly defined animal behaviors used to guide consistent observation and recording.

Ethology The scientific study of animal behavior.

Evaluation The systematic examination of a program or practice to determine its effectiveness or value.

Evidence Information that helps determine whether a belief, claim, or practice is supported.

Evidence-Based Practice Professional decision-making informed by the best available research, practitioner expertise, and client values.

Formal Assessment The use of standardized, validated tools to measure specific constructs.

Human-Animal Interaction Observable behaviors exchanged between humans and animals.

Human-Animal Interaction Scale (HAIS) A structured self-report tool designed to quantify behaviors exchanged between humans and animals.

Infographic A visual summary that combines graphics and minimal text to communicate information clearly.

Informal Assessment A flexible, nonstandardized method of gathering information within everyday practice.

Intervention A structured action or service designed to produce change in a specific outcome.

Journal Article A written report published in an academic or professional journal that presents research findings, theoretical ideas, or practice-based insights.

Line Graph A visual display that shows changes in data over time using connected points.

Literature The collection of published research and professional writing that contributes to knowledge in a field.

Mean The average of a set of numbers, calculated by adding them together and dividing by the total number of values.

Median The middle value in a set of numbers arranged in order.

Measurement The process of assigning numbers or categories to behaviors or experiences in a systematic way.

Measurement Instrument A tool, such as a scale or checklist, used to collect structured data.

Measurement-Based Care An approach to practice that uses ongoing data to guide clinical or program decisions over time.

Mode The value that appears most frequently in a set of numbers.

Naturalistic Observation Observing behavior in its usual environment without manipulating the situation.

Observation The act of watching and recording behavior in a deliberate and systematic way.

Operational Definition A clear description of exactly what counts as a behavior and how it will be measured.

Outcome A measurable result or change associated with a service, program, or intervention.

Overt Behavior Observable actions that can be directly seen or recorded.

Pie Chart A circular graph that shows how parts contribute to a whole.

Practice-Based Evidence Knowledge generated through systematic observation and reflection within real-world practice settings.

Practitioner–Science Evidence Base The collective knowledge created through partnership between practitioners and scientists, where data from everyday practice contribute to research and research helps improve practice.

Pre–Post Measure A method of measuring change by collecting data before and after an intervention.

Program Evaluation The systematic use of data to assess how well a service or program is working.

Qualitative Data focused on descriptions, meanings, or experiences rather than numbers.

Quantitative Data expressed in numbers that can be counted, compared, or statistically analyzed.

Rating Scale A measurement tool that asks respondents to indicate the degree or intensity of an experience.

Reciprocity An observable exchange in which one organism responds to another's action with a related or corresponding behavior, such as returning an approach with an approach.

Reliability The consistency of a measurement tool or observation across time, people, or situations.

Sample A smaller group selected to represent a larger population.

Sample Size The number of participants or observations included in a sample.

Sampling The method used to select which individuals or observations will be included in a study.

SAGA A practical method for data-driven work: Start with a story, Ask a question, Gather evidence, Act on your findings.

Scientist–Practitioner A professional who integrates scientific thinking and evidence into everyday practice.

Self-Report Data collected directly from individuals about their own thoughts, feelings, or experiences.

Shared Inquiry A collaborative process in which practitioners compare questions, methods, and emerging patterns to build cumulative knowledge across settings.

State A temporary condition or experience that can change over time.

Statistical Significance A statistical result suggesting that an observed difference or relationship is unlikely to be due to chance alone.

Stoplight Method A wellness-monitoring framework that uses green, yellow, and red zones to guide participation and protective decisions.

Story A narrative account of events that gives meaning to experience.

Symbiosis A close relationship between two species that involves patterns of mutual benefit, cost, or neutrality.

Systematic Observation A structured method of observing clearly defined behaviors using consistent recording procedures.

t-test A statistical test used to compare the average values of two groups to determine whether the difference between them is likely meaningful.

Trait A relatively stable characteristic or pattern that tends to persist over time.

Unit of Measurement The specific format used to record data, such as frequency, duration, or rating.

Validity The extent to which a tool or method accurately measures what it is intended to measure.

Variable A characteristic or factor that can change and be measured.

Wellness Saga An application of the SAGA method focused on monitoring the well-being of the animalhandler team.

Index

For Product Safety Concerns and Information please contact our EU representative GPSR@taylorandfrancis.com Taylor & Francis Verlag GmbH, Kaufingerstraße 24, 80331 München, Germany